Reflective Practice

Reflective Practice

Writing and Professional Development

Gillie Bolton

P·C·P
Paul Chapman
Publishing Ltd

ISBN 0-7619-6728-1 (hbk)
ISBN 0-7619-6729-X (pbk)
© Gillie Bolton 2001
First published 2000
Reprinted 2003, 2004

Paul Chapman Publishing
A SAGE Publications Company
1 Oliver's Yard, 55 City Road
London EC1Y 1SP

SAGE Publications Inc
2455 Teller Road
Thousand Oaks, California 91320

SAGE Publications India Pvt Ltd
B–42 Panchsheel Enclave
PO Box 4109
New Delhi 110 017

British Library Cataloguing in Publication data
A catalogue record for this book is available from the British Library

Typeset by Dorwyn Ltd., Rowlands Castle, Hampshire
Printed and bound in Great Britain by
Athenæum Press Limited, Gateshead, Tyne & Wear

This book is dedicated to all who heal, care, and educate.

Contents

Foreword

by Anne Hudson Jones

Narrative competence – that is, the mastery of several kinds of narrative skills – has increasingly been seen as desirable for professionals, and especially for those in medicine. One way to foster such narrative skills is the practice of reflective writing that Gillie Bolton describes in her book. This process of writing depends upon the intuitive, linguistic, and imaginative capacities rather than the rational and quantitative modes of thought that dominate much of professional training and practice.

Although the process may sound simple, if practiced well, such writing requires honesty and courage and can lead to unexpected insights and new ways of knowing. The results may improve practice as well as revitalize the practitioner.

As one who has had the privilege of participating in a reflective-writing workshop led by Gillie Bolton, I can affirm the validity of testimonials to its power. I can also affirm this book's opening reminder that the best way of undertaking reflective practice is to do it rather than to read about it. But for those who have not yet had that opportunity, this book offers the next best thing. Read it as a prelude to, rather than a substitute for, engaging in the reflective practice it encourages.

Anne Hudson Jones
Institute for the Medical Humanities
The University of Texas Medical Branch at Galveston

Acknowledgements

This book has been enabled by the many practitioners and colleagues with whom I have worked over the last twelve years. We have explored many new territories together – excitingly and sensitively. You have most generously given time, enthusiasm and insight into the depths of your own experience, knowledge and feelings, and – perhaps most vital of all – human warmth. Thanks seem paltry for the adventures we have had, and for your permission to quote and refer to your work; but heartfelt thanks is all I can offer. I thank the Sheffield University Institute of General Practice Master in Medical Science graduates, Nottingham Community Health nurses, participants in many kinds of medical, nursing, social work and counselling/therapy education and development programmes, and Sheffield University Masters in Education graduates.

There are some in particular without whom I could not even have put my boots on for the journey which has led to this book. Richard Winter is a constant and loved companion; Rosie Field dances hand in hand with me along the most rocky and precipitous paths; Kate Billingham and Amanda Howe illuminate the track we travel together; Nigel Mathers has been a dynamic co-tutor with whom to create an exciting enough course to write about; Nick Fox offered intellectual and post-modern stimulation at the right moment; Sir Kenneth Calman, David Hannay, Steve Dearden, Pat Lane, Tony Warnes and Sonya Yates have given wonderful support; Faith McLellan, Anne Hudson Jones and Trisha Greenhalgh warm advice and insight. Marianne Lagrange has been a model editor. Moira Brimacombe, Jo Cannon, Adam Forman, Tom Heller, Bob Purdy, Helen Starkey, Shirley Brierley, Clare Connolly, Naomi Dixon, Maggie Eisner, Seth Jenkinson, Sheena McMain, Mark Purvis, Becky Ship, Bev Hargreaves, Di Moss and Janet Hargreaves have laughed and cried with me. Sue Gee has generously offered valuable insight into the story-writing process. The staff of Sheffield University Institute of General Practice keep directing me when I get in the wrong lane at roundabouts. Marilyn Lidster, with an unfailing smile and laugh, endlessly picks up the bits of myself I drop all the time, and sorts out machines which never seem to work for me; and Jo Barton and Jan Morrison have been wonderful. Dan Rowland says 'Oh Gillie!' but tells me again what to click on, and wants to discuss anything and everything important with me. Alice Rowland helps me with what to wear, and how not to slip in the mud, or fall over the edge.

Stephen Rowland has travelled this and many other roads with me so closely I am no longer sure whose journey we are on – his or mine. In so many ways this book is one of the milestones in our shared adventure. He not only makes sure I have a warm jersey, compass and whistle, as well as the right map, but also always fills my rucksack with goodies.

Preface: Mind the Gap

In the end I found that the reflective process itself was where the bounties lay, and no amount of reading about reflecting could help me.

This writing allows you to touch things you otherwise couldn't.

This is an opportunity to inhabit the unknown.

Reflective practitioners

If the first speaker above is right you should shut this book now. So why do I want you to read it? Reflective practice is only effectively undertaken and understood by becoming immersed in doing it rather than reading about it or following instructions. But an initial guide can save time; this one will, I hope, enable you to engage in the process as dynamically as he did.

Bank Underground Station, London, is built on a curve, leaving a potentially dangerous gap between platform and carriage to trap the unwary. As a 1960s teenager, I was struck by the loudspeaker voice instructing passengers to 'Mind the gap'. Such a gap is a boundary between train and platform. The notion of *gap* can be used as an image for other boundaries in our lives, such as that between me as a professional and me as a parent. We spend our lives minding gaps in order to protect ourselves from being hit by trains, eaten by bears (Milne 1924, p. 27–9) or falling into uncomfortable situations where we don't know the answers. But these last sort of gaps can be constructive – where we learn things; they can lead to reflective questions being asked, such as a deep and thorough examination of just what made something so spectacularly right, or what went wrong in a given disaster. At such moments of openness understandings can flash. 'Aha' moments of 'oh I see!', and epiphanies of allowing myself to stop thinking, stop carefully being myself, and allow other possibilities to present themselves, can happen. At these times and places the practitioner is open to querying, or potentially querying, situations, knowledge, feelings and understandings. Such deeply reflective questions are like bridges:

> Bridges are sort of the opposite of boundaries, and boundaries are where wars start.
>
> Levi 1988, p. 104

Professional *boundaries* often keep the personal and the professional apart; *borders* and *frontiers* are sensitive politically. We use them to tell us who we are, and the way we will relate to others (friend or family? stranger or fellow-countryperson? colleague or client?). We take on many different roles – lover, parent, chauffeur, academic, supervisor, counsellor, friend – all with uncertain boundaries between them; we strive to clarify our roles for ourselves and others. We also strive to know the answers relevant to our roles: a doctor assumes the patient wants an answer, the parent wants to give the child the right one. It can, however, be useful to say 'I don't know', at least to oneself. In striving for certainty in an uncertain world, for clarity of boundaries, we sometimes forget to ask reflective, personally and professionally developing questions about our boundaries, and the issues found there.

> how difficult it is for professionals in such anxiety-producing work to remain open and responsive (rather than reactive); routinised responses and procedures (though an essential framework for action) can also lead to a rigidity which is inimical to the uniquely personal response needed in the caring professions.
>
> Effective learning is therefore dependent, at least in part, on access to that world of feeling and phantasy, which allows structures of meaning to be recognised, and to be open to change, in a way which facilitates a different (and perhaps more constructive) professional response.
>
> Yelloly and Henkel 1995, p. 9

Reflective Practice: Aesthetic and Artistic

Reflective practice can enable a mindfulness of the gap – an awareness of and willingness to tackle border issues – excitingly, if carefully. Winter *et al.* (1999) maintain that reflective practice is one way of redressing the 'devaluation, deskilling and alienation' now suffered by the caring and teaching professions:

> The late 1980s saw professional staff beginning to experience a sense of having their autonomy reduced, their decision-making mechanised, their expertise fragmented and their 'artistry' abolished. . . .
>
> The reflective paradigm assembles its theoretical resources in order to defend professional values, creativity, and autonomy in a context where they are generally felt to be under attack from political and

economic forces which threatened to transform the professional from an artist into an operative.

Winter *et al.* 1999, p. 193

Working reflectively with our whole selves (holistically) entails harnessing our artistic talents alongside all the others. If practice itself is an art, then the reflection upon it is also an artistic process (Bleakley 1999, Winter *et al.* 1999). Creative (expressive and explorative) writing is an appropriate form for reflective practice as it relies on our habitual communicating medium, words. Writing gives validity, form and coherence over time and space, as well as aesthetic illumination.

This book offers an introduction to effective reflective practice, based on teaching and research experience with doctors, nurses, social workers, therapists, counsellors and teachers. Practitioners write stories, poetry or drama about their work, or their research data, then submit these to discussion with a facilitated group, supervisor, mentor or co- (peer-) mentor. The writing develops and clarifies the writers' understanding of their data or experience; then the discussion draws out issues and locates gaps and queries, extending the learning process for writer as well as group (or mentor). The writer becomes reader and co-critic, and the audience takes on the role of co-author. This critical research also encompasses the reading of as wide a range of appropriate texts as possible, thoroughly and clearly embedding the whole reflective process consciously in the practitioner's wide political, cultural and social/professional context.

About this book

I provide: background information; the how, why, where, who, when, what of the process; a discussion of theoretical educational principles and underpinnings; insight into facilitation and group work; an explanation of writing methods, the learning journal, and different ways or genre of writing; and an examination of queries and problems, including those relating to ethics and values. Principles and practice of reflection and reflexivity are discussed with reference to facilitated group, supervision or peer-mentoring.

' "What is the use of a book," thought Alice, "without pictures or conversation?" ' (Carroll 1865, p. 1). Alice had the wisdom to know that a text had to capture her heart, imagination and spirit as well as her mind in order for it to speak to her fully. It is the same for everyone. This text is fully illustrated and exemplified throughout with original writings from colleagues, students and published material: from education, medicine, nursing, social work and therapy. They are first-hand stories of practice, accounts of discussions about stories, reflections upon the usefulness of the reflective process, and descriptions of methods and processes used and their effectiveness.

A suggested criterion for my Masters students' final assessment is *evidence of enjoyment* (as well as *evidence of substantive reading*, etc.). My pleasure in marking portfolios is increased when the students' enjoyment oozes off the page. We only learn effectively when we are doing what we want to do. I suppose this book concerns effective, enjoyable reflective practice.

The Ah-Ha Moment

Rowing is a precise art. You must have confidence in your boat and oars, but also confidence in your ability to let go and trust your natural instincts.

I will let you into a secret. The best way of introducing this feeling is to take away for a moment the crew's vision. To get them to shut their eyes. This lifts outside interference and pushes back those constraints of *how it ought to be* to *how it is*.

Shutting your eyes and letting those natural instincts take over can be daunting but liberating.

SEE HOW IT CAN BE DONE IF YOU JUST LET GO . . .

Jo Turner

Oars are 'wings that make ships fly', according to Odysseus (Homer trans 1996, p. 464). If we continue Jo's metaphor of rowing for reflective practice, I hope this book will enable you, reflective practitioner readers, to fly, and to find 'goodness there':

Just halfway through this journey of our life
I reawoke to find myself inside
A dark wood, way off course, the right road lost.
How difficult a task it is to tell
What this wild, harsh, forbidding wood was like
The merest thought of which brings back my fear;
For only death exceeds its bitterness.
But I found goodness there.

Dante, *Inferno*, Canto 1 lines 1–8

1

An Introduction to Reflective Practice

We do not 'store' experience as data, like a computer: we 'story' it.

Winter 1988, p. 235

'Begin at the beginning,' the King said gravely, 'and go on till you come to the end; then stop.'

Carroll 1865, p. 104

Stories are the mode we use to make sense of ourselves and our world. This world and our lives within it are chaotic: governed by forces not only beyond our control, but beyond our understanding. We tell and retell episodes both minor and major to our colleagues, to our loved ones, to therapists and priests, even in extremity to a wedding guest – preventing him from joining in the feast (Coleridge 1834). This can merely be a process of tucking ourselves securely under a quilt patchworked out of safe and self-affirming accounts: our stories can only too easily be essentially uncritical. This self-protectiveness can ensure that our stories are not exploring our sensitive issues, but are expressions of what we feel comfortable with, or would like to be.

> One day when Pooh Bear had nothing else to do, he thought he would do something, so he went round to Piglet's house to see what Piglet was doing. It was still snowing as he stumped over the white forest track, and he expected to find Piglet warming his toes in front of the fire, but to his surprise he found that the door was open, and the more he looked inside the more Piglet wasn't there.
>
> Milne 1928, p. 163

Effective reflective practice can be like looking for Piglet: the more you look for it the more it seems not to be there; and afterwards it is hard to describe why it was so absorbing and life-changing – because the insights and inevitable changes they necessitate seem so obvious.

1

Although reflective practice has become a standard in initial and continuing professional education and development, 'how do I do it effectively?' is a cry I often hear.

A story is an attempt to create order out of a chaotic world. But for our experiences to develop us – socially, psychologically, spiritually – our world must be made to appear strange. We, and our students, must be encouraged to examine our storymaking processes critically: to create and recreate fresh accounts of our lives from different perspectives, different points of view, and to elicit and listen to the responses of peers. Listening critically to the stories of those peers also enables learning from their experience. We will never arrive at a 'true' account, one which enables us to see what people 'really' thought and felt in any situation, or what 'really' happened:

> important knowledge about reality always comes out of literature . . .
> but through a . . . transformation of reality by imagination and the
> use of words . . . When you succeed in creating something different
> out of . . . experience, you also achieve the possibility of communicat-
> ing something that was not evident before that novel or poem or play
> existed. But you cannot plan this transmission of knowledge. The
> novel is a reality in itself.
>
> Llosa 1991, p. 79

The process of postulating what the other actors in the situation might have thought and felt, empathising with them and the situation, as well as imaginatively reconstructing the situation in fresh ways, offers understandings and insights as no other process can. For example, a practitioner can retell a story from the point of view of the student or client, reconstruct it with the genders of the actors reversed, or a satisfactory ending in place of a horrible one.

Effective reflective practice meets the paradoxical need both to tell and retell our stories in order for us to feel secure enough, and yet critically examine our actions, and those of others, in order dynamically to increase our understanding of ourselves and our practice (Johns and Freshwater 1998).

Reflective Practice: a Political and Social Responsibility

Reflective practice can fall into the trap of becoming only confession. Confession can be a conforming mechanism, despite sounding liberating, freeing from a burden of doubt, guilt and anxiety. Confessing has a seductive quality; the desire to hold an audience with a 'glittering eye' (Coleridge 1834) is strong. Jennifer Nias, a researcher into the experience of women teachers (Nias and Aspinwall 1992), noted with surprise that all her potential interviewees were keen to tell their autobiographies at length.

Reflective practice is, however, more than an examination of personal experience; it is located in the political and social structures which are increasingly hemming professionals in. Their right to make moral and professional judgements is being eroded daily; they are being reduced to technicians, their skills to mere technical competencies. In order to retain political and social awarenesses and activity, professional development work needs to be rooted in the public and the political as well as the private and the personal.

To this end, a reflective practice examination of personal practice needs to be undertaken alongside open discussions with peers on the issues raised, an examination of texts from the larger field of work and politics, and discussions with colleagues from outside practitioners' own milieu. Reflective practice work can then become politically, socially as well as psychologically useful, rather than a mere *quietist* navel-gazing exercise.

Goodson creates a distinction between *life stories* and *life history*. The latter is the former plus appropriate and challenging data from a wide range of sources, and evidence of vital discussion with colleagues. 'The life history pushes the question of whether private issues are also public matters. The life story individualises and personalises; the life history contextualises and politicises' (1998 p. 11).

Noel Gough (1998) uses a similar method with postgraduate students in education curriculum. He says he *plays* with the method, which he calls *currere* – a term coined by Pinar (1975) and Grumet (1981).

Paula Salvio uses this kind of approach to support teachers in *empathetic enquiry*, a deeper understanding of ethnic minority students. She says we, as teachers, must 'travel into our own worlds' in order to 'travel to those of others', and gain empathetic understanding. This process must include involvement with the emotions, as 'emotional whiteout' (1998, p. 49) will disable this travel into both our own worlds and those of others. This kind of writing, involving the emotions, is what Cixous described as feminine:

all the feminine texts I've read are very close to the voice, very close to the flesh of language, much more so than masculine texts . . . perhaps because there's something in them that's freely given, perhaps because they don't rush into meaning, but are straightway at the threshold of feeling. There's tactility in the feminine text, there's touch, and this touch passes through the ear.

Cixous 1995, p. 175

Re-view

A film or story is a dynamic fresh look through the eyes of more than one actor. Replaying back what 'actually' happened is impossible: any retelling will inevitably be affected by the view of the person doing the retelling. Effective reflective practice enables the exploration of a range of viewpoints and possibilities. As Mark Purvis, a reflective practitioner, has written:

> Stories are a lens through which I view the world to make sense of my experiences and those of my colleagues and patients. In writing some of these stories I am able to focus on complex issues that have previously appeared distorted by time and emotions. Metaphors shed light on subjects that I had been unaware of before, patterns stand out in ways that I had not hitherto understood.

Mark Purvis

Reflective practice is a process of learning and developing through examining our own practice, opening our practice to scrutiny by others, and studying texts from the wider sphere. It is a focusing closer and closer. In the film *Blow-up* the only evidence for a murder is in a photograph, but too indistinct to be distinguished. The hero blows up and blows up this tiny detail until the evidence is there before our eyes. Similarly nothing is too trivial or insignificant to write and think and talk about. These vital details might have gone unnoticed at the time – just as the piece of evidence did in the film *Blow-up*. Reflective practice is 'Oh I see!' kind of stuff, as the detail becomes clear to the writer through the processes of writing, rereading, redrafting and discussing.

Education, medicine, nursing, therapy, social work and many other professions are all processes of facilitating the other to understand elements of their lives and themselves better, and hopefully improve things thereby. A practitioner cannot support another in this way if they are not aware and open themselves (Smyth 1996, Murray 1982). Terry Smyth has further pointed out that if the personal is brought into the professional then the empathy between client and professional will be increased. Aesthetic experience (such as creative writing) can leap over the seeming gap between the personal and the professional self. This can only bring greater unity and wholeness of experience to the practitioner or educator, and greater empathy between them and their client. Job satisfaction will increase, and work-related stress decrease:

> Perhaps the most accessible form of freedom, the most subjectively enjoyed, and the most useful to human society consists of being good at your job and therefore taking pleasure in doing it— I really believe that to live happily you have to have something to do, but it shouldn't be too easy, or else something to wish for, but not just any old wish; something there's a hope of achieving.
>
> Levi 1988, p. 139

Writing stories and sharing them in a trusted confidential facilitated forum of peers, or within supervision, is a way of increasing job satisfaction and effectiveness, and is the process offered by this book. Explorative and expressive writing is pivotal: the writing of a story or poem is a first order activity. The writing, the essential discussions and the writing of additional stories from different angles with the support of the group, is a creative explorative process in its own right – not a tool in professional reflection. Course participants do not think and then write; the writing is the vehicle for the reflection: reflection in writing. Not only does writing enable the most appropriate reflection, but also, as a participant commented, 'one of the values of writing is that you can freeze the film: reflect upon one frame or a short series, then run the film backwards and review a previous scene in the light of reflections upon a later one. This would be difficult to do in talking: it wouldn't make sense; impossible to do during action.' And as Laurel Richardson has said:

> I consider writing as a *method of inquiry*, a way of finding out about yourself and your topic. Although we usually think about writing as a mode of 'telling' about the social world, writing is not just a mopping-up activity . . . Writing is also a way of 'knowing' – a method of discovery and analysis. By writing in different ways, we discover new aspects of our topic and our relationship to it. Form and content are inseparable.
>
> Richardson 1998, p. 345

The psychologist Oliver Sacks studied people who were missing, or effectively missing, part of their brains, and the bizarre things this led to. In his essay *The Man who Mistook his Wife for a Hat*, he studies 'Dr P.' who could see, but had lost 'visual perception, visual imagination and memory, the fundamental powers of visual representation . . . insofar as they pertained to the personal, the familiar, the concrete.' Sacks concludes:

> Our mental processes, which constitute our being and life, are not just abstract and mechanical, but personal as well – and as such involve not just classifying and categorising, but continual judging and feeling also. If this is missing, we become computer-like, as Dr P. was. And by the same token, if we delete feeling and judging, the personal, from the cognitive sciences, we reduce *them* to something as defective as Dr P. – and we reduce *our* apprehension of the concrete and real . . . Our cognitive sciences are themselves suffering from an agnosia essentially similar to Dr P.'s. Dr P. may therefore serve as a warning and parable – of what happens to a science which eschews the judgmental, the particular, the personal, and becomes entirely abstract and computational.
>
> Sacks 1985, p. 19

Reflective practice can learn from Sacks's 'warning and parable', and be open to as much of ourselves as is possible. A reflective practice suffering from agnosia will not get us terribly far.

Effective reflective practice encourages the seeking of understanding and interpretation of principles, justifications and meanings (Morrison 1996). This can lead practitioners to perceive a need for change in their world, their relation and attitude to it, and to seek to change the attitudes of others. One of my students stated: 'this is not an academic module, but an assertiveness training course'. Asserting yourself inevitably involves challenging social structures.

One of the greatest benefits to a student in a learning situation, or a client in any interaction with a practitioner, is the sense of their relatedness to the professional: that they are interested, involved, and care. In medicine this has been called the *placebo effect* of the physician as *healer*: 'the attitude of the doctor can make an appreciable difference to the psychological response of the patient who feels the need to be understood and listened to empathically' (Dixon *et al.* 1999, p. 310). To give the people we work with confidence in us as professionals, we have to be secure and happy enough ourselves in our roles, and not anxious or inhibited.

How can that happen in overworked, overstressed professions, which are getting less appreciated daily? One of the ways of being an empathetic, effective practitioner is to reflect fruitfully upon practice. In order to do this the practitioner has to be reflexive as well as reflective. Being *reflexive* is focusing close attention upon *one's own* actions, thoughts and feelings and their effects; being *reflective* is looking at the *whole scenario*: other people, the situation and place, and so on.

Reflective practice according to the principles and practice outlined here is a valuable developmental process for any teacher, social worker, clinician or student. It can take its camera down to any aspect of practice, with patients, colleagues, administrative and other staff, the interface of home and work, the impact of experiences in the past on present actions. Nothing is too small or big for the zoom or wide-angle lens.

Story-Based Practice

You are watching a film. One of those arty ones starting with a wide-angle lens – hawk's eye view – of an English city. From this height cars and buildings look like toys, and the grid of streets and fields are a pattern – pretty but with little human meaning. People are too small to be seen.

The camera moves in closer, into focus comes one particular street – people walking and talking, everyday interchanges taking place. The camera comes closer and closer – up to one building in particular, and one window of that building. We pass through the glass and into the staffroom of a big secondary school.

Effective reflective practice is the focusing upon detailed stories of practice and life, and upon the thoughts and feelings associated with the actions in them. These stories are imaginative creations drawn from experience. Seen as a set of interlocking plots, the problems, anguishes, joys of practice become comprehensible – material to be dealt with creatively and developmentally. The use of the aesthetic imagination in creating this material provides a screen as wide as life itself, drawing upon all of a practitioner's faculties. Attempting to reflect only upon 'what actually happened', and then to subject such an account to rational questions such as 'how might I have done it better?', unnecessarily restricts what might be explored.

I ask you to return to my film.

A Film of Professional Practice

The camera has entered the big secondary school staffroom. The atmosphere is stiff and almost silent; only one staff member, the head of maths, is humming to himself, the rest look anxious and jumpy. The headteacher enters the room and the quiet deepens; she asks the hummer to follow her to her room as she has something of importance to talk about. He follows her out and the tension in the room shifts, doesn't lessen, but staff are enabled to talk, albeit in low voices. This tension has been building up for months ever since the biology teacher began to suspect the head of maths of having a sexual relationship with one of the pupils.

The camera pans out, circles at hawk level again, and then zooms. This time it focuses on a small terraced house in a narrow street where the houses have no front gardens and tiny back yards. We are in the front room, a distraught mother has run out, thrusting her dead baby into the health visitor's arms. The tiny body is cold – so cold. The little girl wants to play with the 'dolly', and thinks the nurse might be kind and let her, Mummy wouldn't. The health visitor is in anguish as she knows the baby has had an autopsy – a horrifying sight unclothed.

The third time the camera takes us to a high rise block of flats deep in London's East End. It is one of those utterly confusing ones with walkways, where the lifts work sporadically and jerkily, and flat numbers seem to have been assigned by a dyslexic infant. A grey-haired social worker is confusedly studying flat number after flat number as the wind whistles round the corners, blowing crisp packets to reveal a pile of hypodermic needles. She jumps as heavy footsteps interrupt the sound of the wind, and her heart misses a beat as she sees a very dark shape loom round the corner.

What do the practitioners in our films do with the distress, guilt, anxiety, horror, anger, humiliation – which they cannot, or do not express at work? How do they prevent these powerful feelings from draining their energy, disabling them from effective practice? How do they learn from their own feelings, turn all those negative energies round into positive ones? How do they learn from each others' mistakes and successes, each others' ideas, experience and wisdom? How do they learn to empathise with another through experiences which they will never know? A man will never know childbirth, for example; how does he learn the compassion and understanding needed to support a mother in travail?

Our films zoomed in from the distant and impersonal to the close and intensely human. This focusing in close-up on the 'rag and bone shop of the heart' (Yeats 1962, p. 201) is what effective reflection can do. We move from the grand ideals of our practice, to the precise story of a small handful of people who cry and laugh, who shout and tremble silently – and who are involved with people at the thresholds of life and death, at periods of intense change and development.

Our professional heroines and heroes come to terms with their own powerful emotions, learn from their own and others' mistakes and successes, and develop empathy – through reflection – in writing and then in discussions about those writings.

This book is about how practitioners can examine their own stories closely, look at themselves as heroines and heroes in their own real-life films, and the people with whom they work as heroes and heroines also. They take themselves, their problems, griefs and anxieties, as well as joys – seriously.

Vital Details of Practice

I'd like to return to those film plots. All of them are stories of experience, written about and brought to groups by practitioners. They reflected upon them in the writing, and we discussed them further together.

The story of the head of department who was having an affair with one of the pupils very greatly distressed the teacher who wrote about it. She was closely involved with all the parties: the child, the family, other teachers and the community. She felt deeply entwined with the whole drama, as did many of the other staff, but of course she could not talk about it except to her husband, as it was all completely confidential. A reflective practice group where confidentiality was assured was an ideal forum, however. She started writing the story as a romantic love story. I think it was perhaps the distancing and the strong set structure this gave her which enabled her to begin. She then wrote an episode each week during the Masters in Education module. Her small group (a subset of the course group) were agog each time to hear the next episode. Her writing was so important to her that it became powerful hearing; and the discussion and support of the group was invaluable to all of them, so much so that the group continued beyond the end of the module with the members continuing the writing work as a special study module the next semester.

The health visitor did, of course, prevent the toddler from unwrapping the 'dolly' dead baby at her bereavement visit; but she was distressed she had not handled it sensitively to be a growing experience for the child. The group who heard her story were able to help her to unpick it, to see it through the eyes of the child, and to consider carefully how she might have acted, rather than just anxiously ward off the toddler.

The black man who approached the social worker in the East End high rise flat courteously asked her if she was lost and if he could help her find her way. In discussion, the group helped her out of just feeling intense shame at her assumptions when she saw him coming towards her. She was then able to consider her habitual state of mind on home-visits.

Why Practice as Screenplay?

Sharing stories with each other must be one of the best ways of exploring and understanding experience. That is, if Winter is right that what we want and need to say is not just *stored*, but held in our minds as *story* (Winter 1988), and if Goodson is right about their import:

> stories do social and political work. A story is never just a story – it is a statement of belief, of morality, it speaks about value.
>
> Goodson 1998, p. 12

Narrative telling is a vital part of our lives – in the nurses' station, the staffroom, and in our own kitchens. Narrative is a 'source of consolation' (Eagleton 1983, p. 185). Stories offer the fictive comfort of structure with some sort of beginning, middle and end (see Carroll above), and of the closure of our desire. We are involved in an endless search for something lost – God, Lacan's Imaginary, Freud's pre-Oedipal stage, Sartre's 'Being-in-itself', a unity with the mother's body, a sought-after haven where the signified has a direct innate correlation with the signifier:

> something must be lost or absent in any narrative for it to unfold: if everything stayed in one place there'd be no story to tell. This loss is distressing but exciting as well: desire is stimulated by what we cannot quite possess.
>
> Eagleton 1983, p. 185

We relate to the loss or lack in every story because we want to see the good characters gaining their just hearts' desires, and the bad founder. We share their joys and tragedies vicariously. The story has the effect of reinforcing our assumptions about what we might desire and what fear; it affirms our sense of moral, emotional or spiritual, or physical right. We follow Odysseus past the Sirens holding our breath, and when a fair wind brings him back to Penelope, we will him to shoot his arrow straight to prove he is really her husband; and we help Dorothy kill the wicked witch of the West. When Tony Archer's son was on trial for political activity (BBC Radio 4 *The Archers* Autumn 1999), that's what people were talking about in my village rather than the latest news or the football, until they were satisfied the jury had found him 'not guilty'.

The role of the listener to the narrative is just as important as the reader or teller:

> so there is an art of listening . . . Every narrator is aware from experience that to every narration the listener makes a decisive contribution: a distracted or hostile audience can unnerve any teacher or lecturer: a friendly public sustains. But the individual listener also shares responsibility for that work of art that every narration is: you realise this when you tell something over the telephone, and you freeze, because you miss the visible reactions of the listener. . . . This is also the chief reason why writers, those who must narrate to a disembodied public are few.
>
> Levi 1988, p. 35

Reflective practice writers are not writers in this sense. They are writing for an *embodied* set of people; they write for their group, or supervisor/mentor. Practitioners who work with me often point out that the discussion with these colleagues, a process of restorying, is just as much an essential part of the process as the writing and storying.

Reflective practice supports practitioners to see their relationship with their student, client, patient or colleague within a range of possible roles. This is a way of rounding out practice, as well as a response to practice. We speak of the ideal of *holistic practice*: of seeing the whole patient or student or client rather than just a disease or teaching situation or problem. But there is more than this, the practitioner needs to be aware that they themselves also are whole people – they do not leave their personalities, their souls, their senses of humour, their fragilities outside the classroom, consulting room or client's front door. And they need to be aware that they take on different roles at different times, just as we all do all the time.

The possible roles for both professional and client could be seen to be: *I, you,* and *her/him*. The client as 'I' is at the centre of the drama – the subject, the heroine – the story told from their point of view. The client as 'you' is the other in the script – the whole person in relationship with the professional, and the professional is the teller of the story – whether telling it with themselves as 'I' (first person narrative) or 'he/she' (third person narrative). The client as 'her or him' becomes like an object – an appropriate role in some circumstances such as research trials when the patient is only a statistic. But it is wholly inappropriate in others, as when a community psychiatric nurse said 'I encourage the ladies to do their garden, it is good for them'. There were only two 'ladies' in this case – both well known to the speaker: why did she have to turn them into objects in this way?

This poem by a GP explores her awareness of the way her patients can see themselves *centre stage*, as 'I', and the way she handles that:

Performance
This is your stage.
Sit down, compose your face.
Lines rehearsed in the waiting room.
Family can't hear you –
'Leave mum she has a headache.'

Headache.
Muscle ache.
Spirit ache.
Tired all the time.
Tired of the time.
Too much time.

Let me perform for you.
Let me touch you,
measure your blood pressure,
measure your worth.
You are worth my time.
When you get home, they'll ask what I said.
Rehearse the lines.
This is your chance.
This is your stage.

                                                    Jo Cannon

Now what about the practitioner's relationship with her- or himself? A practitioner wrote in her evaluation of a *writing as a reflective practitioner course*: 'Writing weaves connections between my work and the rest of my life, between my inner and outer selves, between the left and the right sides of my brain, between the past and the present.' A trainee said: 'this kind of writing has to have material about who we are and what we stand for'. A GP wrote: 'I'd considered resigning because I'd been struggling with being a doctor and who it turned me into. Creative writing has helped me see what was happening – share it with others and begin to find a way through.' Storying and restory-ing our lives help us to keep pace with the way we change and develop over time. 'Who I am' does not and cannot remain stable:

> It is important to view the self as an emergent and changing 'project' not a stable and fixed entity. Over time our view of our self changes, and so, therefore, do the stories we tell about ourselves. In this sense, it is useful to view self-definition as an ongoing narrative project.
>
> Goodson 1998, p. 11

Why Reflective Practice?

Our stories are inextricably intertwined – with themselves and with those of others. We tell and retell, affirming and reaffirming ourselves in our own and each others' eyes (and ears). The accounts slip and merge as we tell them, developing new twists and losing ones that have served their turn. This urge to recount and recreate each day is strong; but it is only too easy to devalue our own stories because they are unimportant compared with those of powerful others such as pop stars, surgeons, politicians: we have lost trust in ourselves, and owner-ship of our stories.

Reflective practice through writing is a way of expressing and ex-ploring our own and others' stories: crafting and shaping them to help us understand and develop. These stories are data banks of skill, knowledge and experience: much of our knowing is in our doing. We can learn from our own and each others' mistakes and successes, each others' ideas, experience, wisdom, and tackle and come to terms with our own problem areas. Although practice is continually aired – over a solitary coffee or beer with a colleague – we do not tell each other or ourselves the things which are really at our cutting edge of difficulty.

Sharing reflective writings and discussing them in depth enables the development of practice because the outcomes of reflection are taken back into practice – improving and developing it (see Kolb's learning cycle: Kolb 1984). Reflection reaches the stage, as Aeschylus said: 'Words can do no more . . . / Nothing remains but the act' (trans. 1999 p. 115). This gives a 'different way of being', or as another course participant put it: 'It seems like a new country, one which we've all been peering into for a long time.' Rita Charon, a general internist and medical professor, has shared her own reflective writings about pa-tients with them; some patients have also responded in writing. She reports this as having deepened and clarified understandings between herself and the patient (Charon 2000). Quite apart from specific aspects of learning, there are more general ones which reflective practice can offer:

> I have realised that we have to make the day-to-day parts of our work more enjoyable and varied. Writing, and the reflection it allows, has brought me a real pleasure – that's why I used to smile and now I can keep that joy and even the intimacy by writing what I've felt or seen and its ironies too.
>
> Clare

Reflective practice can enable us to:

- study our own decision-making processes;
- be constructively critical of our relationships with colleagues;
- analyse hesitations and skill and knowledge gaps;
- face problematic and painful episodes;
- identify learning needs.

Reflective practice will not provide neat answers to the conundrums of practice. It will not directly answer the question: 'what should I have done?' Yet more questions are likely to be thrown up, such as: 'Why did the maths teacher take so little care to hide his relationship with the pupil; what was going on there for him?' 'Perhaps I could have told the toddler a story about the dead baby in order to help her to understand; what story would have been right?' The episode about the high walkway in the East End was capped by another group member who recounted her own tale of how she turned to face a gang of threatening young people and asked the way (although she knew it); the frightening 'gang' were immediately transformed into kids who could not attack once they had communicated with her as a person. This supported the social worker to reassess her attitude to threatening-seeming people.

There is a paradox at the heart of reflective practice, about effective practice not being certain. We all know colleagues who always know what to do or say, and never say 'I don't know'. They are very rarely effective because of their inflexible need to be the one who knows. I am going to divide this basic paradox into three. In order to acquire confidence as an effective practitioner you:

- let go of certainty, in an environment where you feel safe enough
- look for something when you don't know what it is
- begin to act when you don't really know how you should act.

Reflective practice entails an embracing of: uncertainty as to what we are doing and where we are going; confidence to search for something when we have no idea what it is; the letting go of the security blanket of needing answers. This kind of work will lead to more searching questions, the opening of fascinating avenues to explore, but few secure answers.

> The goal of education, if we are to survive, is the *facilitation of change and learning*. The only person who is educated is the person who has learned how to learn: the person who has learned how to adapt and change; the person who has realised that no knowledge is secure, that only the process of seeking knowledge gives a basis for security. Changingness, a reliance on process rather than on static knowledge is the only thing that makes any sense as a goal for education in the modern world.
>
> Rogers 1969, p. 152

Experienced effective practice is about a willingness to: have faith in your own knowledge, skills and experience; trust the process you are engaged in (doctoring, teaching, etc.); relate to the student, client or patient with respect and unconditional positive regard (Rogers 1969).

It is also about a willingness to subject every action and thought both to reflection *in action* and self-respectful effective reflection *upon action* (Schon 1983). Reflection *in action* is the hawk in your mind constantly circling over your head watching and advising on your actions – while you are practising. Reflection *upon action* is the process with which this book is primarily concerned: a considering of events afterwards so that practice can effectively be enhanced (Schon 1983).

So self-respect plus an ability to stay with both uncertainty and difficult, painful, possibly shaming-seeming issues in reflection are needed. These are the areas to be thought about:

- *actions*: what you did
- *ideas*: what you thought about
- *feelings*: what all of it made you feel.

These three basic foundations have been expressed far more poetically as the basis for life:

> We live in deeds not years; in thoughts, not breaths;
> In feelings, not in figures on a dial.
> We should count time by heart throbs. He most lives
> Who thinks most – feels the noblest – acts the best.
>
> P. J. Bailey (1816–1902) *Festus*

Sophocles has been translated as saying: 'Between feeling and action there is thought' (*Antigone*). Our actions are effective if they arise from both feelings and thoughts. Emotions can too easily be marginalised in professional life:

> There is something rather odd about trying to get help from health workers who have not worked out their own feelings, or who deny them to themselves and others. Where do all those spontaneous feelings go and who is to say what damage they might be doing to the delicate internal workings of our minds if we continue to repress and suppress them . . . The key insights and changes in the way I view myself and my professional work have come through self-reflective work.
>
> Heller 1996, p. 365, 368

Uncomfortable Emotions to Reflect Upon

Powerful emotions sometimes arise within practice and within reflection upon practice. These can be difficult to handle, but it can be more developmental to work through them rather than push them away as inappropriate to a professional enquiry. Very strong emotion can initially appear to inhibit the ability to reflect and understand, however, as Andrew Eastaugh (1998a) found in his research into co-tutoring; he also found it well worth persevering:

> The idea that my emotions are a source of understanding has an exciting and novel ring for me. Exciting because it opens up the possibility . . . that the emotional part of me has a value outside my own personal attachment to it. . . . It is novel because my experience of the world of learning has been that emotions are at best, merely the icing on top of the cake, for decoration, self indulgence and treats, but not the real substance. Too much will make you sick and is unnecessary. At their worst they are a serious barrier to the real business of life – should be pushed aside and ignored.
>
> Eastaugh 1998a, p. 48

Anger can prove to be a useful if uncomfortable focus for reflection. Here is a Masters student reflecting later upon the effect of his reflective practice story-writing and work:

> As a result of reflecting upon these incidents I now understand much better how I have been dealing with anger and the effect it was having on me. I felt unable to express anger because I was afraid of making a fool of myself, afraid of losing control and because I want to be well

thought of. I feel that if I get angry with someone they will not like me. I want to be liked. I therefore tend to push my anger down inside. I have not been consciously aware of doing this and therefore have not been aware of how much anger I have been carrying. I have therefore not been able to explain the unpleasant feelings I have had when it has begun to rise to the surface.

I now know that it is not possible (or necessarily good) to please everybody all the time. I know the difference between telling someone I am angry and expressing the anger itself. I am able to recognise when I am angry, when I am suppressing it and the feelings that this causes. I feel more able to tell people when I am angry with them and that I can do this articulately.

Rod

And a doctor wrote a vehement and dramatic long-term 'diary' about his relationship with his Health Authority; when he later reflected upon it, he wrote: 'I am much less emotionally reactive in all these management meetings I have to go to, and certainly not as nervous!' Lindsay Buckell's 'expression of my passionate hatred of the current climate of fear and blame' (see p. 143) is another.

A GP (family practitioner) trainer, and supervisor for applications to fellowship of the British Royal College of General Practitioners, Keith Collett, encourages the writing of drafts of medical reports, responses to complaints and so on, so they can be discussed, reflected upon and redrafted:

This is incredibly useful to prevent registrars overstating support or condemnation for a patient. . . . They have a chance to reflect on how it will be received by the patient, their relatives, or their solicitor. . . . I encourage the first splenic draft to be written as I feel it has a healing and calming effect, and offers an opportunity for reflection. Too often dictaphones are used and the resultant text signed and sent without reflective reading.

Keith Collett

Anger is often seen to be an inappropriate professional emotion – beyond the professional boundary. Reflective practice is an appropriate locus for exploring it, and the other dangerous-seeming emotions.

Mark Purvis and the Death of Simon

The grown-ups stand around watching.
Grown-ups know what to do.

The grown-ups stand around watching.

Is that Simon lying on the pavement?
He has got blondie hair like Simon's.
The grown-ups stand around watching.

A boy has been run over, another kid says.
Is that Simon lying on the pavement? He *was* walking in front of me.
The grown-ups stand around watching.

Mrs Bailey puts a blanket over him – but I can still see his blondie hair.
She looks at me but before she can turn quickly to the other grown-ups,
     I can see she's scared.
'Send Mark away.'
What have I done wrong?

The grown-ups know what to do.
They send me away.

I run ahead alone.
Trying to find Simon.
I might not recognise him.
Pulling kids by their shoulders – no that's not him.
I speed up when I hear the ambulance siren.

'Simon's been run over.' Pete Williams said.
I run away, trying hard not to believe him.

How can Pete Williams tell who is lying there,
anyhow I saw *him* looking for *his* brother too.
Surely I would have recognised my own brother.

My teacher says 'Simon will be in his classroom'
But he isn't, so she smiles and cuddles me, warm and soft.
'It's alright Mark, they call ambulances for sprained ankles these days.'

When he came into the classroom everyone stopped and looked.
He didn't have to tell me.
I said 'Simon's dead', and he nodded, unable to speak.

                                                        Mark Purvis

Mark's poem concerns his brother's death when they were both small.
Mark (a GP trainer) needed to write about it in a professional
development situation to free himself from the way the unexplored
memory inhibited his ability as a doctor to cope with child deaths.
After he had read the poem to the group and we had discussed it, he
said this:

I had never before in detail talked about what I was feeling at the time when Simon died. Now I have written about it I can and do talk about it.

Simon and I had had an argument about a fortnight before he died. I'd asked Simon not to walk with me to school. You know what it's like, an older brother wants to be with his own friends and doesn't want to be seen taking care of his little brother. Until I did this writing I felt guilty about Simon's death – that it was my fault for not allowing him to walk with me.

In the past my feeling about Simon's death disabled me for dealing with the death of child patients. Everyone finds it difficult; but for me they used to bring all sorts of things to the surface. I remember one child who died, I was totally disabled and unable to cope with consultations with the parents. I cried with them, and told them about Simon and that I was crying for him.

The writing has made me feel completely different about Simon's death, has made me deal with it in a different way. I can now see I wasn't responsible; though my mother still feels very guilty that she didn't drive him to school that day. The time was right for me to write.

I didn't know I was carrying so much guilt. Now I know I don't need to carry it. I will cope differently now when a child patient dies.

Mark Purvis

Focus on Reflection

Mark was able to reinhabit his childish world again – speak in the voice of himself as a child to write his poem. This enables us to hear and empathise with the little boy in his bewilderment and pain. Can you imagine Mark being able to *talk* about Simon with anything like the power of his poem? This is essentially a written piece, in a poetic form. Through writing – a private quiet space – Mark was able to reinhabit his child self, speak once more in the voice of himself as a child.

Film-makers use this device to show a child's point of view: the camera is held at child height. Reflective practice has to do the same. The reflective practitioner has to be able to reinhabit their own skin at whatever time in their lives the event upon which they are reflecting happened; during training perhaps, or some other time way back in their past. They also need to have a go at seeing the world through the eyes of another – a student or patient perhaps. The funny thing is that one *can* re-experience an event, or experience another's vicariously. 'The past is [not] a foreign country. They do [not] do things differently there' (Hartley 1953, p. 1). My son used to think that everything in the past was black and white, and people walked jerkily, because they did in old films. Listen to Cocteau holding his own camera at child height:

> I thought of going along the street from the Rue Blanche to number 45, closing my eyes and letting my right hand trail along the houses and the lamp-posts as I always used to do when I came back from school. The experience did not yield very much and I realised that at that time I was small and that now my hand was placed higher and no longer encountered the same shapes. I began the manoeuvre again.
>
> Thanks to a mere difference of level, and through a phenomenon similar to that whereby a needle rubs against the grooves of a gramophone record, I obtained the music of memory and I discovered everything again: my cape, my leather satchel, the name of the friend who accompanied me, and the name of our teacher, some precise phrases I had said, the marbled cover of my note-book, the timbre of my grand-father's voice, the smell of his beard and the material of the dresses worn by my sister and mother, who were At Home on Tuesdays.
>
> (Cocteau 1930, p. 137)

Why Reflective Practice Now?

The grand stories of patriarchy/patriotism, religion, family and local ties no longer hold society together. We look to counsellors, therapists, teachers, clerics, life partners, GPs or social workers for essential support. Marriages founder and practitioners increasingly experience stress. These relationships now have the burden which a nexus of local and family community used to carry.

Faith in that great god science has also been shaken: 'Science, in my view, is now at the end of certainty' (Prigogine 1999, p. 26). There has been a powerful frontier between science (and the scientific professions such as medicine) and the arts since the Enlightenment. A blinkered view of what constitutes knowledge and experience cannot be held for much longer:

> If any of us are out of touch with any part of ourselves we are in an impoverished state. The dominant culture is scientific, but the scientist who concentrates on this side of themselves exclusively is as impoverished as is the musician or writer who concentrates only on the artistic.
>
> Robertson (Director of Medici String Quartet) 1999

The age of post-Newtonian belief in our ability to order ('master' even) our world is going. It led to the mess we and our world are in: the rise of clinical depression and the spread of the deserts, for example. The assumptions that an objective view of the world (Kantian) is 'grown-up', that we should shed our subjective view along with sand and water play, are being questioned (see also Sacks 1985, pp. 1–21).

The anthropologist James Clifford (1986) points out how the ethnographer can no longer stand on a mountaintop from which authoritatively to map human ways of life. Similarly practitioners cannot confidently diagnose and dictate from an objective professional or scientific standpoint. The enmeshment of culture and environment is total: no one is objective.

Clifford goes on to comment that 'since the seventeenth century, Western science has excluded certain expressive modes from its legitimate repertoire: rhetoric (in the name of "plain" transparent signification), fiction (in the name of fact), and subjectivity (in the name of objectivity). The qualities eliminated from science were localised in the category of "literature" ' (1986, p. 102). These categories are being brought back from that 300-year marginal position, to be embedded alongside the pure scientific approach.

Holistic coherent understandings which might support us out of our alienated mess are increasingly entertained. 'We now see the world as *our* world, rather than *the* world' (Reason 1988). Complementary healing considers our wholeness, not just within ourselves, but also within our environment and community. As Reason puts it (ibid.) 'we seek a knowing-in-action (and thinking-in-action) which encompasses as much of our experience as possible'.

Ideal professionals, gathering data on which to base their pedagogy, diagnosis or care, are rather like social anthropologists. Geertz suggested that successful ethnographers create a 'thick description': a web of 'sort of piled-up structures of inference and implication through which the ethnographer is continually trying to pick his way' (Geertz 1973, p. 7).

This knotted nexus has then to be understood and interpreted to some degree: 'a good interpretation of anything – a poem, a person, a history, a history, a ritual, an institution, a society – takes us into the heart of that of which it is the interpretation' (Geertz 1973, p. 7). An effective reflective practitioner attempts to understand the heart of their practice. Geertz points out, however, that understandings gained in this way are always partial; the deeper the inquiry, the less the inquirer realises they know and understand: *the more you know, the more you know you don't know*. Geertz stresses that it is vital not to generalise across cases but within them. Having got somewhere near the heart of the client's story or poem, the practitioner can then begin to act upon this understanding.

The practitioner writing about their work, sharing it with colleagues in order to offer insight, and relating this to a wider field professionally and politically, are together engaged in an activity rather like Reason's *co-operative inquiry method*, in which researcher and subject collaborate in all the stages of research, including reflecting on the experience and making sense of it (Reason 1988). The practitioner takes a full share of responsibility. All too often professionals act in the mould of traditional researcher; acting *on* people: collecting data, and coming to conclusions in camera.

'In this way, it may be possible to avoid providing care which is dry, barren and – perhaps the greatest sin of all – unimaginative' (Smyth 1996, p. 937). Effective reflective practice can enable the practitioner to provide care or education which is not a working out of their own needs and wants but is alert and alive to the client's or student's needs and wants, whether professed or not. It can enable the practitioner to use their skill, knowledge and experience creatively and lovingly, and to look forwards with a greater confidence.

Making Sense of Experience

Life does not really have a beginning, a middle and an end (Carroll 1865) – that is the prerogative of fiction – drama, novels, film. Writing and telling our stories is never quite as easy as the King of Hearts made out; but if we can have sufficient faith in ourselves, trust in the process, and respectful unconditional positive regard (Rogers 1969) for the people with whom we work, to create a beginning, the rest might well follow. Here is an evaluation of a reflective writing group:

> a different way of seeing: many insights, many views
> a sense of wonder at the creativity of so many people I had seen
> only as professional colleagues
> I am challenged to see others I meet with new eyes.
>
> a different way of hearing: many voices, many themes
> I have been moved by the quality of our listening and by the careful
> and gentle hearing of my own emerging voice.

a different way of being: many persons, an experience shared.
I have found a sense of integration in allowing the creative part of
myself which I had stifled to energise my life and work.
there is empowerment for deeper living in the shared silence,
laughter and tears.

Sheena

The camera focuses upon a drained doctor at the end of a long week.
She reaches into her lowest desk drawer and takes out something
which will enable her to cope, and to continue to see her profession as
growing and worthwhile. It is not a bottle, hypodermic syringe, or
pills. It is a pad of yellow paper and a pen. She starts to write. . . .

2

Principles of Reflective Practice

The sage offered her disciple tea, but did not stop pouring. 'Master, the cup is full!' 'You are just like this cup: overflowing,' the sage replied, 'there is no space for you to learn.'

Story from Chuang Tsu

We teach and write to become what and who we are. . . . The function (of pedagogy) is to invent the conditions of invention.

Wen-Song Hwu 1998, p. 37

Reflective practice is an educative process, often undertaken with a tutor. Tutors and students relate to each other within a particular paradigm, or model of teaching and learning, whether they are aware of it or not. This chapter examines and critiques a range of such models, and offers one which seems to work for reflective practice. The vital relationship between tutor and student is also addressed. At times the educational process is supported by a tutor, facilitator, supervisor or a peer either individually or in a group. At times the practitioner is reflecting alone on an issue, either in their reflective diary, in the car driving home from work, or in the middle of the night. This chapter addresses educational relationships, and finally the context in which teaching and learning takes place, and some ways in which this can be understood and handled.

A Muddle of Models

Any involvement in education, whether as teacher or learner, can only be undertaken from within a particular approach or understanding of the processes, and the end-products expected or hoped for. Sometimes the parties concerned are only too aware of their own image, metaphor or model of education; sometimes they accept a 'given' model without knowing what it is. In order to be involved in an effective, consistent educational process, I suggest it is invaluable to be

24

aware of the model used. The following is a description of some well-known ones, and the one which this book is recommending.

The chalk and talk model

This is a traditional view, one which we all recognise from our schooling and much of our university education. Paolo Freire called it the banking model (1972), Fox the transfer theory (1983), and Rowland (1999) the didactic model. This is when teachers who know the answers attempt to funnel them directly into the heads of students who don't know. Another way of expressing the didactic model is to call it the 'moulding theory' (Fox 1983) in which the learner is like a piece of putty to be formed by the educator. The tutor retains control of the learning situation; the learners are not considered with respect and are not expected to have creative ideas of their own. A hierarchically determined system of knowledge and social status is reinforced in such a system, and the impact and body of that knowledge is predetermined.

Rocky path model

This has also been called the 'exploratory model' (Rowland 1993), or the *fofo* way of teaching (f*** off and find out). Rowland quotes a DES document as describing it thus:

> The broad objectives of the work were discussed with the (students) but then they were put in a position of finding their own solutions.
>
> DES 1978, para 3

The student in this model is being respected (possibly) and given autonomy, but probably not enough guidance and support; the tutor is not primarily involved in the processes of learning.

Hey presto model

We live, teach and learn in a consumer culture with a market orientation in which people, practitioners included, are bombarded with new practices and new ways of being all the time. It is a time of individuation: appearing to celebrate difference yet fostering conformity. We can choose to change and mould our lives (even our bodies) in ways never before possible: to fashion new identities for ourselves. Outward signs (packaging) are important: what things are called, what they look like. Market-place understandings dominate. We can buy 'care' these days, even 'love' according to adverts of a particular pal-liative nursing organisation as I write. And the word 'Trust' is used of those who hold the purse strings. This has had a huge impact upon education. Organisations 'deliver' courses on the assumption that the commodity bought will directly improve their service, as if it were the latest fertiliser.

Competencies, skills, and fully developed reflective practice abil-ities all do need to be acquired by practitioners. But in this system they are seen as products or commodities – *things* like bricks or vitamin tablets – to be bought with education currency without primary atten-tion being paid to fundamental educational *processes* which enable their development, such as tutor–student relationships and the learn-ing environment.

In this system teachers are assessed on the *value* they offer the consumer. But the *objects* the students consume are all too often *signs*, communicating social position and worth. *Who I am seen to be*, and *what I can get as a result of this course* (e.g. a better job) have become more important than the innate value of the intellectual enquiry un-dertaken. This reminds me of a social worker's client who bemoaned she couldn't take up jogging for the sake of her health, although she dearly wanted to, because she could not afford the gear. She had to be seen to be doing it right.

Giving students set proformas, lists of prompts, questions or areas which must be covered in reflective practice will stultify them, make them passive and feel unrespected. Reflective practice can become mere training if the questions about practice being asked and an-swered are created by others. It can appear to be liberating – understand yourself and learn and be more effective – but in fact it means understand yourself in terms of those in authority and mould your practice towards the wants and needs of the system.

Testing and checking up on students to see if they have acquired the required competencies will only endorse this subordinate sense. I cringe whenever I hear a tutor/facilitator say 'I get the students to. . . . In this situation the student is manipulated in what might appear as a situation in which they 'choose'. In fact the scenario is set, the student only has to paint the right bits the right colours, or join up the dots; they are not respected as autonomous beings. The 'shopkeeper' who is delivering the 'package' of the course ends up with a neat pile of pigeon-hole sized submissions with predetermined areas accounted for: evidence that the students have learned this, this and this –

products which can then be consumed by both practitioner and assessor. It has quite probably been a paper exercise only; but that does not matter as there is no continuity between course and practice – no one to see practice has changed or developed; what matters is the product: the neatly ticked boxes look right.

Our *problems* cannot be *solved*, however many *problem-solving* exercises we undertake. Problems, issues, relationships can all be aired and examined constructively, but to see the process as a straight line from *identification of need* to *problem solved* is effectively to prevent any constructive learning.

The values basis of this functional competence model is technical-rational, utilitarian and instrumental. Students in such a situation will always be short-changed and manipulated. A full educational process has to be undergone with everyone, however painfully and expensively. There are no short cuts, no prestidigitation. But this next model, for all its wonderful features, is not The Answer either; but of course there is no Right Answer.

Path to freedom model

Carl Rogers described a process of *personal* liberation in his writing about education and psychotherapy (1969). Paolo Freire developed a model of effective education which he called *problem posing:* a liberating *political* process (1972) (it must be remembered Freire was working in a politically revolutionary situation in the 1960s):

> Authentic reflection considers neither abstract man (sic) nor the world without men, but men in their relations with the world. . . . That which had been perceived objectively but had not been perceived in its deeper implications (if indeed it was perceived at all) begins to 'stand out' assuming the character of a problem and therefore of challenge. Thus men begin to single out elements from their 'background awarenesses' and to reflect upon them. These elements are now objects of men's consideration, and, as such, objects of their action and cognition. . . . The banking method emphasises permanence and becomes reactionary; problem-posing education – which accepts neither a 'well-behaved' present nor a pre-determined future – roots itself in the dynamic present and becomes revolutionary.
>
> Freire 1972, pp. 55–7

A group of my students echoed this when they called a course 'consciousness raising'. And such reflective practice can lead to very real change – both to the individual and to the organisation or state upon which they might act. Freire was right that education should be rooted in the present, and should pose problems about our lives here and now: this is the stuff of reflective practice.

Effective reflective practice is a critical process – active and dynamic in a wide sphere. Practitioners question and problematise themselves, their roles and those in authority over them – the political, social and professional situations in which they find themselves. Once they are doing this they will hopefully no longer be able uncritically to accept a situation, nor just moan about it. The role of reflective practice is to encourage them to *do* something about it, and that means not just keep the fridge in better order so the wrong injection is never given again, but question whatever aspects of the system they can. One of my group members during one of her very first 'six minute' writings realised she had to change her job. She not only got one much more suited to her, but also one in which she could and did implement significant change for her staff.

Marx recommended a 'relentless criticism of all existing conditions, relentless in the sense that the criticism is not afraid of its own findings and just as little afraid of conflict with the powers that be' (Marx 1962, p. 212). Carr and Kemmis (1986) with their theory of critical social science and *praxis* of *action research* drew upon the work of Marx and Freire. Based on the work of the philosopher Habermas, this is a political-social understanding (critical theory) rather than the personal one developed by psychoanalysis or therapy (as in Rogers, for example):

> The purpose of critique then is to provide a form of therapeutic self-knowledge which will liberate individuals from the irrational compulsions of their individual history through a process of critical self-reflection. . . . Critique is aimed at revealing to individuals how their beliefs and attitudes may be ideological illusions that help to preserve a social order which is alien to their collective experience and needs. By demonstrating how ideological forces generate erroneous self-understandings, ideology critique aims to reveal their deceptive nature and so strip them of their power. . . .
>
> Action research is simply a form of self-reflective inquiry undertaken by participants in social situations in order to improve the rationality and justice of their own practice, their understanding of these practices, and the situations in which these practices are carried out.
>
> Carr and Kemmis 1986, pp. 138–9, 162

Action research, as its name implies, is more research based than reflective practice, with a 'self-reflective spiral of cycles of planning, acting, observing and reflecting' (Carr and Kemmis 1986, p. 165), but it does offer a model for reflective practice.

So what's the problem?

It seems an unwarranted certainty to consider that the 'compulsions of (participants') individual history' *before* they begin on a 'process of critical self-reflection' are any more 'irrational' than those they will be enabled to arrive at *after* the process. It could also be said that *all* 'beliefs and attitudes may be ideological illusions that help to preserve a social order which is alien to their collective experience and needs,' *however* they are acquired – through reflective practice or otherwise.

Freire was certain, in the political sphere, Carl Rogers in the personal (see below), and Carr and Kemmis in both, that progress is taking place towards a particular goal of personal or political productive change and development. This model asserts that reflective practice (or critical action research) will automatically bring people in a upward curve from ignorance to knowledge, from political passivity to effective action. But this certainty is based on nothing more than an assumption that a greater understanding of ourselves or the world will make things better. In the personal sphere this model asserts that these can be *self-actualising* processes in which each practitioner will find the *real me*, the *me* they were intended to be.

The very notion of *me* is problematic, however. *I* am not a static entity, but in the process of being created every day as social and political forces impact upon me: *I* am a story I tell and retell every day, with fresh facets and new viewpoints each time. *I* am not so much a thing – static in shape, form and time – but more a verb – not *me* but *to me*. I was always fascinated by the ability of *Startrek* heroes to travel by transforming their physical selves. Perhaps I too can say 'beam me up Scotty', since my self (even if not my body) is in constant flux.

Reflective practice has, contrariwise to the 'path to freedom' model, been accused of being a way of encouraging practitioners to accept their lot, however bad – a form of quietism. People cannot be 'empowered' or 'given a voice' by a more powerful other (tutor, for example); they can only give it to themselves – *take it*, that is. According to this critique:

> We become active knowing subjects but now we subjectify ourselves rather than being subjected by others. We think we have mastered the power that imposes itself from 'outside' only to find that it is now

'inside'. We have the power, indeed the obligation, to exercise our 'freedom' but we are not thereby empowered to affect our social and political environment.

                                                        Usher *et al.* 1997, p. 87

Practitioners can become trapped in that they learn to control themselves to work according to the wants and needs of the system, rather than responding to exterior control. Power is a slippery, omnipresent thing, and does not necessarily do what it *appears* to do. The practitioner, the tutor and the curriculum designer have to be sensitive to undercurrents and meta-levels in education: 'the most effective forms of power are those which are not recognised as powerful but as enabling or "em-powering" . . . The drive for emancipation may itself become oppressive' (Usher *et al.* 1998, pp. 87, 190). And:

> Practices of 'freedom' or 'authenticity', or search for a 'real' self are in fact rule-bound examples of governance of self by self through self-surveillance. While advertised as a route to liberty or autonomy, [they] offer strictly coded forms of self-governance and regulation.
>
>   Bleakley 2000 (in press)

Another critique is that if people feel they are being accorded time and space and facilitation to examine their problems and fears, they will feel grateful to their employers for being so thoughtful. The very examination itself may defuse the strength of their potentially rebellious feeling against an autocratic or unjust system, and they will become complaisant. They may reflect upon a narrow range of professional issues, change their practice and feel they are doing their job better: their clients are more satisfied, and their managers are getting value for money from their labour. British Victorian Quakers made millions from chocolate, by managing their staff paternally and indulgently – telling them they were treated particularly well, thus creating a docile work team who felt it was worth working hard for their masters. Another anti-reflective practice argument might be that tying practitioners up in a web of stories half remembered from their working lives, combined with conflicting views of colleagues about their practice, is far from liberating, but increases guilt and confusion.

Carr himself called his project 'essentially an enlightenment project' (Carr 1995, p. 121); such a project assumes a knowledge of what *rationality* is: we do not have this knowledge. The very notion of *enlightenment* maintains a confidence that the 'light' I am in now is any better than the 'dark' I was in previously, and that what my tutors tell me is 'light' is 'light' indeed for me.

The reflective practice educational process is one of constant reflexive self-examination – actions, thoughts, feelings, motives, assumptions. In order to be critical of my own personal, social and political situation I have to be able to stand outside it – to some extent. Of course I can't do this fully, whatever contortions I attempt. No one can critique one paradigm while within it: no sailor can propel a yacht by blowing into the sails. We all wear culturally tinted lenses through which we view the world: there is no way we can take off our emerald (or crimson or aquamarine) spectacles and see the world, our actions, and those of others *as they really are*. Perhaps Alice was the only one who managed fully effective reflexivity and critical emancipation: by crawling right through the looking-glass and experiencing herself and her world from the other side – not an action we can imitate.

No tutor (facilitator or supervisor) can guide anyone else towards their own emancipation, no one can have this wisdom or power; nor can it be an aspect of the curriculum. There can be no specific way of working (however wonderful reflective practice may be) which supports another to 'free' themselves from their social, political and psychological constraints. Educative reflective practice can yet lead to greater agency, responsibility, self-understanding and self-confidence.

Through the looking-glass model

The previous models made assumptions which, I have suggested, we need to shed, and missed out other vital elements. Effective education is based upon both tutor and learner being able to make as many aspects as they can of their situation, and themselves, strange and different – in order to study them. The model I am suggesting here is more like a question than a theory. It uses themes from the other models but leaves the ends open.

This is an approach in which the learner is encouraged to be as reflexively aware as possible of their own social, political and psychological position, and to question it, as well as their environment. In this dynamic state things will appear to be strange, back to front, and to operate in unusual ways: they should do so. One of my students called it 'making the ordinary extraordinary'. It is this very strange-seemingness or extraordinariness which will enable students to formulate their own questions about the situations in which they find themselves (reflective), and the self they find there (reflexive). These questions are almost bound to be different from the ones they thought they might ask before they undertook the reflective and reflexive processes. The questioning will be undertaken in a spirit of enquiry which will lead to a process of more specific, usefully appropriate and meaningful questioning. Interim answers will appear, but will still be markers along the way rather than finishing posts.

Learners are supported to discover ways of finding out what they feel they need to know at any point (from literature, from knowledgeable others whether other students or external authorities, from the tutors themselves). This can be as widely understood as the students wish – popular culture, as well as literature and so on – all carry vital data.

Many of the elements of the previous models will come into play in an eclectic way in this one. There is no comfortable beginning, middle and end to this process, and the *characters* and *places* are not clearly delineated and set, as they are in the classic stories (myths, fairy stories). Individuals keep taking on different roles – the tutor may be didactic teacher at one point, and equal friend along the way at another; a colleague may be the enemy at one time and fascinating authority at another. The student may think they are well on the way to understanding something, and then realise they have to stand one step back and view the matter from a fresh standpoint and begin all over again with a new set of questions.

The student and tutor are both engaged in a process, and their roles are far more equal than in the other models. Knowledge and understanding are seen as something they are constructing together according to the wants and needs of the student. Their relationship and their roles will constantly be under reflexive review.

Three foundations

Three of the foundations of the *through the looking-glass model* are:

- certain uncertainty
- serious playfulness
- unquestioning questioning.

Certain uncertainty: the one thing we can be certain of is uncertainty. In a reflexive, reflective process you begin to act when you don't know how you should act. Any interim goals are constructed in the light of material arising from the process, rather than there being a predetermined goal: a creative, dynamic situation, though perhaps less comfortable than having a clear road mapped out ahead. Participants on a course, or supervisees, who are not used to experiencing the uncertainty of not having a structure provided, may feel they have a 'right' to demand such a structure. Staff may need time and gentle encouragement towards gaining the confidence required to create their own structure of appropriate and stretching enquiry. This confidence is only acquired to a degree – 'good-enough confidence'.

The confident, effective practitioner is the one who is able to respond flexibly and creatively to a range of influences, needs and wants of clients or colleagues, and unforeseen events and forces. A practitioner who thinks they know the right answers all the time is bound to be wrong. To people willing to 'not know' all the time, all sorts of things are possible.

Serious playfulness: the only way to make this uncertainty dynamic is by being playful and willing to try a range of things: accepting reflective practice as a process of looking for something when you don't know what it is. An adventurous spirit leads onto that trackless moorland which education has come to be, rather than a walled or hedged field (Usher *et al.* 1997, p. 3), and discover some pertinent questions. Sacred positions are not taken seriously here: anything and everything is brought into question – even ourselves – leaving no room for self-importance. There is, however, only so much we can do to alter our own situation, that of others, and the wider political one, by reflexivity, reflection, or education: our power is unlimitedly limited. This playfulness is essentially serious: we are talking professional and personal development, not Ludo.

Unquestioning questioning: we accept, unquestioningly, that the process will be one of questioning. It is our questions which determine which way we will set out across the moorland, and therefore what we are likely to find along the way. These findings beget more questions. Reflective practice is a process of laying open to question our own and others' daily actions, and those of the organisations in which we work: a willingness 'to risk abandoning previous "truths" and sit with *not knowing*' (Gerber 1994, p. 290). This 'not knowing' is active and enquiring – rather like the small child's iconoclastic eternal *but why?*

Paradoxically the way to find out about ourselves is through forgetting ourselves. This is a creative letting go of everyday assumptions about who we are, in order to be open to the discovery of other possible selves – the myselves of whom I am not habitually aware, the myself I might be, and the selves I am becoming. Only when 'the cup is empty' can the practitioner receive, hear what is being said, perceive what is happening.

These three oxymorons underpin an aesthetic and ethical approach to education rather than a logical or instrumental one. The approach assumes and requires 'artistry' (to use Schon's word) from the reflective practitioner. It is a way of telling and retelling one's story, in relation to the stories of others and that of the situation in which the writers of these stories find themselves.

Socrates' pedagogic method was based on just such oxymorons; here is Meno struggling with Socrates' ruthless method of enquiry into the nature of 'virtue':

Meno: Socrates, even before I met you they told me that in plain truth you are a perplexed man yourself and reduce others to perplexity. . . .

Socrates: It isn't that knowing the answers myself, I perplex other people. The truth is rather that I infect them also with the perplexity I feel myself. . . . So with virtue now. I don't know what it is. You may have known before you came into contact with me, but now you look as if you don't. Nevertheless I am ready to carry out, together with you, a joint investigation and inquiry into what it is.

Meno: But how will you look for something when you don't in the least know what it is? How on earth are you going to set up something you don't know as the object of your search? To put it another way, even if you come right up against it, how will you know that what you have found is the thing you didn't know?

Plato trans. 1958, pp. 127–8.

Looking-Glass Ways of Being

Alice did not stop to study her reflection before she went through the looking-glass. Had she done so her reflection would merely have been a back-to-front image of her accustomed self. But having crawled right through the glass she encountered a world where everything 'was as different as possible' (Carroll 1865, p. 122). She learned a great deal from the way familiar things and situations being so different ensured she could not take anything for granted. For example, when she wanted to reach an attractive small hill, she bumped into the house again every time. She learned to walk away from anything she wanted to reach (Carroll 1865, pp. 132–6).

A reflective, educational process does not allow anything to be taken for granted. We need to walk away from things in order for them to come into focus. Why?, how?, what?, who?, where?, when? need to be asked of everything – all the time. Alice had to ask these questions because nothing worked as she expected; we have to push ourselves into this state of incredulity.

Through the looking-glass education requires self-respect in both learners and tutors; a willingness and ability to work either autonomously or in collaboration with whomever – as appropriate; and the confidence to ask questions which might lead anywhere. It tends towards the aesthetic rather than the purely functional. The very questioning playfulness, rooted in uncertainty as to where the process will lead, is essentially non-functional (however valuable its outcomes might be) because to be functional it would have to know what the goals were from the start. It is a physical (rather than purely cognitive), passionate (rather than purely intellectual), context-bound (rather than goal-driven) artistic process requiring flair, style and intuition. It is therefore aesthetic because both learner and tutor appreciate and explore the nuances of people's sense of themselves, their environment, and their experience. Winter has defined the imagination and the aesthetic in this context as: 'a universal capacity for the creative interpretation and representation of human experience' (Winter *et al.* 1999, p. 199).

It is pleasurable, as one would expect of an aesthetic experience – rather exciting even: come to my party. But, of course, in keeping with all I have said about the *through the looking-glass model*, and as I stated above, we can't totally make things strange (or extraordinary) by viewing them reflexively and reflectively. We are all culture-bound – physically, socially, psychologically and spiritually. We might change that culture, but can never make ourselves culture-free. Nor can we be fully uncertain, playful or questioning – our lives would fall apart. But we can do a great deal in that direction: in a game of *what if. . . .*

We have examined the educational situation at a *meta* level: that is, some of the assumptions both teachers and learners make about the processes in which they are engaged. We could call this the kind of plot or story line of education, which is being constructed with a certain set of characters in a particular place. We will now look at (a) the characters within the teaching and learning situation – the relationship between teacher and learner; and (b) the place in which they are working – the context.

Educational Relationships

The role of the teacher is not to tell others what to do, not to issue edicts, nor to assist in the constitution of prophesies, promises, injunctions and programs. The task of the teacher is not to affirm prevailing general politics of teaching but to question critically the self-evident, disturb the habitual, dissipate the familiar and accepted, making the strange familiar and the familiar strange. . . . The classroom is therefore a place of invention rather than reproduction.

Wen-Song Hwu 1998, p. 33

Carl Rogers maintains it is the relationship which ensures the success or failure of a teaching and learning situation:

The initiation of such learning rests not upon the teaching skills of the leader, not upon scholarly knowledge of the field, not upon curricular planning, not upon use of audiovisual aids, not upon the programmed learning used, not upon lectures and presentations, not upon an abundance of books, though each of these might at one time or another be utilised as an important resource. No, the facilitation of significant learning rests upon certain attitudinal qualities that exist in the personal relationship between the facilitator and the learner.

Rogers 1969, p. 153

This opinion was borne out by a group of community nurses in training for reflective practitioner facilitation. One said 'the person of the teacher is the vehicle' for the learning, and another that it is the 'being' of the tutor which creates the success or failure of the teaching and learning situation.

I had asked the group to tell each other, in pairs, about significant teaching and learning situations in their lives: both effective and dreadful. There was animated agreement about the underlying principles of good teaching; these were when the tutor:

- is able to create a relationship with each student which feels 'special' even when it is known to be one-way, i.e. the student knows the tutor does not feel specially about any particular student;
- 'gives of themselves', not just taking on the 'role' of tutor, but being a whole person;
- engenders confidence and respect;
- wishes to challenge both students and themselves as tutor, at the same time as valuing, being respectful of, being patient with, and offering praise to the students: an unconditional positive regard (Rogers 1969);
- makes the learning pleasurable, clear and significant; to do this they must love their subject.

The group turned to the qualities which they felt made for a destructive rather than a positive teaching and learning relationship. These cause students to close in on themselves and feel negatively about the subject, possibly lastingly. They were when the tutor:

- has no understanding of or interest in the student;
- bullies, humiliates or even abuses the student with personal intrusions, generally wields power negatively;
- has a set, inflexible agenda, a mission with no regard of the needs of the student;
- lacks confidence in the student as a person;
- transfers their own anxiety onto the student.

These lists were created by one group of eight nurses in half an hour, demonstrating how we feel intuitively we know effective teaching from bad: this transcends any cognitive understanding or articulation of methodological models. The best teachers and practitioners are reflexive and reflective. These qualities can be enhanced and fostered by education.

The issues of fundamental importance for the success of a teaching and learning situation are the environment the tutor is able to create, and their relationship with the student – one of trust, respect, openness, confidence and security – both ways. Of course we are here talking about a *good-enough* relationship: every tutor is only human, but if the foundations are there, then inevitable tutor errors and misjudgements are much more likely to be forgiven; and it might prove a learning situation for both.

Peter Abbs laid greater emphasis on the role of the student than that of the tutor, but still stresses the same principles:

> Education is not primarily concerned with the accumulation of facts and techniques but rather with the expression and clarification of individual experience. The centre of education resides in the individual. If we are to achieve a genuinely human education we must return again and again to the person before us, the child, the adolescent, the adult, the individual who is ready, however dimly and in need of however much support, to adventure both further out into his experience and further into it, who is ready, in some part of himself, to risk himself in order to become more than he now is. The teacher, the tutor can provide the conditions and the support for such a journey – but the journey itself can only be made by the assenting and autonomous individual.
>
> Abbs 1974, p. 5

I think this is very similar to Rogers' view. After all, if the tutor wants to 'return again and again to the . . . individual' then they must be the kind of tutor my group wanted, and Rogers endorsed.

My own team of Masters (Medical Science) tutors asked an Education colleague to run an in-service training reflexive (and reflective) session with us. We each drew how we viewed our role as educators. One drew a candle – the educator as lighting the darkness; one a map and compass – teacher as guide through rough places; one a church – initiating others into the holy of holies; and another a gardener watering a tree. These are all metaphors for educational practice in which the educator nurtures, supports and initiates the weaker other; the tutor is *enlightened guide*. I remember my drawing was of me with my arms outstretched inviting everyone to come to an exciting party. Alan Bleakley has added to this list: 'I have always imagined my own teaching in terms of contemporary jazz (post-bop): opening theme with chorus – long improvisation – chorus – coda. I like the idea of strange harmonies, dissonances combined with resonances, melodies that lose themselves in improvisation but are echoed throughout, and then restated at the end of the piece' (personal communication).

Modelling

One role an educator takes (often unwittingly) is that of model: whatever a teacher is teaching they are providing a role model to their students of their side of the relationship, and their expectations of the student side. This is a powerful process; the lists above of good and bad learning situations show how students do not forget their model best and the worst teachers. They may spend the rest of their lives unconsciously attempting to emulate and be unlike these vital figures in their development. My best teacher was very matter of fact and straightforward but not motherly, and humorous: she taught biology and I shall never forget her impassioned account of earthworms copulating under the moon. She brought the subject alive with stories and images. My worst teacher was a real chalk and talk didact and we dared hardly move, cough or hiccup during her lessons, let alone ask a question; she managed to make a fascinating subject boring with her flat instructive tone. To this day I think historical romances must be turgid: she recommended us to read them to widen our understanding of the era about which she was instructing us. The influence of those two is probably clearly discernable in this book.

The teacher is here seen to be our most important companion in education. I now wish to turn to the terrain we explore together.

Landmarks on the Syllabus Moor

A country area with no paths can seem to be a confusion of walls, sheeptracks and tors. If a walker was looking down from a helicopter, the small area would seem to make more sense – walls joining up to make comprehensible fields with a gate for each, for example. If our walker took a trip in a light aircraft, higher up in the sky, then clarity of the whole walk could be obtained. Adult education has recently been likened to 'moorland', rather than the 'field' it used to be called (Usher *et al.* 1997). The helicopter or light-aircraft view offered by a heuristic model, or a meta-understanding of the situation, can be useful here.

Stephen Rowland (1999, 2000) has suggested that under all circumstances both tutor and students might understand their resources for learning as a triangle of three areas:

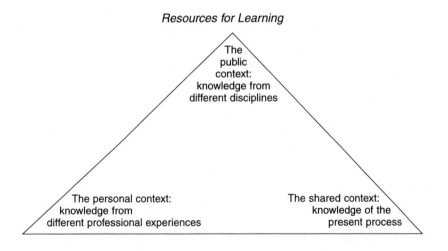

Resources for Learning

Adapted from Rowland 2000, p. 61

The *public area of knowledge* is, in principle, open to everyone through public texts, whether government documents, or professional and academic papers and books. Interpretations of these may vary, and some professionals will be more knowledgeable in certain areas than others. But if an area is disputed, the text can be referred to as arbiter. It is vital that reflective practice be embedded within this public arena, that it does not become a merely confessional personal journey.

The *personal area of knowledge* is private, known only to the individual. Much of the material of reflective practice belongs in this arena. These are the things that happened to the individual: knowledge of the situation, people involved, and the thoughts and feelings involved, belong in the mind of that individual. The process of examining this area might be the reflective one of laying any aspect of the situation open to question; or it may be reflexive: questioning one's own impulses, attitudes, assumptions and so on. The individual is the authority on these matters.

The *shared area of knowledge* is the 'process of the group's work', or that of the teaching and learning pair. Each individual within a group or duo has their own private set of stories of their own lives – personal and professional: this is the personal area of knowledge. In association with the other(s) a shared set of stories, assumptions, principles and so on is built up. All those present remember how they struggled to grasp the difference between reflection and reflexion, for example; or when Sue shouted at Bob for assuming she was late because of childcare; they feel they have their own group way of doing things – tacitly understood – for example, sitting in silence reflecting deeply when appropriate rather than rushing to come up with immediate answers. This knowledge and understanding is available only to the group members, but is shared within that group – no one member has more information or rights over it than another.

The *shared* area is often missed out for reflexive consideration. Yet addressing it, whether in a 1:1 situation like supervision, or in a group, can be invaluable. People can only learn when they are confident, respected and valued, and to an extent control the process of learning. Exposing the educational process (including the role of the tutor) to scrutiny can enable participants to take a degree of control: say what they want out of a teaching and learning situation, and attempt to redress anything which they feel is going wrong. The tutor can be enabled to adapt their methods or syllabus to the needs and wants of their student(s). This can be an invaluable area for any reflexive and reflective practitioner to develop within their practice, enabling them to gain and act upon effective feedback from colleagues and clients/patients/students.

The focusing on any one of these areas will clearly be different in different situations. Within reflective practice the *personal arena* may be the one mostly concentrated upon, though material from the *public domain* will usefully be drawn upon to develop or extend ideas and critique existing ones, and ensure their burgeoning understandings are embedded in the wider social, professional and political sphere. For example, my reflective practice students pursue information about areas in which they've realised they are particularly interested and don't know enough about – the ethics of an area, for example, or a particular form of analgesic in childbirth – by seeking journal papers or books, or consulting others (authorities whether by experience or academic/professional prominence). A reflexive examination of the *shared domain* – the process which is being undertaken with the tutor (whether group or 1:1) – can provide a model for a similar examination of any process in which learners find themselves.

A tutor who is aware of these three contexts can harness and drive them to both their own and their students' advantage. A student can use them to broaden their awareness within, and response to, learning situations.

Awareness of different ways of functioning within the three contexts can further enhance understanding and ability to maximise teaching and learning efficacy and interest. Within the *public* context, *reason* comes to the fore. Within the *shared* and the *personal* contexts, actions, thoughts and feelings are all appropriate for consideration. Examining what was done, thought and felt about a specific situation will help to explore dark corners in personal professional experience, shared group experiences, and in the political situations in which we work.

> Reflective practice is the public recognition and interrogation of the *e*ffects of *a*ffect within action [emphasis in original].
>
> Usher *et al.* 1997, p. 220

Conclusion

Marilyn Pietroni gives a useful set of 'nature and aims of professional education' (1995):

- to provide a containing environment in which individual practitioners are given the opportunity of recovering or establishing creative individual thought
- to offer partnerships in learning between educators and learners
- to provide a learning environment in which the log-jams and messiness of day-to-day practice can be faced and scrutinised in detail

- to provide continuous workshop environments (Schon's practicum) in which new ideas and approaches can be explored before and after their use (the double-feedback loop)
- to enable the nature of the organisational structures and defences that frame the work to be examined in relation to identified tasks
- to educate for a context of continuous change in which professional categories and languages, and organisational structure, are constantly by definition under erasure.

Pietroni 1995, p. 48

This chapter has gone some way towards examining some of the underpinnings of educational situations: the relationships, the context, and the structure of assumptions within which learner and tutor might be working (or playing) together. There is no one way of getting the education business right: eclecticism is a valuable approach. But attention to these vital areas, in particular to mutual respect and authority, and to a genuine openness as to end-product, are likely to enable effective reflective practice:

A disciple, who went to learn at the feet of the great master, became frustrated because she never knew how long meditation would last. The master always rang a bell – sometimes after five minutes, sometimes five hours. The disciple became so infuriated that one day she grabbed and rang the bell when *she* wanted meditation to end. The master bowed to her. She had learned.

3

Pushing to Creative Limits

You understand how to fly using wings, but you have not yet seen how to fly without them. You understand how to act from knowledge, but you have not yet seen how to act from not-knowing. Look at empty space. It is in emptiness that light is born. If you are open to everything you see and hear, and allow this to act through you, even gods and spirits will come to you, not to speak of men.

Chuang Tsu trans. 1974, p. 68

The term *reflective practice* is not a terribly useful one. The metaphor it embodies is limited: a mirror reflection is merely the image of an object directly in front of it – faithfully reproduced back-to-front. The process explored in this book is a creative adventure right through to *looking-glass-land* the other side of the silvering. Such reflective practice can take us out of our own narrow range of experience and help us to perceive experiences from a range of viewpoints and potential scenarios. It can do this by harnessing a vital human drive – to create stories about our lives, and communicate them. This chapter discusses the *through the looking-glass process* of reflective practice, the role of stories and fiction in our lives, and an introduction to how to use them in reflective practice.

Perhaps this approach should be called *flexive*. Flexion means 'alteration, change, modification', and 'a bend, curve, and a joint'; whereas reflection means 'the action of turning (back) or fixing the thoughts on some subject' (*Shorter Oxford Dictionary*), with the associated definition of the inverted reproduction of an image. This makes *reflection* sound as dynamic as *rumination* – a goat chewing smelly cud.

The mirror image model of reflection suggests there is a me *out there* practising in the big world, and a reflected me *in here* in my head thinking about it. If I think about it constructively enough I will be able to alter my practice and my relation to you out there in the big world. This model is located in Cartesian duality: *this* in dialogue with *that*, *in* and *out*, or *here* and *there*. Here is an ancient Zen text:

> You must first forsake the dualities of: self and others, interior and exterior, small and large, good and bad, delusion and enlightenment, life and death, being and nothingness.
>
> Tsai Chi Chung trans. 1994, p. 95

The model I am suggesting involves far wider potential interactions, opens up more developmental reflexive and reflective space than is possible with a Cartesian-based one. 'Reflection is the central dynamic in intentional learning, problem solving and validity testing through rational discourse' (Mezirow 1981, p. 4). Yes, true, but there is an awful lot more than just the 'rational' for us to explore. Professionals cannot fully crawl through the looking-glass – only fictional Alice could do that. But they can still explore the wide and rather perplexing other side of reflection.

Through the Looking-Glass

> Alice was through the glass, and had jumped lightly down into the Looking-Glass room. . . . Then she began looking around and noticed that what could be seen from the old room was quite common and uninteresting, but that all the rest was as different as possible. For instance, the pictures on the wall next the fire seemed to be all alive.
>
> Carroll 1865, pp. 122–3

Effective reflective practice is a process of making the ordinary of one's experience seem extraordinary, making it 'as different as possible'. At the same time it makes the extraordinary, the foreign, of another's experience more comprehensible, and close. It is storying which enables this to happen. Actions, interactions, professional episodes, memories even from long ago, spiritual elements, thoughts, ideas and feelings *are*, or are about to become, 'all alive' – both to the story-teller and to their audience.

Practitioners open themselves to relating to a wide range, within both their own experience and that of others, through this dynamic process. They recognise that we have many different ways of knowing things, all of them valid. Nothing is irrelevant, however insignificant or personal it might appear to be: assumptions as to what is relevant or significant thwart the process.

> When I realised my mother's cancer was terminal I considered resigning my job to help care for her. Realising that wasn't possible I then had to consider how to survive over the next few months. I'd

considered resigning because I'd been struggling with being a doctor and who it had turned me into. Creative writing has helped me see what was happening, share it with others and begin to find a way through. I discovered that I could barely engage with my own emotions and fears any more. I had developed a protective shell through which I couldn't feel but which allowed me to keep going. The reality of a very significant loss in my life meant I had to feel it and understand my self again.

Clare

We do not practise with one part of ourselves, and live a personal life with another: all the elements of ourselves are each a part of the other. They might be linked in surprising ways, moreover, by irrelevant-seeming factors. The insignificant-seeming incident, which has oddly always been remembered, may well be the most vital one for a practitioner to explore.

The *through the looking-glass* reflective and reflexive process can enable the practitioner to gain access to layers of reflective material, as well as the possibilities of what they might do with that material, an aesthetic and creative process:

Roland Barthes made [the difference] between *ecrivante* and *ecrivain*. If I remember, he said an *ecrivante* is someone who uses language only as an instrument, an instrument through which a message, any sort of message, can be transmitted. And an *ecrivain*, a writer, is someone who uses language as an end in itself, as something that in itself has justification.

Llosa 1991, pp. 114–15

It requires the practitioner to engage in 'that willing suspension of disbelief' (Coleridge quoted by Schon 1983, pp. 296, 363), to open themselves to uncertainty as to what needs to be learned, what is wanted, and what it is possible to learn or find out. This uncertainty, or knowledge of lack of knowledge, is an educative state of mind – in which space has been created in the vessel of the mind for insight, intuition and credulity. Alice was instructed by the White Queen in 'living backwards', and told to practise believing up to six impossible things before breakfast every day (Carroll 1865, p. 173) (Alice had already learned to walk *away* from whatever she wanted to reach (pp. 132–6)). Last week I congratulated a novelist friend on having made me believe in impossibly extraordinary characters (Glaister 1999). Her response was immediate: 'the more you can believe the better'. Well, that is pretty well what effective reflective practice demands of us.

> I never thought I would write poetry, let alone be bold enough to share it out loud with a group of (colleagues). Somehow the process of being part of the reflective writing group has helped me to dig down to new layers of depth and understanding within myself. It has been a journey rather like an archaeological exploration through ancient layers of protective and professional gubbins. I knew there was something stirring deep down, but never gave myself the time, or quite found the mechanism to bring it into the light of day. The discipline of the process, we have to prepare a piece of writing for each session, and the supportive and wholly empathetic group who share the experience, have touched and refreshed my personal and professional depths. It also seems to help my ways of getting wider issues into perspective and seeing the real value of things. My advice to you all is to try it. Write down what you think, how you feel and the stories of the day. Share these writings with others if you can possibly find the courage.
>
> Heller 1997, p. 29

> During the course's monthly meetings, (professionals) contribute by reading aloud pieces they have written in the intervening weeks. This can be a subject of the member's own choosing or one that has been suggested by the group. These are kept intentionally vague, such as *a time of uncertainty*. Each piece is discussed by the group. An observer seeing the group in action – with members enthralled and, at times, moved by both sadness and mirth – would appreciate that the age-old art of storytelling is alive and well. In these meetings people's prevalent emotions are laid bare, whether of humour, pain, cynicism or sadness.
>
> This course has encouraged me to be more aware of each day, and is making me more observant. Emotionally charged events no longer make me gulp and bottle things up. I now tend to write about what has happened and how I feel about it. I now keep a jottings pad on my desk and even a notebook in my car. I can be seen scribbling away in a lay-by.
>
> Brimacombe 1996

> It is easy for (practitioners) to work in almost total professional isolation, even in a friendly partnership, and it can be hard to admit to mistakes, vulnerability, sadness and even occasionally, joy. If you can commit some of these thoughts to paper, then not only can it be personally therapeutic, but by sharing them with others you may bring insights that can strike a chord and be of benefit to others.
>
> Purdy 1996

Is Reflective Practice for All?

People do not all naturally reflect; some are better at getting on with the job and leaving the thinking about it to others. Ferry and Ross-Gordon give a comparison of those teachers who do reflect, and those who don't (1998). Copeland *et al.* found that teachers are reflective to very different depths at different stages of their lives and careers and feel this should be catered for in education and training. They also mourn that the 'opportunity, time and assistance from others are often lacking in typical teacher education programmes' (Copeland *et al.* 1993, p. 357). Truscott and Walker found, however, that 'despite the opportunity for critical reflection, student teachers appear to focus on technical skills' (1998, p. 291).

Tutors of reflective practice report very different levels of success, and different experiences. I imagine this difference relates to the way the process is introduced, facilitated and supervised. For example, Clarke (1998) found that student teachers write reflectively on *themes* rather than on *incidents* or single events. I find asking people to write about *a time when* . . . focuses them upon an event. I do also find that journal work lends itself to the kind of in-depth longitudinal thematic musing to which he refers.

Yet reflective writing portfolios (including such material as poems and 'freewrites') for preservice science teachers have been found to be very useful for: 'encouraging positive attitudes towards science, developing an understanding of science concepts, providing embedded diagnostic information and creating "natural" opportunities for curriculum integration.' In addition, it 'seems to help students become aware of their own growth and beliefs regarding science' (Deal 1998, p. 244).

Levels of Reflection

Reflective stories, additional stories, journal writings, discussions, and wider researches can be undertaken without: set questions, such as, 'why did I intervene as I did?' (Atkins and Murphy 1994); reference to levels or stages of reflection (e.g. Mezirow 1981); or writing guidelines (e.g. Tripp 1995a, b) other than the writing and group-work support. A reliance on the writer's inherent ability to deconstruct their own practice makes the writing process organically synthetic, and close to the *writing of the body* of the feminist post-structuralist writers (Flax 1990, Moi 1985). Reflective writers can follow the train

of their own deep knowledge, experience and understanding leading to professional and personal cognitive, affective and spiritual
insights.

An analysis of reflective practice can be useful as a way of
understanding the process for the tutor, or for the practitioner
once deep reflection has been established, in order to help them
identify the processes they have been undergoing. Van Manen has
reported Dewey's five steps (van Manen 1995). Keith Morrison has
derived a four-stage process of reflective practice from Habermas
(Morrison 1996). Tripp uses an extensive list of items for the creation
and analysis of *critical incidents* (Tripp 1995a, b). Johns has developed
Barbara Carper's four ways of knowing: empirical, ethical, personal
and aesthetic (Johns 1995). And then of course there is Kolb's learning cycle (1984). In her final journal entry Masters student, Ann,
asserted:

> Looking at the discussion of the previous week and thinking of the
> Mezirow stages finally made the whole thing click into place for me.
> What is hard about the reflection is that it is so multi-layered. Analysis
> is of the actions, motivations, perceptions, etc. of the individual players
> in the story along with making links to other situations in the players'
> own past histories. But connections are also made at a more political
> and theoretic level of analysis which makes you then re-look at the
> original incident from another angle. No wonder it all takes so much
> time.
>
> Ann

And I could add: no wonder it all takes so much trust in the group, as
well as a degree of self-confidence and faith in the professional self.
These also all take time and nurture.

Guidance or Control?

Just as there are severe drawbacks in *structuring* a practitioner's reflection for them, so too there are inherent potential problems in *guiding* it.
Reflective practice is most effective when undertaken with a discussion group (or pair) of peers. Open discussion can widen the experience of the reflection and reflexivity politically and socially. *Guidance*
cannot take the place of this discussion: to be reflective and reflexive
effectively practitioners must question and be brought up against
political and social aspects rather than, or as well as, being subject to
the interpretation and direction of a superior.

An examination of daily practice undertaken under guidance may well transform practice by creating a more effective and self-satisfied workforce. But this workforce may be regulated from outside (by the supervisor and line-manager) as well as from the inside. The practitioner internalises the instruction of the supervisor relative to the practice as discussed. The practice which was once private and formed by their own ethical and professional judgements is now public – open to scrutiny and guidance. The professional is now controlled from without *and* from within.

Responsibility

An effective reflective practitioner takes responsibility for their own learning. Careful support by facilitator or mentor is useful to help them be brave enough to stay with the uncertainties, and feel they are strong and intelligent enough to develop their own questions.

If we always think we know what we know, or know the foundations or parameters for what we know, or the type of thing we want to learn about, there will be no room for development – no room for the 'aha moment', the 'epiphany', the 'dropping of the penny', the sunlight to come through the window. Similarly, wanting safe, understood structures for our learning leaves no scope for effective learning. As you read further chapters in this book you will meet practitioners who say such as this in evaluation:

> I felt to begin with that the course was slightly wacky and flakey – surreal. . . . I felt uncomfortable and a bit insecure at first. . . . But now I feel this process is empowering.

This was said with hindsight – her criticism at the beginning might have been better described as 'lack of structure and analysis'. These assumptions, however, did not close her off from having a go at the process to which I was introducing her. But I have often found that articulate course participants, those used to telling other people what to do, will try to prevent us getting to the most 'uncomfortable' and 'insecure' bit of the process – the parts where they will have to begin believing unbelievable things, and questioning givens. A group of nine senior doctors last week were like a naughty class of infant lads in using delaying and warding-off tactics. Some of them would far rather not have tried to practise believing any impossible things – they thought they wanted structure, to be told what to do and think. We did get somewhere in the end – but it was exhausting.

In the more didactic nursing and education literature, practice is problematised and teachers or nurses are asked to isolate small areas of experience to be described and then dismembered for answers to such questions as: *What did I do right here?* and *What could I have done better?* (Atkins and Murphy 1994, Tripp 1995a). In these texts, as in other such structured work, the practitioner is even sometimes given a fictitious situation on which to reflect.

Yet: 'Argyris and Schon remind us that the ego-protecting function, as well as the relative implicitness of some theories-in-use, might make their access through reflective exercises very difficult indeed' (Greenwood 1995). So these exercises are likely to lead merely to a musing on action or a telling of anecdotes which largely review obvious points. It can also be merely a reiteration and strengthening of attitude and perspective, which might be prejudice.

Such reflective practice, furthermore, takes apart incidents in order to reflect upon them. This is essentially necrophylic: taking an organic entity apart will necessarily kill it; only a dead creature can be dissected.

There is an assumption in much of the reflective practice literature that material for reflection is accessible, e.g.: 'practitioners must first select what aspects of the situation to attend to' (Greenwood 1995). If practitioners are 'selecting' in this conscious way, they will not be able to stand outside their own actions and view them creatively. In fact, how can they 'select' in this way when, as she also asserts: 'the problems of practice do not present themselves ready labelled for solution; the knotty problems of practice inhere in messy indeterminate situations of uncertainty, instability, uniqueness and value-conflict'. A muddle in the model, I fear.

Another problem with reflection, as reported in the literature, is lack of clarity about how it can be facilitated:

(I have sought) out again some of the literature on reflective practice. I realise now how varied this is in quality, scope and depth. On one level some people talk about reflective practice as if it was just a chat about an incident over a cup of coffee.

Ann

Fear of Going Through the Looking-Glass

A protectiveness against setting off into the unknown of oneself arises from the fear people have of uncovering things they don't want to know about within themselves. This has given rise to such stories as: Dr Jekyll seeing wicked grotesque Mr Hyde in his mirror (Stevenson 1886), Dorian Gray and his mirror portrait ageing before his eyes (Wilde 1891), Hesse's Steppenwolf (1927), and 'The student of Prague', whose reflection stepped out of the glass and committed terrible crimes in his name (1929 Conrad Veidt film).

Freud built on this fear in his theories of the *ego, superego* and *id*. The *id* has been seen as the 'animal instinct' part of ourselves – potentially ungovernable, and in need of control by our conscious *egos*. If our *superego* – conscience – failed in its function of directing the *ego* in the right way, we could well be in terrible trouble as our devil side – *id* – might take over our conscious mind. Pat Barker explored this, in her study of shell-shock and fugue in the First World War (1991).

Although reflective writing for practitioners is exciting and deeply educational, such fears are not unfounded. Dynamic development can be as troubling and unrestful as unquestioning lack of change can be boring and depressing. But expressive and explorative writing is a trustworthy, paced reflexive and reflective process, if allied with carefully facilitatated group- or paired-work. Participants get what they pay for: those who are willing to pay by expressing and exploring deeply will receive the most. Practitioners will involve themselves in the process according to their strengths, wants and needs. Those who are not so ready will only go as far as they can and need at that time. There are often those whom I wish could have taken themselves further. It is always their choice, whether conscious or not.

This process is personally demanding, and has to be. It enables practitioners to view their practice in a far wider way than before. It can offer insight into the motives, thoughts and feelings of others, and suggest a range of possible actions which could never have been envisaged before. This is likely to change practice, and the relationship of the practitioner to their practice, dynamically – a politically and socially unsettling process. But it can't *transform* practice with the wave of a *hey presto* magic wand, without a deep personal investment. No education can offer definitive answers, and betterment is never unalloyed. The wish for *transformation* in this way can be as uncritical as Midas' wish that everything he touched might turn to gold. Here is the voice of Midas' unenchanted wife:

Look we all have wishes; granted.
But who has wishes granted? Him. Do you know about gold?
It feeds no one: aurum. Soft, untarnishable; slakes
no thirst. He tried to light a cigarette: I gazed entranced,
as the blue flame played on its luteous stem. At least,
I said, you'll be able to give up smoking for good.

Duffy 1999, p. 12

Even if we could wave the magic wand, the gain is likely to prove unpalatable, as it was for Midas, based as it would be on uncritical, unquestioning assumptions. Myth is full of such accounts as these: telling us to take full responsibility for our own lives and learning, to have our eyes clearly open to the drawbacks as well as advantages, errors, blunders as well as successes of our educational journey. Here is a special story:

Malcolm

One morning we were doing number work. Malcolm was struggling to recognise sets of two. He was troubled by the book in front of him and sat slumped on an elbow.

I had one of those 'bright ideas' teachers tend to get. Let's make it more practical. 'Malcolm,' I said. 'Look at Darren. How many eyes has he got?'

Malcolm looked at Darren. Pointing with his finger he slowly counted in his deep voice, 'one . . . two.'

'Good, well done,' I said. 'Now look at Debbie, how many eyes has she got?'

Pointing carefully again Malcolm intoned slowly, 'one . . . two.'

'That's great, Malcolm, now look at Tony, count his eyes.'

'One . . . two.' Let's take this a step further I said smugly to myself.

'Now Malcolm, look at Matthew. Without counting can you tell me how many eyes he has got?'

Malcolm looked at me as if I had gone mad. 'OK that's fine Malcolm, you just count them like you did the others.'

Relieved he slowly repeated his methodical counting: 'one . . . two.'

There is a magical moment in teaching, when the penny drops, the light goes on, the doors open. Success is achieved. I was starting to worry. We weren't getting there!

'Malcolm, how many eyes has Naheeda got?' Malcolm counted slowly, as if it was the first pair of eyes he had ever seen. 'One . . . two.'

'Good, you're doing really well.'

We carried on round the class. Eager faces looked up to have their eyes counted. I was growing desperate as we ran out of children. Was I leading Malcolm on an educational wild goose chase? Were we pursuing an idea that was not yet ready to be caught?

The last pair of eyes was counted. 'One . . . two.' The finger carefully went from eye to eye. There was only me left. 'Malcolm,' I said, trying to hide my desperation, 'how many eyes have I got?' Malcolm studied my face carefully. He looked long and hard at my eyes. I waited expectantly in the silence. His brow furrowed. Finally he spoke.

'Take your glasses off.'

Kevin Marsden

Kevin, a special school teacher, and Masters in Education reflective practice module student, read this to his established subgroup of five teachers. They trusted each other as well as feeling confidence and respect for each others' professional abilities and views. Kevin was able to share his sense of frustration and failure, and the rest of the group learned a great deal about the methods, joys and problems of special school teaching. The group were able to explore the probability that Malcolm had had a different understanding of his task than did his teacher, Kevin. Possibly Malcolm, for example, thought he was being asked to count the eyes, rather than 'guess' how many each had. To do this he would have had to ask for spectacles to be removed so he could see clearly. The situation of a mismatch between the intention of the teacher and the understanding of the child must happen so often.

Variations on a Theme

'You've made things really difficult for me, you have. I shall never be able to teach the way I used to again' (Rowland and Barton 1994, p. 371) Taking responsibility for practice can be uncomfortable yet creative and exciting. Different practitioners have experimented with a range of variations on the theme of reflective practice.

I have run on-line postgraduate CPD courses for general practitioners: each member compiles a portfolio of reflective writings, reflections upon the writings, responses from other group members, and evidence of discussions with colleagues (team members, for example), and research they have undertaken (Internet, or literature search, for example). All communication is electronic in a closed email group; each member writes accounts which are read and commented upon by the other members, who also make research suggestions. This mode of communication inevitably has distinct advantages and disadvantages; it is particularly appropriate for busy, reasonably articulate clinicians, but requires careful facilitation. A group member reflected how it 'enables you to *meet* colleagues you would probably never meet otherwise'.

A student science teacher 'Barbara' was supported by her tutors in reflecting on how her practice 'did not mesh with her beliefs about how she wanted to teach' (Abell *et al.* 1999, p. 133), and what to do about it.

> What we have learned about our students led us to take action on the elementary science methods course. . . . Interestingly our finding that methods students lack an understanding of first graders' abilities mirrors our lack of understanding of the preservice teachers. While our students were observing, writing about, and discussing the actions of first graders and their teacher, we were learning about them.
>
> Abell *et al.* 1998, p. 506

School students are being encouraged to use reflective writing too. Caroline Keys encourages her science students to write creatively and expressively 'to help students acquire a personal ownership of ideas conveyed in lectures and textbooks' (Keys 1999, p. 117). And: 'it promotes the production of new knowledge by creating a unique reflective environment for learners engaged in scientific investigation' (ibid., p. 119). She calls the process *writing to learn*. Phye tells how school students write reflective portfolios in a similar way (Phye 1997). Bonnie Meath Lang tells of her deaf students writing journals in the classroom, sharing them with each other and with their teacher. This, she says, helps them to know each other better and communicate more effectively (Meath Lang 1996).

A remarkable university-wide reflective practice project was undertaken at the University of Innsbruck, with lecturers across the disciplines engaged in action learning. 'They articulated their own *practical theories*. . . . It was only when faculty members learnt to accept what they regarded as strange and different in their colleagues' attitudes, that processes of collective reflection and mutual understanding could develop' (Schratz 1993, p. 130).

Reflective practice commonly seeks to support practitioners to: develop their practice (Schon 1987); pass on their experience to others

(Benner 1984); and create a growing, developing environment for their clients/patients/students (Boyd and Fayles 1983). Going *through the looking-glass* can support the practitioner in gaining a view out of the box of their habitual world.

Out of the Box

The philosopher Zerubavel writes that we live within very tightly confined mental boxes but the walls to these boxes are made of glass. While we sit happily inhabiting the same old space we look out at the world through the glass walls and imagine we are free of bias and preconception. Only when we try to get up and move to another mental space do we bump into the glass walls of these prisons and become aware of their existence.

Bell 1992

Jill Bell is speaking of learning to read, write and speak Chinese, adding that 'it simply never occurred to me that in attempting a new literacy, I might be entering a new way of looking at education . . . I never questioned whether for instance (the Chinese) notion of progress might be different from mine.' She had to learn also that 'the form of a text is inextricably linked to the content': that 'balance and concentration' are essential mental and physical prerequisites to the learning of the language. Jill Bell effectively (and surprisedly) saw the walls of her own 'cultural box', and the outlines of another.

Reflective practice could lead to too much introspection, to pushing the practitioner more firmly and unquestioningly *into* the box of their cultural position. The value of reflexivity is to problematise the self, and one's role professionally, socially and politically. The support of a critical group (or co-mentor) of peers, and the searching out of material (professional, political and social texts) from as wide a sphere as possible will enable the reflexive process. Effective reflection and reflexivity examine emotions, experiences, thoughts and actions both of the self and of trusted confidential peers as embedded within the global situation.

Teams can usefully examine themselves as well as individuals. The 'story of a course' in a later chapter tells how reflection enabled a group of individuals to become a team. Barry *et al*. have written most persuasively about their use of reflective writings in developing their team researching doctor–patient communication (Barry *et al*. 1999).

To study the self (or the team) is to forget the self. Letting go of our everyday assumptions about who we are, in order to be open to the discovery of other possible selves – the myselves of whom I am not habitually aware, the myself I might be, and the selves I am becoming, the team in development. Listening creatively to the voices within us, and those without, and responding creatively is effective reflective practice.

4

Group Processes and Facilitation

Socrates: It isn't that knowing the answers myself, I perplex other people. The truth is rather that I infect them also with the perplexity I feel myself.

Plato p. 128

The process of running a group for reflective practice has to be considered in its own right. A group has to be formed with care, looked after knowledgeably, and terminated thoughtfully. The role of a good facilitator involves Socrates' attitude – that of not knowing the answers but being willing to enter into a joint investigation and enquiry.

The work of a good facilitator is often transparent: the group members are often not aware she/he is doing very much. But the role involves constant awareness of what is happening in the group (both verbal and non-verbal) and fine judgements as to the timing and wording of reactions and suggestions. It might not be noticeable, but it's certainly vital:

Reflection is a real key to change, but facilitating good reflective learning experiences is probably more difficult than many anticipate.

Ann

This chapter is useful for both group facilitators and members. Participants can usefully be aware of group processes as well as the facilitator, in order to support the process productively. This does not mean being 'teacher's pet'; it may even involve challenging the facilitator if they feel appropriate actions are not being taken, or reminding her of forgotten elements (for example: 'do we have ten minutes for this activity as well?'; 'Might it be useful if we introduced ourselves first?'). An aware group member may, for example: stop speaking when they know they have said enough, and draw out a silent member of the group instead; set out the chairs beforehand rather than waiting for the tutor to do it; be brave enough to break an awkward silence, or conversely to hold a productive silence instead of nervously and ineffectually breaking it.

An effective group is run *for* its members. Participants are encouraged to consider and express what they want and need, right from the start, to find out and be encouraged to meet their own learning needs. The facilitator's job is to orchestrate this discussion and support the group in developing a process which enables them all reasonably to get what they want. Occasionally a member is lost during this process: they want something so different from the others it is clear they can never get it from this group. It is much better for this to be clear from the start and for them to make their decision to stay and do what the majority of the group wants – with slight modifications perhaps – or leave. I well remember one man who came to a group early on in my facilitating career, saying he wasn't going to write, he only wanted to talk about how writing can help: he hadn't realised that's what *interactive workshop* meant. He stayed the whole day, and disrupted the working of the group. I now know I should have been firmer in stating the aims and objectives of the day, and eliciting the support of the rest of the group. It should have been clear to him he either left, or joined in fully.

There is always a *hidden curriculum* in any group. This will be different for each member and for the facilitator. Everyone brings expectations, hopes and fears which combine with unspoken elements within the group to create *curricula* which are not stated and might be either productive or harmful. An awareness of this, and sensitivity to participants' sensitivities is invaluable. It also helps to know that, partly because of this, what the tutor thinks she is teaching may be very different from what the participants take away with them. A poet told me he never could tell what children would ask him, when he worked in schools. The questions were rarely about poetry, but about things like his shoes.

A group will test boundaries during the first few sessions, and decide how they wish to function, and what it is they wish to do. The facilitator's job is to guide them in this process. Trust, respect and confidence will increase in each meeting, if the ingredients are right and mixed carefully.

We learn from our tutors, teachers and lecturers; we can learn far more from our peers. An effective group is one in which participants feel confident enough to create the discussion. The facilitator is there to keep them from straying from the task in hand, timekeep, support a reasonable balance of contribution from everyone, and so on. An audience to our writings can offer particular insights from group members' own experience. They can also help us understand what our writing is trying to tell us.

Writing in this way, and sharing it, can be deeply personal; feelings and emotions can be raw and exposed. This kind of writing can bring out confidences normally only drawn forth by supervision or therapeutic processes, or in a trusted friendship. Careful facilitation and confidentiality can make all the difference.

Principles

I felt like I'd been given something – real parts of other people.

Elaine

Respect, shared responsibility, confidence and confidentiality are vital cornerstones (I will return to confidentiality under *groundrules* below). There will be a wide range of different abilities, interests and confidence in the group, as well as possibly nationality, ages, types of social background, and both sexes. Respecting these, and respecting the contributions of everyone, ensures the group will gain from variety. Some people talk readily, others are naturally quiet; a balance of contribution is also important.

A group can be powerfully facilitative if it can create its own rules of behaviour and function – like a relatively safe warm island in a choppy sea. Issues can be raised tentatively and even hesitatingly at times, aired supportively, and then taken out into the big world when both individuals and group are ready. Participants share a specific part of themselves and their lives with each other; group relationships are even more partial than others in our everyday working, social and family lives. Miranda realised there was a world outside her own small island when she met shipwrecked people (Shakespeare's *The Tempest*). These strangers arrived at just the right moment for her to be ready to encounter a greater width of contact and experiences. Her immediate response was: 'O brave new world, that has such people in it' (V. i. lines 183–4). There are many ingredients for creating the right kinds of boundaries to offer a sense of confidence and relative safety. Two are: members taking each other as they experience them within the closed social system of the group; members relating to and supporting each other through discussions of the writing without seeking to question beyond the boundaries of that writing, and the group.

Both these help participants to write about and share important issues with each other. A group member is not relating to another member as *doctor*, or *senior lecturer*, but as Sue or Phil. They are not exposing *themselves*, but their writing. Members will have had time to write, reread and think about the sharing of that writing before they do so. It can be helpful if participants treat each writing as a *fiction*. The discussion will then remain focused on what the writer intended to share with the group, on the writing rather than the hinterland of the account. Questions like 'did you *really* . . .?, 'And what happened next . . .?', 'Why did you perceive your senior partner like that . . .?' can lead the writer to say far more than they intended.

If the writing is considered as fiction, then there isn't a *'really'*, nor is there a *'what happened next'*: characters don't walk beyond the page and do anything. A question will be asked sometimes which strays beyond this rule, but accompanied by such as: 'I'm going to ask you this; please don't answer if you don't want to, but I think it might help.' A group respects a 'no', just as a decision not to read a piece because it feels too personal is respected.

Groundrules

- A sense of the group's **confidentiality** fosters the development of trust, of this being a safe forum. Belonging to such a group, hearing important reflective material, is a privilege. The writings belong to the writers, and the discussions to the group, neither should be shared outside the group without express permission. I remember one group even requesting we did not share anything even with our life partners (husbands/wives, etc.).

- A sense of the group's **boundaries** helps create confidence that probing questions will not be asked in order to extend the information given in the writing. Again the viewing of each writing as a *fiction* is useful here. Many professional groups create further boundaries for themselves, such as choosing only to write about and discuss work issues. A further boundary is to outlaw apologies, many are nervous at exposing their creation: instituting an imaginary £5 fine for any apology about a writing can defuse this effectively and humorously.

- **Respect and mutual trust** are facilitative. An attitude of 'unconditional positive regard' (Rogers 1969) cannot be demanded in group members, but the facilitator can model it. Even if a disagreement has arisen about a particular issue, the discussion can still hopefully be undertaken in a spirit of mutual respect. Discussions will be constructive and friendly if comments are either kept positive, or if negative elements are always expressed gently, along with definite appropriate constructive suggestions.

- **Silence** is powerful in any group. In an interactive confidential group, discussing deeply held principles and problematic practices, this is particularly true (for a useful exploration of this see Rowland 1993, pp. 87–107). 'The leader must learn to allow for different sorts of silence – the reflective, the anxious, the embarrassed or puzzled' (Abercrombie 1993, p. 118), the angry, the portentous, and so on.

Silence can be felt to be confronting and aggressive, especially if people feel the responsibility to break it belongs to others. Silence can be used fruitfully for deep reflection when individual group members feel responsible for their group. If no one in the group has anything particular they need to say, then no one needs to say anything. The silence will be broken when a participant knows or feels what they do want to say. A silence might be used, for example, to allow previous words to sink in, and an appropriate ensuing response sought. Understandings and clarities do not necessarily emerge through argument or discourse. Here are two evaluation comments:

> Sharing our writing weaves connections between members of the group. The special attentiveness as we listen to someone reading their work, and especially in the silence afterwards.
>
> Maggie

> Silence is but a feeling silence. Someone has just finished reading their contribution – perhaps a difficult encounter with a patient or a partner or even memories of training and hospital days which still have the power to hurt. The group has lived through that moment with the speaker, shared the emotions, and for a few minutes there is nothing to say. We are amazed at the power of each others' writing. Certainly when we come down to discuss, with Gillie's help, there are ways that the writing could be made more telling, but the inspiration comes from the group. It is not afraid to face the feelings aroused daily in medical practice and is learning in the safety of the group to translate them into words.
>
> Naomi

More can sometimes be said in silence than any words can manage, as Sophocles knew: 'a long heavy silence promises danger, just as much as a lot of empty outcries' (*Antigone* line 1382), and Aeschylus pointed out that safety and discretion can reside in silence: 'Long ago we learned to keep our mouths shut/Where silence is good health, speech can be fatal' (*Oresteia* trans. 1999, p. 29).

Function of the Group

A reflective practice group exists to support practitioners in their own professional and personal explorations and expressions to: understand more clearly the import and implications of the experiences they choose to share; think of fresh reflective writing avenues to try; enable them to discuss sensitive issues with involved and supportive others who are on similar voyages themselves, yet are 'disinterested' (are not 'interested' parties such as line-managers). A group can also reinforce the self-confidence and self-esteem which writing tends to bring ('I really felt involved in that story – it's a great piece of writing in its own right'), and help a writer out of the occasional inevitable bog of loss of confidence, reflective writer's block, and lost way.

The purpose of the group is for the participants to decide before they start: more or less what they are there for, how they are going to do it, why, where and when. The group is likely to be organic: develop its own specific working aims, objectives, patterns and relationships over time, but some agreement from the start is useful. A great deal of hassle, disappointment, and possibly pain is avoided by an initial sharing of ideas with an attempt at clarity as to purpose. Deciding what the group is *not* can be useful. It is not:

- a *writers' workshop* in which the form rather than the content of the writings are constructively criticised in order to help the writer improve the text (e.g. story, poem or play) with publication in mind – the content of the writing is not considered in such a forum;

- a *therapeutic writing group*, where the content of the writing is focused upon, but in order to support the writer in psychotherapeutic explorations;

- a *chat group* where the writings are read out, and the response is such as: 'how nice, now that reminds me how my Auntie Gwen used to . . .'.

What is the Group Going to *Do*?

There are two basic possibilities: to discuss material which has already been written; to generate new writing. The former will clearly always be undertaken, and has been discussed; the latter sometimes. Some people find the time and subject constraint and presence of others creative and liberating when writing together in a group; some, on the other hand, find it threatening, or just not conducive.

Creative writers tend to be addicted to these; I must have run hundreds and participated in a fair few exciting experiences. There are so many creatively facilitative stimuli to use with a group, far more than I have been able to include in this book. A resourceful facilitator will invent ones tailored to the needs and wants of the group. Nurses coming together for a dayschool should not be asked to write about *The worst experience of my life*, for example, but perhaps *A turning point*, or *A person who influenced me beneficially*.

When writing during the group, beginning with the *six minute free-intuitive writing exercise* (see Chapter 8) can ease the writing process. Resulting writings are not for reading out: this gives permission for anything to be written. The exercise puts something on the white space of the paper, possibly captures fleeting inspirations, and stores those distracting thoughts (*horrible* traffic getting here/what shall we eat tonight?). Specific stimulus can then be offered for a further piece of writing, followed by time for rereading, altering, and making connections.

An awareness of the possibility of reading to the group allows participants to bear this in mind when writing; the security of feeling they can opt not to read, or read only a fraction, can, however, free them up to write what they need to write. Ample time for private rereading of new writing in order to make additions, deletions, alterations and decisions of how much or little to share offers the chance to acquaint themselves with what they have written before making anything public. Reading aloud will give a deeper experience than talking about the writing can; but occasionally when a participant has indicated they do not wish to read, then talking about their material can be a great deal better than contributing nothing from their writing.

The Life of the Group

A closed group with the same members at each meeting (allowing for occasional absences, of course) will be the most effective for reflective practice work. Trust and confidence can be enabled to grow, as well as skill in drawing out useful themes from events depicted in writing. The experience of being in a group is different at different stages – a courtly dance, then jive, quickstep, country dance, or tarantella.

A group is rather like a story, with a 'plot' of *beginning*: boy meets girl, *conflict*: boy falls out with girl, *conflict resolution*: boy and girl kiss, *mission*: lovers win over their parents (or don't), *end*: lovers sail off into the sunset (or die), and *mourning*. What makes a story a story is the way the characters and the situation, and the readers' view of them, change and develop. A group will not continue to get better and better; the duration and shape of the 'plot' will vary for different groups (*Romeo and Juliet* or a cheap romance):

- At the **beginning** members begin to see themselves as a group rather than a collection of individuals. This involves finding out about the other members, and being willing to become a group member rather than just an individual.

- **Conflict** is the traditional 'middle day' phenomenon when the group has constituted itself and perhaps felt rather congratulatory. Members provisionally sort out their roles, flexing role muscles and jockeying for leadership perhaps, or wishing to push their own preferred objectives. People can become quite badly hurt in this process if it is not handled carefully. But it is an important stage, even though an initially harmonious course may appear to disintegrate angrily. Some very creative thinking can take place, such as: precisely what are we doing here?; who am I in this group?; what do I want to get out of it?

- **Conflict resolution** is a process of creating a group identity and rules, developing a sense of commitment, as well as wanting to nurture and care for it and the individual members.

- In **mission** the group has tackled each other, uncovered quite a few prejudices to sidestep, and strengths and skills to harness. They have a reasonable group feel for who they are, what it is they are doing, why and how (as well as when and where) they are doing it. They work well together, and are doing whatever it was they set out to do (or possibly something else which has become more important).

- **End** is when the group has done its work and is ending gracefully – with regret hopefully, but optimism about the next stage of action for each participant. Members leave – once more individuals. A 'rite of passage', such as a shared lunch, can ease the parting.

- **Mourning** is a period of which facilitators are not always aware. An effective supportive group is bound to leave a sense of regret at its passing.

A reflective writing group may not initially know how long they need. One way of handling this is to set a time limit, say six sessions, review the situation at sessions four and five, and decide on a further six, if appropriate.

I have set out these stages simplistically, as for any model. Of course, a group is not a story written by one author, but a story authored by all the group members. The stages will probably get mixed up, and earlier stages, even if undergone thoroughly, may recur. For example, conflict may arise at any time and need to be dealt with, and conflict resolution undertaken and hopefully reached (lovers do continue to have tiffs and need to kiss and make up). New rules and guidelines may well have to be considered and put in place. The group may even go back to elements of the first stage and need to get to know each other again in areas which did not seem important to this group in the initial *beginning* stage.

The *mission* stage of mutual understanding and shared knowledge, trust, forbearance, support and effective listening will only be reached after at least some elements of the previous three stages. The beginning stage is characterised by reserve, avoidance of conflict and politeness; few personal risks are taken, and views and feelings are withheld. During the conflict stage people are defensive and assertive, distrustful and suspicious, and not listening to each other. At conflict resolution members are supportive, receptive, and attempting to avoid conflict. By the time they are set on their mission they are open, trusting, listening well, and willing to take risks. All these, of course, are within the boundaries of the group: individuals meeting each other outside the group's boundaries may still stick a knife in each other or go to bed together in reaction to whatever personal or professional situation they are in.

So the relationships which obtain within a mission group are not a model for those outside between the participants. However, I have often been told that being in a reflective writing group, even a one-off session, positively affects later working relationships. I ran a single morning session in an academic medical department one Christmas. They were a large, wonderful, fascinating group of people; the writings and discussions were extremely fruitful. I later discovered they don't normally have smooth working relationships with each other: but more than one reported to me up to a year later how they could still sense the improved working relationship engendered that morning.

Characters

A story relies on characters just as much as it does on plot: the talkative and exuberant, the shy and quiet, the silent but anguished, the dominant and bossy, the analytic reasoner, the facilitative, the divergently creative thinker, the moaner, the kindly and motherly, the frustrated rescuer, the frightened pupil, the babbler, the lurker, the catalyst, the logical structurer, the teacher's pet, for example. Troubles sometimes arise when a group contains two or more people who are used to being the dominant one, for example; different problems arise when too many are shy and quiet (or even worse anguished and quiet). Facilitator awareness of these roles can enable a gentle and subtle encouragement to move beyond the one adopted by certain participants.

Different roles may be played in different groups, just as in life – mum one minute, teacher or lover the next. One student was described as 'facilitative' in a reflexive group discussion. She was astonished, a bit fearful, and kept referring to this. We all supported her in thinking it was all right for her to be facilitative to others. Until then she had clearly only seen her group role as being the whacky one who had creative ideas but had to have the more serious elements of the course explained carefully. The 'game' which had led to this enlightenment on her part was one in which we in turn all said what animal each other reminded us of. We then gently and cautiously teased out what we thought our metaphorical animals 'meant'.

The facilitator also takes on different roles at different times, as appropriate. These roles should be played with discretion, she needs to be a 'good-enough facilitator', take on each character just 'enough' of the time. She may be:

- **Teacher**. Giving a keynote talk on an essential issue, for example. It's quite often a relief to group members when this happens. But too much of it makes for a passive group which will find it difficult to take responsibility for their learning at other times (as in *chalk and talk model* in a previous chapter).

- **Instructor**. Giving instructions for a set task, for example. The group can undertake to do what they're told. This approach is useful when asking people to undertake a revealing task, such as asking people to write to a certain theme for a certain length of time. Responsibility for everything else other than the content of what they are writing about is removed. They are freed then to be creatively explorative and expressive in their writing. That is if there is an environment of enough trust and support; if not, then the writing will not be worth the paper it's written upon.

- **Interpreter**. The facilitator may reflect back a group member's contribution, repeat it in her own words in order to clarify and ensure it has been heard. This can increase member confidence, but must be used with care as it can irritate, or reduce the autonomy of the member. She might also interpret what is going on between people, or other behaviours in the group. She may make connections or linkages between concepts or ideas arising from the group. This pattern-making or -perceiving can be creative and constructive.

- **Devil's advocate/confronter**. Once more this approach is the right one in certain circumstances. Groups need to be challenged – enough. If the facilitator is confronting one member they must be reasonably confident in the way the individual may respond – tears and anger can be very fruitful, but not when the facilitator has engendered them by mistake.

- **Compatriot/discloser**. A group in which the members are revealing themselves, but the facilitator never does, will not work. Nor will it work if the facilitator reveals all the skeletons in her cupboard – and takes up the group's emotional space and time. A doctor in one of my groups called this latter *boundary sickness*.

- **Consultant**. The facilitator is likely to be more experienced and knowledgeable than the members. She may respond to a particular wish or need of the group for some information or advice from this greater skill.

- **Neutral chairman**. The chairman makes sure the group keeps to the point, to time, that everyone has a chance of a say, that the subject is appropriately thoroughly aired, that sexism, racism, doctorism (professorism, big white chiefism) do not happen, that the groundrules are adhered to, that the discussion is appropriately recorded, and so on. But the chairman is not primarily involved in the discussion or activity.

- **Participant**. The opposite role to chairman. This is a useful role on occasion – creating a warm and coherent feeling; the skill is knowing when to draw back and become chairman or whatever. Quite often a member who knows nothing about group processes thinks the facilitator is being a participant much of the time – they do not notice the chairing, interpretive, confronting, and some of the directive functions.

- **Manager**. All the essential but unexciting tasks of organisation and management are undertaken by the manager role. The participants need to arrive at the right time and place and with the right papers and expectations.

I have delineated these roles simplistically in giving only a few obvious ones. They do not in practice have clear boundaries but tend to merge and slip. A group will often not realise an experienced facilitator is moving between them. But moving from one to another appropriately and smoothly is not straightforward; even a skilful tutor can confuse, anger or devalue a group at times, or alienate one participant.

Authority and power

The facilitator is in a role of authority within the group, and always is. An awareness of the extent of this authority, power even, is useful:

> Trainers need to give considerable thought to what backing they need to enable them to face the full extent of their managerial authority and of the potential impact of this on the functioning of participants. The more they know about their own authority, the less are they likely either to deny it and collude with participants in avoiding powerful learning experiences or to wield it unthinkingly and impose rigid, unresponsive courses. Our argument has been that the more open trainers are about the extent and limits of their own authority, the more open they can be to the professional and personal authority of course participants.
>
> Hughes and Pengelly 1995, pp. 169–70

Transference, counter-transference, projection, introjection

These are all terms from psychoanalysis and refer to the dynamics of people interrelating. We *transfer* onto others elements of other relationships – for example, the facilitator being seen as parent. This can be a problem in the case of anger, hurt or great need in the relationship with the actual mum or dad; the facilitator may therefore find they are receiving bewildering emotions which do not belong to them. *Counter-transference* is when the facilitator reacts similarly to group members: finding they are mummying or bullying, for example. *Projection* is when one's emotions are *projected* onto another, for whatever reason; 'I'm sure you are getting at me', for example, might mean 'I really wish I could get at you'. *Introjection* is when feelings, such as anger, are swallowed and not expressed, possibly leading to the bottled feelings erupting in painful or awkward ways later.

All of these phenomena are a perfectly normal part of everyday life – part of our playing out of character roles. It is useful, however, to be aware of them, and take them into account, especially if things go wrong in a group – when anger or tears erupt inexplicably, for example.

Group Management

Groups don't happen, they are created and nurtured. These elements are useful:

- The group and facilitator doing what they decided they wanted to do.
- Everyone knowing everyone's name from the start. Beginning the first session with a game to learn names is a good *icebreaker*, and helps everyone to feel individually valued. Beginning the second session with a name check is useful: I often just suggest those who don't know a name ask the person across the circle. It's quick and leads to laughter and companionship, rather than embarrassment, as we are all doing it at once.
- A *formative evaluation* at the end of each session: a simple check to see if members are getting what they want. If they have other ideas then a discussion might ascertain who would like a slight (or large) change, and whether a majority do – if this is feasible.
- *Timing*: each member having a fair share of time for their piece of writing and discussion – running out of time so one writer takes their piece home unread could be disastrous; the session beginning and ending when expected. This confidence in both *time sharing* and a *time boundary* help create the sense of a safe island.
- *Open questions* rather than *closed* ones, e.g.: 'how did you feel about that?', rather than 'did that make you angry?'
- *Personal pronouns*. People often say 'you' when they mean 'I' ('you get tired of saying it over and over again', they mean 'I get tired . . .'). Sometimes 'we' might be used instead of 'I' – an assumption that the rest of the group agree with the speaker. Sometimes 'they' is even used for 'I'. The use of 'I' by each speaker can help the group

to own and be responsible for what each of them say. I have worked with groups who make such a rule and insist everyone sticks to it.

- Using people's *names* whenever possible and appropriate. This can make for a sense of value and inclusion.
- An awareness that *sub-groups* can form within groups, constructively or destructively.
- A supportive yet stretching relationship to the *roles or characters of group members.*
- *Verbal contributions from as many group members as possible.* Silent or quiet (for whatever reason) participants can fruitfully be encouraged to speak, for example by working in pairs or small groups, or taking it in turns to participate.
- *Problematic participants* can usually be coped with by the group – with careful facilitation. This can lead to greater group cohesion in the long run.
- *Non-verbal communication* (facial expression, posture, gesture, blushing, sweating, laughter, crying, and so on) can tell participants and facilitator a great deal about each other.
- *Listening to, commenting on, and eliciting comments* reflectively on the written experiences of others is usually a skill to be learned and practised tentatively.
- *Learning how to take the comments and discussions of others,* about one's own work, equally needs practice. People, to begin with, do not know what to expect, do not realise there are no *magic* answers, and that ideas will come as much from themselves and the rest of the group as from the facilitator, if not more. I have been asked: 'now are you going to psychoanalyse me?', when someone has finished reading: the writer expecting to be a passive recipient of my judgement. It is the role of the group and the facilitator to support the writer to extend and clarify their *own* ideas about themselves, not to impose their view.
- *Who comments first, and when* after a story is read? In my groups it is never me; as the leader I can so easily dominate, and always have quite enough to say about a piece; so I speak after everyone else. I ask for someone to respond quickly: waiting after you have read can be an agonising time – seconds seem like hours while you imagine everyone thinks your writing is awful, and you a pig. Silence can be facilitative, however, in a group which has been meeting for some time and is more confident. A deeply thoughtful pause while a writing sinks in to its audience, and they reflect on what they want to say, can prelude a fruitful discussion.

- *The door-knob*. Issues people find difficult or painful to talk about are sometimes put off. Just as the facilitator is beginning to make moves to end the session (has her hand on the metaphorical doorknob) the most disturbing or important details or information may be blurted out – invariably issues which need time. The facilitator is now forced to decide they must wait, or allow the group to go over time. An awareness of this potential scenario can to an extent prevent it happening. Being very firm about time boundaries can prevent participants feeling space will be made, and aiming normally to finish the business in hand before the end-time can help – leaving some space for dealing with such matters. If none arises, the time can usefully be used for a recap of the session, or a reflexive period.
- *Variety of group size and organisation* can offer a refreshing change, and an alteration in dynamics. Paired work and smaller group work can enable a situation of closer trust. With an audience of only one, and to a lesser extent three or four, a quiet or well-defended person can feel emboldened to say more.

Practical Issues in Group Management

Arrangement of furniture affects a group. King Arthur thought a circle helps everyone to feel equal, but a centre table can give too much security and can be a barrier. A circle of chairs can create more confident intimacy. I think for this to be the case, the chairs have to be comfortable ones, so people don't feel they are balancing with nothing to lean on. When schoolroom chairs are all that is available, then packing people in close round a table can be really great. By the time they are all leaning forward, they are quite close enough to create a gathered circle.

Having just the right number of chairs for everyone makes the group feel complete; if fewer people arrive than expected, it is worth removing the unneeded chairs – though if the group is a strong, gathered, trusting one, then leaving the chair of the absent member can retain a sense of their presence within the group. I had a lovely experience of this with a group of primary healthcare workers (health visitors, GPs, nurses, etc.). Jenny was expected, but not present, so we left her chair. The group referred to her empty chair as if she was there. Then, when she came in apologetically late, slipping into her waiting chair was a warm and wanted experience.

- Any necessary equipment, such as an overhead projector, being in place beforehand saves wastage of valuable time.

- Punctuality and regular attendance can offer a sense of respect to the group and its work, as well as saving time and frustration.

More Practical Issues: Housekeeping

These small details are much more important than one might think:

- *Numbers*: size affects the group dynamic considerably. I think eight is a lovely number; twelve is the ideal maximum I would take for this purpose; four is too few because there will be times especially in winter when one or two may be unable to attend, but four may be perfect for a short introductory one-off session.
- *Funds*: who pays what, when, how, how much, to whom (if appropriate).
- *Venue*: is it the right one?
- *Coffee time*: important because people get to know each other. But when, where, how, how long?
- *Dates and times*: people like to know at the beginning when they will get their breaks (coffee, tea, lunch) and when they will finish. One parcels out one's energy and commitment unconsciously for the allotted time – surprises in this area are not useful. An unexpected hour on the end of a session, when the energy has been used up, is as unfacilitative as people coming to the finish time before they are ready – they could have invested more energy and commitment earlier, had they known.

Di Moss's Game

Di designed this game to help practitioners appreciate the value of being reflective and reflexive about actions, thoughts *and* feelings. The facilitator will need: six eggs in a box with a number painted on each; plastic floor covering; a small hammer; writing materials; and a watch:

1. Place eggs in the centre of the group circle.
2. Explain that one egg has been hard-boiled.
3. Ask group to study the eggs without touching, and decide individually which has been boiled – without conferring.
4. Each group member to spend five minutes writing the number of their chosen egg, and why they chose it.
5. Make a performance of putting down a plastic sheet and producing the hammer.

6. Make individuals ill at ease by saying you are to choose someone at random to test out their choice – what a mess if the choice is wrong!
7. Ask group members to write how they feel about being offered the hammer, and its possible consequences.
8. Confess that no one is to hammer an egg, and none of the eggs is boiled. Their first paragraph is an example of being reflexively reflective about actions and thoughts, the second about feelings.

Juggling

A course facilitator juggles with co-ordinating these three areas:

Needs of the group

Needs of the individual   *Needs of the task/organisation*

Conclusions

I keep six honest serving men
    (They taught me all I knew);
Their names are What and Why and When
    And How and Where and Who.

Kipling 1902, p. 83

These have served me well for years, too. I call them *can-opener questions*. Used as a checklist in planning and writing, they help ensure I have covered everything.

An array of issues for both participants and facilitators to consider have been suggested in this chapter. Yet a skilled facilitator, just like any expert practitioner, is consciously aware of very few of them in practice: they are skills to pick unwittingly from the toolkit at the appropriate time. But even an expert facilitator makes mistakes, has to learn a new method or technique. And it can feel like a dangerous business, as emotions, feelings and opinions can be expressed and felt with vigour. One of my participants once said: 'the responsibility for encouraging reflection is awesome'. But if effective learning is to take place, that responsibility needs to be taken:

> Effective learning is therefore dependent, at least in part, on access to that world of feeling and phantasy, which allows structures of meaning to be recognised, and to be open to change, in a way which facilitates a different (and perhaps more constructive) professional response. Great emphasis is placed . . . on the learning environment, particularly

on the need for space and for containment. . . . High value is given to creating a space which is somewhat apart from the everyday world, where a reflective mode and a slower pace is promoted, and where it is permissible to allow vulnerability to surface (a view somewhat at odds with the dominant ideas of competence and 'mastery').

Yelloly and Henkel 1995, p. 9

Facilitating an effective group offers immense satisfaction: experiencing people developing and growing and reaching fresh understandings, as well as learning how to support each other. Effective groupwork is rather like a group of people who have learned to drum in rhythm with each other:

Drumming

Rhythm, seamless, breathless, captivating. Ah ha! We do have rhythm. We can do it! Circle of faces, my friends.

Rhythm of the heart, of the step, of the circulation of the blood. Change of the seasons. Night and day. Springtime and harvest. Marching, dancing, walking, skipping, running, jumping, talking, poetry.

Jenny Lockyer

5

The Creation of a Team

Shape clay into a vessel;
It is the space within that makes it useful.

Lao Tsu trans. 1973, p. 11

Sunlight's a thing that needs a window
before it enters a dark room.
Windows don't happen.

R. S. Thomas 1986, p. 53

This account offers a picture of reflective practice facilitation. Issues raised, as well as principles and practices, are covered more fully as the book unfolds.

An Apprehensive Beginning

Seven people were sitting on easy chairs when I entered the long, narrow room with huge venetian-blinded windows overlooking the car park. Unlike me, they were used to the warm atmosphere I had walked through, where old people moved slowly, one shuffle at a time with the aid of a stick or frame, between tea table and telly. They were officers in charge of this and the nearby old people's homes, all strangers to me, apart from their area manager who had set up the group. He had experienced a similar course and wanted one for his staff feeling it would be *for them*, and about *their situation*, and might bring these isolated professionals together to form a collaborating supportive group. Wonderful chocolate buns, fresh from the oven, and piping hot coffee did much to relax me after my long January drive over the moor.

My new colleagues, I was later to discover, were even more nervous than me and they didn't know each other very well either. We eyed each other, thinking: what have I let myself in for? They later shared their difficulty in perceiving what they might get out of the course when they started: they needed to do it in order to understand. They asked me, as so many others have: 'writing is so difficult, why can't we just discuss these issues with each other?' One member commented in her final evaluation:

> First day – not too keen. Did not know what to expect – wasn't going to be really clever – I am not an academic type person.

In at the Deep End

But the new group couldn't reflect upon their anxieties about writing, and about sharing vital issues with each other for very long, because they were almost immediately plunged into the process. We (including me) were to pick up our pens and start to write. For six minutes we wrote whatever came into our heads in whatever jumbled order – without stopping. Since this writing was not to be shared with each other, we could put down a list of the morning's irritations, a shopping list, a diatribe against an impossible colleague/family member, last night's unshareable nightmare – anything at all in fact. If we ran out of ideas we were to repeat the last word written. A new thought would pretty soon arise.

This *six minutes* ensured that marks had been made on the paper – a beginning of writing made. It also allowed the busy business of whatever was uppermost in our minds to surface, be recorded, and hopefully put on one side; or perhaps a flash of insight to be recorded. I then immediately suggested we write for a further ten or twenty minutes – a story about *a time when something vital was learned*. This might be a personal thing from way back such as discovering that Santa was only Mum, or something from yesterday; or a completely made-up event. We wrote in a similar fashion to the *six minutes* without stopping to think. Thinking can block the inspiration and flow of this kind of writing. The difference was that we would share all or part of this writing with each other, if appropriate.

Resting aching wrists and fingers relievedly on their pads, all six expressed a realisation they could all write; pens had scribbled frantically. The next task was to read both pieces of writing privately with attention, to acquaint ourselves with what we had written, and to look for previously unnoticed connections. We then picked out a passage, or all of it, to share with the rest of the group, if we so wished.

Some Boundaries

Before we read our pieces to each other we established initial groundrules to underpin the discussion. My suggestions were:

- We will be trying to tease out professional and possibly personal issues embedded within the stories, and draw out related, underlying themes that are of concern to the writer and the group.

- We will be doing this in a spirit of support and respect for each other.

- A thoughtful silence often arises after a piece has been read. As facilitator, I will never break this silence, as I could so easily do all the talking. The silence may be felt as supportive and reflective; but it may be experienced as unnerving to the waiting writer. Someone must take responsibility for breaking it.

- While you are listening, be formulating your discussion queries/ points, which will probably be provisional and might take the form of a question, a suggestion, or a request for specific further information.

- When you read you may feel hesitant, but the group will not perceive the imperfections of your writing as you do. They will be interested and involved.

- Everyone's thoughts are of value: yours *and* theirs must be heard.

- These pieces are fictions, although they may seem to slide along what appears to be a fiction–faction–reality continuum. The extent of this is not our business; fiction preserves confidentiality. Writers may wish to share more during or after the session, but this is up to them.

- Confidentiality is essential: anything written or said in the group belongs to the group and cannot be spoken of outside without express permission.

Building on these, the seven of us thought out and expressed some of our fears and anxieties concerning the sharing of writings. The processes of writing and discussing that writing can bring up material and emotions which can be hard to face and share, requiring sensitive facilitation. Group members might feel I appear to say and do little; but I always finish extended, attenuated and exhausted.

One of our groundrules concerned careful timekeeping: everyone was to have their turn without transgressing beyond the agreed finish time. We felt no one should be under any pressure to contribute at any one time, whether in writing or discussion, and I suggested I shouldn't take up group time by bringing my own writing to ensuing sessions. Everyone recognised the need to be warm and involved on the one hand, but cautious and incurious on the other – laughing at ourselves despite the tension: what a tightrope to try to walk!

A Sharing

Everyone read out a snippet, a paragraph or all they'd written that morning. The discussion was wide ranging and rewarding, if careful, after our boundary-creating session. Group members were generous in the personal information they shared through the writing, much of which related to how and why they became involved in such demanding and potentially stressful work. Most of the group felt immensely relieved afterwards: this course is about something I can do, and I *think* I might even be going to enjoy it. The unanimously experienced shadow, felt then, but not expressed until later, was: *everyone but myself is a brilliant writer.*

And Next

Time was running out. I had learned already that this is in short supply for these officers, so they said they would try to keep a journal of brief entries after and before each session. Previous courses had taught me the value of this. Before the ensuing week everyone was to write and bring a new piece which could take any form. For this first time I suggested a topic, but for ensuing sessions the group evolved themes as part of the final discussion. I suggested *A Clean Sheet* – to be understood literally or metaphorically. One took this in a novel way, writing in the voice of a sheet fresh from the laundry in the home she managed:

A Story Within a Story
A Clean Sheet

Here I am again on the laundry shelf, and it's lovely and warm in here with all my companions. Light goes on – just when I was feeling drowsy too – someone is picking me up – what rough hands she has got – I wish she wouldn't hold me close like that. Am being carried along – what's that tune she's humming, I'm sure I've heard it before.

Now I am being unfolded – what a shame to disturb my lovely creases and folds – up into the air. I hover – just for a second. The sun is shining through the window although it is frosty and misty outside the world looks different today – an air of mystery surrounds the home. Funny how mist and mystery go together – sense of excitement but forboding. Well I've landed now on the bed, her rough hands are smoothing me out and tucking me in all around the mattress. Oh heck! Here comes the duvet, what a monstrosity – covering me up – suffocating me – oh well I can't do anything about it – must grin and bear it.

Hours have passed and now someone is coming into the room – three people in fact but one of them is very frail. She is being undressed by the other two – now she is being washed – they are doing their best to converse with this old lady but she does not appear to understand what they are saying to her. They lose interest in talking to her and start to talk to each other about the day's happenings. What a pity they have not time to talk to this old lady.

She is now lying on top of me and is being covered by the duvet, one of them has at least taken the time to make sure she is comfortable and has kissed her goodnight.

All is quiet now, her breathing is slowing down and I can feel her relaxing as she is getting warm. What's that she is saying – she is now talking about bygone days – as though she is young again – and talking to a young soldier. She is walking with him down sunny lanes and is feeling really happy – now a tear falls from her cheek and lands on me – a salty stain spreads albeit a small one – I am touched by this emotion – what can I do – what is she thinking about now?

She moves slowly with a slight moan, and then goes quiet – she is sleeping now.

The writer had felt extremely uncertain about her ability to write, but had managed to overcome her fears by setting her alarm and scribbling for fifteen minutes and no more, in note form. I always hoped that she might continue it as she had originally planned – until it ended up in the laundry again. She did write briefly about the dirty sheet, warning of the dangers of washing bacteria-laden sheets alongside tea towels at a temperature less than boiling. I feel this kind of writing could be used as excellent training material for new assistant staff who, like me, have no idea of what to expect at an old people's home. The following week another group member brought a story she had written to be used in just this way. Hearing it, I can imagine that it made effective training.

This story fitted into the group's ongoing discussions about the way their staff related to residents. They were all concerned that the old people should have more than their bodily needs seen to, and that this should be done with grace and loving care. The *Clean Sheet* writer brought a wise yet humorous slant on all this, as her contribution always did.

More Stories

All the group members read their pieces aloud. *It felt like opening windows on themselves for each other*, I wrote afterwards. The writing the group brought over the weeks proved to be equally valuable and rewarding in a range of ways. The suggested headings for ensuing pieces included: 'dilemmas', 'leadership', 'changes', 'aspirations', 'perceptions', 'a conflict of loyalties' and a 'frustrating episode'.

As week succeeded week there never was enough time for sharing the immense range of work and work-related personal issues. There were long-term difficulties which, despite the full support of area managers, were very trying. One group member commented on the wealth of potential writing topics: as though fate had laid on a fortuitous series of calamitous events. We thought about this, and decided their lives were probably always so, but the course offered space and support to examine and, to some extent, come to terms with these crises: therefore causing them to take more notice of them.

Time was found to write about some past, unsorted-out issues, as well as present problems, such as the suicide of clients. This led to a long discussion about death and dealing with it in a dignified and loving way in a home for older people. I was impressed, as I was time and time again, by the thoughtful and caring professional attitudes expressed.

Some Gains

The six gained confidence exponentially in their ability to express themselves in writing. They felt happier and more confident with writing regular reports and other in-service needs. But for the purposes of this course, there was never any feeling that the writing had to be clever or literary, only a gathering sense that they could express things that might be difficult or impossible to take elsewhere. I was often taken off guard by touching or searing material.

The trust and confidence that grew in the group was one of the most vital outcomes. It led to supportive relationships radically altering their working experience, particularly those fresh to it, or taking on role changes. Each had been struggling with daily problems with staff, equipment, inspections, disciplinaries, new rules from the top and so on and on – all of which they were now able to share.

The writing and discussions on this course confirmed my opinion that studying, evaluating, sharing and therefore taking greater control over professional experience in this way undoubtedly enhances freedom and self-respect. Thinking of life as a story, and having the opportunity and courage to tell that story oneself, offers some measure of control.

Evaluation

A brief formative evaluation in which members reviewed the ground rules, format and content concluded each session. On one occasion, for example, they got out their diaries to set up a series of meetings for after our final date. The one thing they really wanted was to continue. That was their evaluation. I undertook a summative evaluation, with the group members writing about their experience in a structured, collaborative and brief form. One of the comments was:

> Coming each week has been a great source of strength and support to me. Sometimes I have come away feeling a more valued member of 'the team'.

Before the group there was no 'team', only a handful of people in the same area doing much the same job. One fear was: 'I hope we don't lose it all!' They did not need me in order to continue. Feedback since has been that they are still supporting each other through further problems and challenges.

6

Assessment, Evaluation, Mentoring and Values

How can we know the dancer from the dance?

Yeats 1962, p. 128

No man can reveal to you aught but that which already lies half asleep in the dawning of your knowledge. . . .

If he is indeed wise he does not bid you enter the house of his wisdom, but rather leads you to the threshold of your own mind.

Kahlil Gibran 1926, p. 67

Professional reflective practice and its facilitation covers a wide and deep range of issues which it is helpful to address. It is not cosy, but rather the pearl-grit in the oyster of practice. As one reflective practitioner commented:

I have come to realise through the process of writing about this incident that reflection is not a *cosy* process of quiet contemplation. It is an active, dynamic, often threatening process which demands total involvement of self and a commitment to action. In reflective practice there is nowhere to hide.

This chapter looks at: the problems of assessment and evaluation; what mentoring and co-mentoring have to offer; and issues of values, ethics, forgiveness and risk.

Assessment

A perennial problem of reflective practice tutoring is that of assessment. Can such sensitive material be assessed and how?

There is no widely accepted means of identifying or assessing reflection. Nor is it clear whether attempts should be made to assess the degree of reflection demonstrated by the developing professional. . . .

The relationship between the ability and willingness to be reflective about one's professional development, and one's ability and willingness to write reflectively is unclear.

Sumsion and Fleet 1996, p. 122

Sumsion and Fleet conclude from their study that 'reflection appears unsuited to quantitative assessment', though they fear this makes 'reflective practices vulnerable to criticisms about their credibility'. Beveridge (writing of mathematics undergraduates) maintains: 'there is a real danger that creating assessment criteria will have the effect of killing off the spontaneity and individuality of the exercise' (Beveridge 1997, p. 42)

Beveridge feels tutors are in a cleft stick with assessment: without it students don't see the process as being sufficiently worthwhile; the effect of it, however, can be to prevent them from expressing themselves freely. He points out that the reflective journal provides not only an opportunity for the student to offer their own assessment of their development, but also a useful evaluation of the course. Beveridge has found reflective journal material to be invaluable feedback on his teaching, and has materially altered his course structure in the light of students' reflective journal material. I have found that the qualitative data from such portfolios provides incontrovertible proof of the value of this work. Students writing their own marking criteria is also valuable in my experience.

David Boud (1998) considers it inappropriate to assess reflection, that assessment will destroy 'raw reflection', i.e. disable students from involving themselves in the process of 'raw reflection'. He also points out that effective reflective practice needs to be unboundaried, which makes an assessed formal learning context, where clear boundaries are necessary, inappropriate. A formal assessed learning context can only too readily lead to instrumental or rule-following strategies, which apart from stultifying the reflection, can also unethically seek inappropriate levels of disclosure and confession. My own way of dealing with this dilemma on my only assessed reflective practice course is to ask my students to *draw upon* their reflective journals and stories for their portfolios, certainly not to require them to hand in 'raw reflection'. This feels better than to have no reflective element in their Masters degree. There is no need to create any parameters for their reflective work other than the assessment criteria, and the facilitation they receive. We do, as a group, discuss the ethical parameters of reflective practice, and the way this is impinged upon by the preparation of a portfolio.

Winter *et al.* do not tackle the issue of assessment affecting, or even destroying, the students' confidence in expressing themselves freely and exploratively, nor the ethical problem. They point out how it is always difficult to assess work presented in a new format, and that, despite explicit criteria, examiners always have to make, and cross-check, interpretations, and be guided by 'tacit knowledge'. They conclude that:

> in the end these difficulties can be resolved, and they are essentially not very different from the problems of academic assessment in general. As with any assessment decisions other than those involving multiple choice tests there is an inevitable component of subjectivity. But if assessment is explicitly based on the professional criteria [below] (or an equivalent specification), and if examiners devote time initially to sharing and discussing their responses to groups of texts, judgements *can* be agreed as to whether the work fulfils the given criteria and with what varying degrees of success.
>
> Winter *et al.* 1999, p. 148

Assessment criteria are directly related to learning objectives. An effective tutor introduces these to their students and facilitates their use throughout the process of learning and practising the writing of reflective accounts and journals. Moon points out the 'need to decide whether the student is being assessed on content or on the writing, the process of the writing, or the product of the learning' (1999b, p. 34), which again should be clarified in assessment criteria, and in teaching. Moon offers a set of assessment criteria (1999a). The assessment criteria for Richard Winter's reflective writing course were designed to synthesise professional and academic educational objectives as follows:

- careful detailed observation of events and situations;
- empathising with the standpoint of other people;
- noticing the various emotional dimensions of events and situations;
- addressing the complexities of issues, events and situations;
- making connections between different events and situations, and between specific details and general principles derived from a range of professional knowledge;
- demonstrating learning, in response to both professional experience and the process of reflecting upon/writing about it.

Winter *et al.* 1999, p. 108

Evaluation

Evaluation is feedback from participants on the experience of a course – advantages and disadvantages – supporting a facilitator in improving practice. Summative evaluations are at the end, summing up participants' experience of the whole course; formative evaluations are undertaken throughout, at the end of each session, for example, and help form the remainder of the course. These latter can often take the form of five minutes' discussion at the end of a session: 'how do you feel we're doing?' An anonymous formative evaluation procedure, however, can increase participants' confidence in giving more accurate feedback.

Students will gain more from a course if they are supported in being 'brave', and tackle negative thoughts and feelings at the time, rather than brood on them and complain pointlessly after the event. Co-mentoring (see below) can help this process as participants can share their doubts about aspects of the course with a peer before venturing to express them to the facilitator and the rest of the group.

Many summative evaluation methods are printed forms, the dullest being multiple choice, slightly better when comments on aspects of the course can be squeezed into little boxes. Some method for ensuring everyone fills these in is necessary – such as having to do them before the end of the final session.

After short courses I often ask participants to write anonymously *what was good* on one piece of paper, and on another *what could have been better*. This gives useful information speedily. When I have a little more time I ask them to spread their positive comments on one table, negative on another, and go round reading them all, marking each one with a tick (if they agree), or a cross (if they disagree), or another comment.

This method can also be used to advantage at the very beginning of a course for the sharing of hopes, expectations and fears, or personal objectives. The comments can then be transferred to a flipchart sheet, or typed up and fed back to them as part of the evaluation at the final session: 'did you achieve your objectives?', 'to what extent were your hopes and fears borne out?'

Writing a brief (ten minute) evaluative *story* at the end of a reflective writing course is useful. The group are used to expressive and explorative writing, and use the same approach for evaluation. We read them back in turn to the group, with no comments. Participants are less forthcoming about the negative comments (so I usually use anonymous evaluative method as well), but are generous and open with the positive. This has the extra advantage of being an affirming and warm way to end a course – because the stories tend to refer to the life of the group as a whole.

Evaluation ideas are inventive. One I liked, but have never used, is to hand out a picture of a tree with fat little people drawn on or in it. Participants circle whichever figure they feel approximates to their experience of the course. One is gleefully at the top; another on the tip of a topmost branch all hunched up and looking frightenedly alone; one is falling from the very top with another trying desperately to help them; one is frowning flat on his belly on the ground below – 'I'm not having anything to do with all this!' another clinging to a bottom branch; some helping each other at various levels; two sitting companionably and safely on a middle branch; one sitting in the middle with their back to the viewer; one who's got part way and clearly does not want to go any further; and so on.

Drawing one's view for formative evaluation has been pioneered in Sydney Universities for a range of disciplines and courses (McKenzie *et al.* 1998). The drawings gave different information, inventively and informatively, from the written evaluations participants also made. One drew a juggler juggling a variety of commitments, for example, another falling at the last of a succession of high hurdles. Anonymity can be obtained by, for example, a postbox to collect evaluations. I think the evaluation process needs to be useful to participants, rather than just a chore.

Out of the Box: Mentors and Co-Mentors

The first mentor was a goddess. Telemachus, son of Odysseus and Penelope, is mentored by Pallas Athene in human form: ' "For you, I have some good advice, if only you will accept it.' . . . 'Oh stranger,' heedful Telemechas replied, 'indeed I will. You've counselled me with so much kindness now, like a father a son. I won't forget a word." ' (Homer, pp. 86–7.) And of course, in following *Mentor's* advice to the letter, he ably supports his father in returning to his throne and queen.

No mentor since then has been a god, and should never be thought they are. Mentoring is usually a situation of a more experienced professional supporting a less experienced in a learning process: at its most informal a very normal aspect of working life – the offer of a supportive hand.

The mentor helps the mentee step 'outside the box of his or her job and personal circumstances, so they can look in at it together. It is like standing in front of the mirror with someone else, who can help you see things about you that have become too familiar for you to notice' (Clutterbuck and Megginson 1999, p. 17). A mentor asks the questions one does not, or cannot ask oneself. A mentor can act as role model, enabler, teacher, encourager, counsellor, befriender, facilitator, coach, confidante, and supporter in 'unlearning' negative habits or attitudes (such as apologising for oneself, and a sense of lack of self-worth, for example). These roles inevitably overlap, but research into *helping to learn* relationships shows that clarity of role expectations makes for greater effectiveness (Clutterbuck 1998). The pair need to be aware of whose interests are being pursued: a mentor or supervisor who is also a professional superior can be seen as (or even be) controlling. It is also important for them to realise when a matter is beyond their relationship, and help sought from another quarter.

Mentoring deals with the whole person of the mentee; the difference between this and counselling is that it is professionally based, and concerned with professional issues. A mentor often offers empathy and non-judgemental acceptance. The mentor helps the mentee examine and reflect upon the relationship between the emotional, intellectual and behaviour content of issues. But the mentor is there to challenge: the behaviour not the person, their assumptions not their intellect, their perceptions not their judgement, their values not their value (Clutterbuck and Megginson 1999).

Mentoring is a relationship in which vital, often confidential issues can be shared: uncertainties, hopes and fears, anxieties and angsts, shame or guilt, wants and aversions, the influence of intense emotions – whether positive or negative, tentative suggestions for action, lack of or partial understandings, questions of role, personal or career ladder issues, repeated errors or inadequacies, and stories of success, failure or conflict. Everyone needs support, reassurance and challenge with such issues, even (or perhaps particularly) those at the very top:

> Now don't please,
>   be quite so single-minded, self-involved,
>   or assume the world is wrong and you are right.
>   . . . such men, I tell you,
>   spread them open – you will find them empty.
>   No
>   it's no disgrace for a man, even a wise man,
>   to learn many things and not be too rigid.
>   You've seen trees by a raging winter torrent,

how many sway with the flood and salvage every twig,
but not the stubborn – they're ripped out roots and all.
Bend or break . . .
it's best to learn from those with good advice.

                                     Sophocles, (trans. 1982) pp. 95–6

Reflective practice can effectively be supported by co-mentoring: pairs of peers. Much of the above work can be done in this way with no problems about payment, control, or danger of god(dess) worship. My co-mentor and myself feel the process gives us clarity about who we are at work, and how to tackle issues.

Courses, and support for practitioners, in co-tutoring in general practice (family medicine) are offered in Britain: 'a system of peer supported learning based on a relationship of parity, whereby participants facilitate each others' thinking and reflection to enable them to address the problems that are pertinent to their individual situation' (Eastaugh 1998b, p. 2).

My Masters students have always found co-mentoring relationships support them through the challenge of the course, and portfolio writing. Each pair creates a working contract – many read and comment on learning journals and assignments-in-progress, and discuss appropriate issues. The students also spend time together as a whole group without us, their tutors, in group co-mentoring activities. Professional students quite properly learn widely from each other; co-mentoring structures this effectively.

Ethics and Patients, Students or Clients

Reflective practice raises serious ethical considerations: concerning the practitioner, the population with whom they practise, and the organisation for whom they work. Ethical elements of practice are, furthermore, very properly aired in reflective practice. The partiality of either or both parties (practitioner and facilitator) may confuse or distort appropriate discussions or decisions concerning ethical issues. I will deal with these areas in turn.

A practitioner's response to material thrown up by the reflective process may be unexpectedly emotive (angry or distressed, for example), or present them with unexpected issues to sort out. John, a Masters student, commented: 'this really made me realise the learner is *not* in control when exploring new ideas'. Inexperienced facilitators, furthermore, may find the content of a student's reflection raises issues or emotions of their own, which may otherwise have remained buried. Hargreaves has examined the ethics of requiring nurses to undertake this activity (1997, and see below). Effective facilitation of reflection can support the practitioner in appropriately sorting out issues which arise; a supervisor similarly supports the facilitator.

When a reflective practitioner lays bare a situation, they often expose confidential material about the population with whom they work. A semblance of confidentiality is maintained by not using the full real name of the client or student, and altering other details. Practitioners do all in their power to discuss cases with respect. But sometimes the need to release feelings overtakes this. I well remember one group of doctors falling about with hilarity about a dead body being dropped, and being unpickupable in snow and ice. No disrespect was intended, but the situation was too horrific to be countenanced until some emotion had been released. I understand paramedics and police officers respond in similar ways.

Practitioners need to develop their practice by discussing specific issues rather than generalities. As a user of services myself, I would far rather think I was discussed among colleagues – in whatever way was appropriate – than feel I was treated by an unreflective practitioner. But these are issues which can effectively be addressed during facilitation.

Reflective practice is an appropriate arena for the discussion of ethical practice. Anne Hudson Jones describes how narratives of practice are used to teach 'narrative ethics', offering 'richer ethical discourse for all' (Hudson Jones 1998, p. 223). Ron Carson maintains that both the study of one's own stories of practice and the reading of literature are the best way of studying and maintaining ethical practice: 'literature shapes sensibility by giving form to feelings and by revealing the narrative structure of experiences of love, loss, loyalty and the like' (1994, p. 238). Reflective journals, and discussions upon them, have been used sensitively and carefully to support student palliative care nurses:

> The diary sessions are in-depth critical discussions and comparisons of clinical situations where logical and rigorous analysis of moral and ethical concepts takes place. Through this analytical process, assumptions made by health care professionals, patients and relatives are uncovered and examined. This leads to the revelation of attitudes, stereotyping, prejudices, preconceptions, philosophical ethics, frames of references, cultural influences, and the nurse's predisposition to act

in a certain way: 'reflecting on clinical situations made me aware of my beliefs . . . and the assumptions I make . . . the uniqueness of people and their rights.'

Durgahee 1997, p. 143

The process the groups undergo is clearly not restricted to the 'logical and rigorous', but a fully rounded reflective process involving emotional responses and synthetic functions.

Ethical dilemmas may arise when a practitioner reflects upon another's faulty practice. A facilitator, supervisor, or other group members may feel ethically beholden to report the bad practice even though it was disclosed to them through confidential reflection. Where does the responsibility of the interlocutors to such a disclosure lie? (This is discussed with reference to nursing in Cutcliffe *et al.* 1998.) What would I have done had my teacher student (pp. 8–9) not made it clear her school was dealing with the colleague who was having a sexual relationship with a pupil? There can be no hard and fast rules made in the abstract about these issues: careful one-to-one discussion with the practitioner who had disclosed the case would be the starting point.

Values

Reflective practice supports, demands even, that practitioners think about values, particularly story-based reflection:

> If we had asked people to talk about their values in abstract terms, we would have received generalised responses. By asking them to tell [write] stories about important experiences, we were able to see something of how values reveal themselves in a complex, varied and shifting way in practice.
>
> Pattison *et al.* 1999

Much of our practice relies upon tacit knowledge and understanding based upon experience. We don't habitually question, or analyse the values which underpin our work. This is one of the reasons reflective practice can lead to dramatic changes in people's lives: brought face-to-face with an issue, they sometimes feel: *I've got to change this!*; and change it they do. This might not be easy, particularly if they realise an action has been against their own ethical code, or that they are in an untenable, but unalterable situation (see Rowland 2000, Chapter 8).

Examining such fundamental areas requires a supportive, confidential, carefully facilitated environment. Practitioners bring their whole selves holistically to reflective practice; and that whole person has vulnerabilities. Reflective practice, to be effective, does not shy away from the emotional aspects of issues. The feelings aroused by a situation are just as important as the actions and thoughts. There would be little chance of a practitioner hoping to work with a whole student, patient or client (holistic practice), if they could not bring their whole person to the work.

Aspects of therapeutic theory and practice have therefore been brought into reflective practice. Carl Rogers was a therapist who advocated this way of working in education (Rogers 1969), and Jane Abercrombie was an academic biologist who brought therapeutic group work principles into higher education teaching in the 1960s (Abercrombie 1993). A basic tenet of this way of working is respect and 'unconditional regard' (Rogers 1969) for the student.

A reflective practice facilitator is not a therapist; but an understanding of therapeutic ways of working can offer greater powers of empathy and facilitation, and greater confidence handling emotive situations. A reflective practitioner may discover therapeutic needs through the reflective process which cannot be met within reflective practice, and must be sought through appropriate channels.

Pre-service students are considered by some to be more likely to uncover material needing therapeutic support. Young students (undergraduates, for example) in my experience, however, tend to tumble in and out of being emotional in reflective practice; I have not experienced them as any more vulnerable, but yet have known extremely experienced doctors break down and need support.

I have, though, noticed undergraduates making definite statements about themselves and each other; 'I'm the sort of person who . . .', 'that's just like you, you always . . .'. Young adults are finding out who they are, and the location of their personal boundaries. Lewis Carroll explored this in *Alice*: the poor lass never knows what size or shape she will be next, nor what life will face her with (though she does stay remarkably cool when 'a mile high', about to have her head cut off, or on becoming a queen).

The positioning of checks and balances in reflective practice facilitation can help prevent distress in either facilitator or practitioners. A facilitator's own supervisor/mentor is the appropriate person with whom to deal with problems or anxieties. Co-facilitating group sessions can enable one to be tutoring while the other is observing and keeping an eye on developments within the group, and in individuals. Group reflexivity and an awareness of Rowland's 'shared context' (pp. 39–40) in a learning situation is also invaluable. The group can be facilitated to take responsibility for its own processes; they will observe if a member needs extra support or to be handled sensitively and will alert the facilitator if necessary. Each member has responsibility for sharing any distress or anxiety before it becomes too big for the group to handle.

Clarification of groundrules of boundaries and confidentiality can help reflective practice groups or pairs deal with such issues. An additional dimension occurs when the supervisor is also in a position of authority over the practitioner, who may be justifiably cautious about what and how they will disclose. This is an institutional issue, and must be dealt with at that level.

As reflective processes are a likely aspect of professional supervision, ethical and power issues need always to be addressed. The area is clouded, however, by differing assumptions of what *reflective practice* and *supervision* mean. Fowler and Chevannes stress 'there are potential disadvantages in making the assumption that reflective practice should be an integral part of all forms of clinical supervision' (1998, p. 379). Marrow *et al.*, however, write of effective supervision, where the sister of a busy accident and emergency unit offered effective supervision to her staff focusing on reflective diaries, which she read (1997). And Judy Hildebrand describes deeply reflective and reflexive supervision of family therapist trainees (1995). Here is Janet Hargreaves' reflection:

> One of the interesting reflections for me in writing about nursing, reflection and ethics, is how an idea forms and where it comes from. At what point does it become something tangible?
>
> It happens with this particular idea I know when I first thought it all out in one go. A routine occurrence of a weekend at my parents.

> *David is playing football with Richard, on a field near the river – an activity which rarely captures my interest for more than a few minutes, so I wander away and walk along the river in the quiet Sunday morning sun. I do a lot of good thinking in this situation – planning lectures, reflecting back, evaluating. As I am walking all of the bits of this idea just plop into my brain – reflection, nursing, ethics. Suddenly I realise that I am forming something new – not a regurgitation of all of the things I have read, but an idea of my own which is growing out of them.*

But the idea did not just start there, out of nothing, it can be traced back over months, or even years, the factors were:

- Facilitation of post registration nurses in undergraduate study using, amongst other things, reflection as a medium for development.
- Study for an MA in Health Care Ethics, broadening my understanding of ethics and challenging previous views.
- Running a session on the ethical and legal issues in reflection on an MA unit in reflective practice.

Issues of confidentiality are a concern in recording reflections, which are often personal and may be controversial. There are also a small number of cases where a reflective diary has been used in a legal setting as 'evidence'.

But once I really started to think about all this I realised that these were not the really important questions. They presuppose that reflection is given: they challenge some of the consequences of reflection, but not the act itself. The really important issue was why were we encouraging nurses to be reflective in the first place? What is it for? What does it achieve? Once I started asking these questions everything changed. Mezirow (1981) talks of paradigm transformation, and this is what happened to me here – a sudden realisation that if I looked at the same thing from a very slightly different angle – I would see a completely different picture. Reflection is not without moral significance, for example:

- Reflection is emotionally demanding for the person who is doing it. Can we insist they do it?
- On reflecting the reflector may feel more pressured to act to change a situation, thus disturbing the status quo.
- If you then share those reflections with others verbally then you expose a part of yourself, and divulge information about unsuspecting third parties.
- If you write down those reflections as part of an assessed course they are read by at least one other person, and are given into that third party's custody for safe keeping. Also in doing this there is an obligation to reveal part of yourself which may usually be private in order to gain academic credit, and to use the experiences of your (non-consenting) patients as the medium for your achievement.

In themselves none of these things is awfully shocking, but they are not without moral worth. Consequently to justify them there has to be some perceived gain. What is it? What can we clearly say has been achieved, or is achievable through reflection, what is the end that is gained via these means?

The justification can be that it makes better nurses, or happier nurses, or better people generally – but all of that would be pretty difficult to prove. It leaves a need to reflect on the nature of the good nurse, and the lack of literature regarding the value of reflection.

I put my ideas together for the Nurse Education Tomorrow (NET) conference, and then for the *Journal of Advanced Nursing* (JAN rather than NET) (Hargreaves 1997).

My moment by the river has been like a starburst, helping me to see the issue differently. What might be interesting too would be to reflect on my own ability to reflect – does it make me a better teacher/a happier teacher, or a better person generally? – if it does – then can that be translated to other things like nursing?

Janet Hargreaves

Forgiveness

Reflective practice can enable a shift in attitude to events, relationships and values in professional life, whether institutional or relative to clients. Forgiving others and oneself can be an element. A connectedness with ourselves, each other and our world tends to have been lost in a world obsessed with measurement and evaluation, external success and appearance, and a belief that people can shape their world by making conscious plans. This connectedness has been replaced by anxiety around relationships, and a fear of each other evidenced by such phenomena as road rage.

Mercy has been marginalised, being viewed as rather soppy and/or religious. Blake's description of mercy as having a 'human heart' (Blake 1958, p. 33) and Portia's powerful plea (Shakespeare's *Merchant of Venice*) have too often been forgotten. 'Given this situation it is no wonder that people are flocking to various mental health practitioners with chronic guilt, shame, resentment, dis-ease, and feelings of estrangement' (Rowe and Halling 1998, p. 227). The goddess Athene says of forgiveness:

> Let your rage pass into understanding
> As into the coloured clouds of a sunset,
> Promising a fair tomorrow.
> Do not let it fall
> As a rain of sterility and anguish.

(Aeschylus trans. 1999, p. 184)

'The failure to forgive . . . stands in the way of our development as persons who are free of unnecessary restraints from the past and illusions of human perfection' (Rowe *et al.* 1989, p. 233). Practitioners have found a capacity to forgive colleagues, clients and themselves through reflective practice, in my experience. This forgiveness is like the letting go of a weight which has been carried, often for years; it can come accompanied by grief (Bauer *et al.* 1992). Forgiveness of oneself and of others go hand in hand and are both vital; the letting go of remorse and hatred or anger with another cannot be planned for, nor directed by a facilitator, however.

Forgiveness is like a gift which comes with increased understanding. The example I shall always remember is the midwife who was still furious with a mother, years after the birth. She wrote the story – angrily – from her own point of view. The reflective practice group (Masters degree module) and I then suggested she wrote it from the perspective of the mother. When she returned the following week with her second story she said humbly: 'I don't feel angry any more. I don't *know* why she behaved so badly, but if it was like in my story she was as hurt as I was, if not more so.'

Risk

This kind of work comes with its own anxieties, doubts, fears and sense of risk. Those who gain from the process feel: *nothing ventured, nothing gained*. I would like to explore the issue of risk with reference to one reflective writing group: an educational principles and practice module on a Master in Medical Science course.

This group had been working together for some time, discussing and learning about education. But this was the first time they were to expose their thinking and understandings *in writing* with each other. It is one thing to say something tentatively in discussion, and then develop or alter it as the subject evolves and mutates. It is one thing to sit silent, or only venturing the odd expression while the more verbal and confident develop their ideas through discussion. It is quite another to put yourself on the line and stand by your written words. The group members knew I would be asking them to write very quickly without forethought – not merely as *rational discourse* (Mezirow 1991), but also to write from intuitive knowledge, understanding, and memory of experience.

One asked: 'Are we just going to sit here and write? How do I know which incident to choose?' I replied I would be facilitating the session; every step would be very carefully explained and agreed to. There was a sigh of relief: the facilitation itself would be strong and straightforward. The process of writing explorative and expressive texts, and sharing them (albeit in a well-formed and effectively performing group) needs, I feel, a supportive, clear, facilitative, interactive tutor, to offer confidence and trust. The growth and development of this kind of work can only too easily feel unsafe and confusing: as much safety as possible and as much respect for confused feelings and seeming muddliness needs to be facilitated. The members need to feel that whatever they write is the right thing for them at that time, and will be respected as such by the rest of the group, as will seeming contradictions and changes of mind. They need to feel the con-fidentiality and possible privacy of writings are respected.

The ensuing week, I assured everyone, we would pull apart my facilitation style and skills, for the sake of their educational under-standings – and we did – but that is not the story here.

The group understood this would be *hot* writing (improvised, rather than played coolly from pre-planned ideas). But they still needed me to explain how to allow words to flow from their pens; after all their heads were empty of ideas, or full of apprehension rather.

The students were asked to trust themselves to go back to the very first stages of writing. The stages of writing without thinking. Those initial stages are the breath of creative life to poets, novelists, play-wrights, autobiographers, but are missed out by academic writers.

Everyone wrote for six minutes without stopping, putting on the paper whatever was in their heads (like a stream of consciousness). This was not for sharing (but could be if the writer so wished): to clear our heads; or capture whatever floating thoughts and ideas were there; and to get the pen flowing untroubledly (or perhaps feverishly fast) over the page. Liz wrote:

> (One group member) has just left the room, obviously upset, and I think that emphasises just how powerful this can be. How does this 'power' get dealt with without leaving more scars?

This element of risk, which the students rightly discerned from the start, is of course, as Liz so rightly judges, the seat of the *power* of this kind of writing. It can seem like a tightrope to a beginning student. Having facilitated a very large number of such sessions, I know that writing these things, although so powerful: is also well-paced, people do not normally write more than they are able to cope with at that time. It is important to give the writer sufficient time to read and acquaint themselves with their own writing before sharing anything with tutor or group. From Elaine's journal:

> The facilitation allowing the group to respond to the writings primarily

and giving permission not to disclose any part of the writing made the group safe and gave responsibility to its members.

This is different from a talk-based discussion group when it is easy to blurt things out and then regret at leisure (Hulatt 1995). Sonya (NHS Senior Nurse Manager) commented in her journal on her own six-minute-writing:

> this seemed to spring from nowhere and resulted in me actively seeking a new job!! All based on a few minutes' thought!

We then wrote about 'a time when I learned something vital at work'. Ann, (herself an experienced educator) wrote about a disastrous session with a group of young disadvantaged mothers which she had facilitated many years ago. From her final portfolio:

> When I began to write this critical incident I started with a series of descriptive words. They mostly related to emotions, both mine and those I had felt from the other people involved in the incident. Then I began to write the story. As I began to write I was unsure about why I had chosen this incident. It had happened some years ago and I felt that as I had discussed the incident with a number of people at the time, that I had understood and analysed it sufficiently. Perhaps that was why I used it – perhaps I felt I had the answers ready to be neatly inserted into the story. Nevertheless I had been instructed to write about the first incident which came to mind and this was the one. As I wrote, the situation was re-created before me. I could see the room, feel the atmosphere, although parts of the sequence of events were hazy in detail. What I did remember and what hit me again was the emotional force of feeling, both those of the women in that room on that day, but more particularly my own feelings. As I wrote I couldn't believe how much there was to put down. I had to force myself to stop after all the others had finished. When I read the piece to the group I was overwhelmed by the emotional force and couldn't complete the reading. All those emotions. And I thought I had 'dealt with' this incident.

Writing in this way can enable practitioners to begin to listen properly to some of the different voices within themselves. This is risky because it takes the writer into a marginal state where certainties dissolve. These certainties are in fact like professional straitjackets, though they can tend to feel comfortable and secure. Within the marginal writing state, the writer loses their confidence in who they are: the characters in the different retellings of the story, or the person they thought they were before. The narrator can become the narration; they cross over that threshold of certainty, of knowing how they should respond in given situations and into the unknowingness of uncertainty. The feeling of riskiness lies in the possibility that through this process the writer may: face issues which had been buried as *unfaceable*; begin to doubt their practice; become confused (how will I know who I am if I bring my basic practice into question?); require themself drastically to alter their practice, to alter their world, even to feel they must attempt to alter the worlds of others.

They do all these things – hopefully. Before they start, however, the students can only perceive the dangers of these changes. Later they realise the exhilaration and increase in self-confidence and self-determination. The job of the facilitator is to ensure this happens at a pace and depth, and with sufficiently created boundaries so 'this "power" gets dealt with without leaving more scars' (Liz, above).

The next stage was to read the writings to each other and discuss them. I wrote and read out alongside the group, though I always make it clear I don't want to hog the discussion and accordingly will keep my verbal contribution until everyone else has had a say. The discussion was not directed except to avoid mere anecdote-capping (unlikely with this group), and to support it towards deeper reflective levels. And we did work within clear guidelines and boundaries set by the group.

Jessica's story concerned a knotty, ongoing work situation, which she unflinchingly brought to the group for them to wrestle with together. She took her fresh understandings back to the work situation, and implemented them immediately: 'I don't believe I could have done it without the learning opportunities I have been given'. Her stories can be read elsewhere (Bolton 1999a).

The group also worked in *peer-mentoring* pairs, as well as a whole group without their tutors. This enabled discussions which were additional to the ones with myself as facilitator. One commented he could discuss issues with his peer-mentor which he would never have been able to expose to the whole group.

The group wrote additional stories and reflective passages to go with their original *core story*. Many suggestions were made by group members as to how fresh writings could be undertaken, many of them imaginative and deeply helpful to their writers. Here is a reflective extract from Ann's journal:

> I surprised myself with both the subject of what I wrote and the power of emotions it provoked. I hadn't realised I had so many unresolved feelings about the incident despite having talked about it to others many times. On reflection I feel that Gillie is right: there is something in

the writing that gives another dimension. Seeing the words on the page gives an added intensity to the power of the feelings. There was a lot of honesty in the group this week, although some people understandably chose to use a far less problematic incident than others. I feel I have learned a lot from hearing the others in the group talk through their incidents. What have I learned? . . . I have learned about the power of the written word. I have thought about trying to do sharing of critical incidents with primary health care teams and feel it could be very valuable. I'm sure every group finds its level of exposure.

Ann felt the group were not sufficiently critical in the discussion, that they supported her too much to feel she had acted out of the best intentions. She wanted to face the possibility that having good intentions just wasn't enough. She noted six weeks later, however:

> I can see that I had still not been able to put this incident behind me and therefore was cross with others for trying to help me to do that. I feel rather embarrassed now by my reactions to the group. It was, of course, not about them but about me. . . . I can now forgive myself for this incident, understand it and accept that everyone gets it wrong sometimes.

She also later wrote her impressions about our discussions around our second story (on gender issues – a theme chosen by the group). She commented that on that occasion we had had more time, and were more confident about what we were doing. She was more positive about the depth of reflection we reached. To me it seems no bad thing that a group starts off very sensitively and gingerly supportive when discussing such writings. Also Ann could not fully take into account, then, the effect her evident emotion had had on the group.

Liz rewrote her piece as a series of *thought bubbles*, thoughts which had not been expressed in the writing. These were the thoughts of the character in the story who was herself, but they could equally well have been more fictional ones of the client as well.

Elaine wrote about a frustrating session with a client at her clinic. She had felt anxious about the event, and responsible for things not going better. After the writing session her strong desire was to put the writing away, never read it again, nor think about that client. On the suggestion of the group, however, she rewrote the event twice, fictionally; from the client's point of view; and as a win:win situation, that is as an occasion when both client and nurse felt in agreement about a positive outcome. From Elaine's journal:

> I was amazed at the reduction of anger when I wrote the win:win situation towards the client and myself. I was also struck by the lack of

centrality of my position in the clinic compared to the wide complex circumstances of the client's life. . . . Writing a win:win situation enormously reduced the overall anxiety and power which caused both myself and the client to OVERACT and OVER-REACT.

Both Elaine and Liz stressed in their journals how the writing, rewriting and discussion helped them to become more objective about the incident, and to separate out responsibilities. Both realised they had taken on responsibility which really was not theirs, some of it belonging to the client. Elaine commented in her journal that the writing and discussion: 'helped change my emotional response to the situations and be more mentally open to all options rather than solving it in a specific way'.

Endnote

Ethical dilemmas, a sense of professional and personal risk, and judgements about values are inevitable within reflection upon the caring and educational professions. More than inevitable, they are cornerstones, and as such need to be supported by effective evaluation, facilitation, supervision, or mentoring, as well as carefully and sensitively assessed if appropriate.

7

Why Use Story and Poetry?

Wherever we walk we put our feet on story.

Cicero

I'm not sure I can tell the truth. . . . I can only tell what I know.
Cree hunter in Clifford 1986, p. 8

Why story and poetry rather than thinking, talking and discussing, or writing 'critical incidents' or 'events' or case notes? Story structure assists understanding and memory: we listen to stories attentively, and remember them afterwards, such as Clough's powerful story about special educational needs (Clough 1996), and Landgrebe's about care of the dying (Landgrebe and Winter 1994). 'The deceptive power of [story] lies in the fact that single startling cases stick in the mind' (Macnaughton 1998, p. 202). And the study of our own stories enables us to work constructively with our own experience:

> Many hold their failures inside, allowing them to smoulder and decay; others step into self-destructive habits; others tell [and write] stories.
> Borkan *et al.* 1999, p. 11

We are brought up surrounded by stories: they flow through us and ratify us from birth, telling us who we are and where we belong, what is right and what is wrong. Many are traditional, whether or not they have been given contemporary dress. Tales in which the wicked step-mother receives her comeuppance explain that mothers can be horrid quite often, but good will ultimately conquer over evil (Bettelheim 1976). Lévi-Strauss (1978) tells us our myths offer us ways of classifying and ordering our society. We do not tell our mythic stories, they tell us. They are a language created each time they are told (Bettelheim 1976), providing ways for us to deal with our complex, strange and often scary inner psychological worlds.

Even small children (Rowland 1984) are clear about story structure. No parent or friend can cheat a child by stopping telling a story before the end even if the child does not know the specific story – they know what kind of thing constitutes a story, and an ending in particular. Their imaginative play is often continuous story, and their first writings have a good grasp of structure. Anyone who has asked a small child about their drawing or painting will know how a child will tell the story of the picture, rather than describe the images. We too live our lives by telling stories about them: 'A man is always a teller of tales, he lives surrounded by his stories and the stories of others' (Sartre 1938, p. 61). But life as it is lived is not structured like an *adventure*; adventures only happen in stories. And the story has to be communicated: told, or read. It cannot take place just in thinking:

> 'Is that the end of the story?' asked Christopher Robin.
> 'That's the end of that one. There are others.'
> 'About Pooh and Me?'
> 'And Piglet and Rabbit and all of you. Don't you remember?'
> . . . .
> 'I do remember,' he said, 'only Pooh doesn't very well, so that's why he likes having it told to him again. Because then it's a real story and not just a remembering.'
>
> Milne 1928, p. 31

Stories are the mode in which our culture is transmitted, from history books to *The News*, or bedtime readings. Stories create the way we see our place in society, and the way we perceive it as moulded around us: telling us what to expect of each other and ourselves. They shape and make sense of our world by reiterating the social order. Every soap opera, every reseeing of Shakespeare or replaying of Henry James or Jane Austen as a 'costume drama', tells us what is good and what bad, what is likely to succeed and what fail.

These meanings are usually implicit. The New Testament parables are perhaps the closest to didactic story telling we have – meanings are not implied, but made explicit – Jesus often explained what he intended the story to teach. Aesop's Fables are similar. But had Jesus and Aesop omitted the story, the lessons would not have been remembered for millennia. We can all remember that we should sow our corn on good fertile ground rather than among stones; that if we assume the unattainable bunch of grapes we had lusted after is probably sour after all, we won't feel so bad about not having it. Similarly we aren't likely to forget that killing your father and marrying your mother, as Oedipus did, is unlikely to lead you to much good. The meanings in these powerful ancient Greek plays are all implicit, just as they are in fairy stories and *EastEnders* or *Home and Away*.

But no story has only one meaning. The writer, when relating to their story, may perceive certain meanings clearly, and formulate specific questions. Different readers will perceive other meanings, and pose different questions.

> The ambiguities of a fiction may be thought of as representing (in some sense) the ambiguities of the author's and the reader's personal awareness. The questions posed by the text are questions about the writer's and the reader's own experience and values.
>
> Winter *et al.* 1999, p. 23

Questions and theories about meanings may seem to conflict. That stories are ambiguous, in this way, is one of their great strengths. A discussion following the hearing or reading of a story can be so fruitful because everyone has their own view of its message. Many insights into a story's implicit meanings will be new to the writer, and will widen their view. The readers or listeners to the story and the writer may disagree, but this very disagreement can only throw light for all of them.

Each reader views a story from their individual viewpoint – often refreshingly different from that of the writer. Our perception of our experience and our self is conceived, enmeshed within the frame of our own social, political and psychological understanding – we cannot know ourselves and our experience independently. Individual experience has been described in the reflective practice literature as *raw* and *authentic* (*true*); yet it is no more and no less than another story; a story which others will cap with their own, or their own view. Greenhalgh and Hurwitz (1998), Montgomery Hunter (1991) and Brody (1987) have explored the fundamental importance of narrative and story to medicine.

Music also tells stories. There are few people who do not find music supportive, restful or invigorating – a different way of communicating from speech. A piece of music will work musically through tensions, conflicts and mood changes, towards a resolution; these relate to each other just as characters and events do in a written story. The cellist of a well-known string quartet explained they practise by working out the plot and characters within the piece, and which belongs to which instrument at which time. They then play as if each of them is a character at any one time, communicating as the plot unfolds.

A classical composition contains certain combinations of notes needing to resolve into certain other combinations. A listener needs no musical understanding or ear to hear this. As a non-musical person, I often feel better off than knowledgeable concert-goers as I can concentrate on this rather than be caught up into musicality.

Some reflective practitioners use poetry to express what they need to express. This, I think, is because poetry's conciseness enables it to reach the parts that prose cannot, leaping straight to the heart of the matter. Poetry is an exploration of our deepest and most intimate experiences, thoughts, feelings, ideas and insights: swift but minutely accurate delineations of these and our world, distilled and pared to succinctness, are the soul of poetry. Grammar, spelling and prose form are out of the window, so the writing is not hindered by such niceties as a sentence needing a verb. Poetry is also lyrical, and relies to quite a large extent on imaginative and insightful image, particularly metaphor. All these make poetry a deeply satisfying and memorable way to express vital matter.

Story and poetry are similar modes of expression and understanding in that they both have an intuitive and imaginative structure (which Sacks 1985 calls *narratology*), rather than rational (Sacks' *schematic*). They both belong in the realm of the aesthetic rather than the functional. Oliver Sacks, a psychologist, describes Rebecca as he first encountered her in his clinic, and then by chance in the garden:

> When I first saw her – clumsy, uncouth, all-of-a-fumble – I saw her merely, or wholly, as a casuality, a broken creature, whose neurological impairments I could pick out and dissect with precision: a multitude of apraxias and agnosias, a mass of sensorimotor impairments and breakdowns (and) limitations of intellectual schemata. A poor thing I said to myself. . . .
>
> She was at home with poetic language. . . . I found myself thinking of her fondness for tales, for narrative composition and coherence. Is it possible, I wondered, that this being before me . . . can *use* a narrative (or dramatic) mode to compose and integrate a coherent world, in place of the schematic mode, which, in her, is so defective that it simply doesn't work? And as I thought, I remembered her dancing, and how this could organise her otherwise ill-knit and clumsy movements. . . .
>
> It was perhaps fortunate that I chanced to see Rebecca in her so-different modes – so damaged and incorrigible in the one, so full of promise and potential in the other – and that she was one of the first patients I saw in our clinic. For what I saw in her, what she showed me, I now saw in them all.
>
> Sacks 1985, pp. 170–3

And I am saying in this book – I see this in *us all*. Not that we are defective, but that we use only a fraction of our 'promise and potential' professionally if we do not harness the creative story-, poetry-, drama-making and musical aspects of ourselves.

> Stories do not carry currency in modern (practice). Stories are not easily quantified or coded and are frequently dismissed as mere 'anecdote'.
>
> I have been able to take the opportunity to share my stories outside the reflective writing group. I was invited to open a palliative care conference with a session entitled *Problems faced in keeping patients at home*. A glance down the programme showed that the other speakers were experts in their field, and that we would be told about new drugs, syringe drivers, and ways of accessing benefits. I read a story about my involvement as a GP with a dying man. The story belongs to John, his wife, his children and his carers. But it belonged to all of us at the study day too. Benefits, syringe drivers and new drugs *are* needed, but we need to put them into context.
>
> Mark Purvis

Rosemary Willett's Two Stories

Rosemary writes of clients from her social worker experience:

Evelyn

Only her father understood Evelyn. Only he knew that there were times when the noises and voices in her head made her angry and she wanted to lash out. There were times when she could not stand the people and bustle in the day centre. Then he took her to sit at the side of the canal while he fished, or to walk in the woods and look at the birds and animals.

Her mother had died when she was ten. Her four brothers and sisters, envious perhaps of her special place in the family, got on with their lives, and Evelyn stayed with her father.

Then, quite suddenly, he was gone. Admitted to hospital for a routine operation, he had a heart attack and Evelyn was alone.

She had to live with people she did not know; there were too many of them and they did not realise that she needed her routine, her space, her time. And she missed her father's comforting presence desperately.

'Evelyn is violent, dangerous. Evelyn has challenging behaviour,' they said. So they locked her up; she was terrified.

Later, she went to live with a family. Happier at first, the toddler's needs competed with her own and she wisely asked to move.

She moved again after she threw a table; she had been accused of lying by staff. Evelyn knew that she was not lying, only saying things as she saw them.

'Evelyn is a gypsy. Evelyn needs to move,' people said. 'Evelyn needs to learn Anger Management.'

The new place was smaller, quieter, more tolerant. Now she has been there for four years. She spends her days travelling alone. When she is tense, she walks by the canal.

She looks after her bird. 'Roy is happy,' she says.

Mary

Mary sits in her pretty pink bedroom and listens to the trains going by. She finds that their rhythm is comforting. It is the first room of her own that she has had in her 50 years and she is so proud of it.

Mary weeps for her dead brother. 'I love him and miss him,' she says. She grieves for the birthday card with its five pound note, and for the occasional casual encounters on the bus. She did not see him when he was ill with cancer or go to his funeral.

Mary was put away when she was three; rejected because she was backward and spastic; since then, only people who are paid have given her attention and love.

Mary is well known because she goes round the district asking for cigarettes and cups of tea. She holds up the traffic by being handicapped. At least she can control that.

Mary gave me a plaque for Mothers' Day. 'You're like a mother to me,' she says.

Rosemary's account of the stories

I came to this job after some years away from much contact with people with Learning Disabilities, and was immediately profoundly affected by their interesting, poignant and sometimes dramatic life stories which are not always reflected in Health or Social Services assessments or academic research.

Working as a social worker in a multi-disciplinary team our major role is the assessment, co-ordination and review of services for our users and their carers. We become involved in people's lives offering them clarification, support and some continuity, and possibly most important we give them our time.

In order to provide the services needed, maximise choices and maintain the quality of life which is everyone's right, it is clearly appropriate to evaluate a range of strengths, needs, skills and behaviours. However, it seems to me that during this process we categorise people in a way which overlooks or denies significant parts of the reality of their life experience, and their feelings about that experience.

Some of the language in these stories is deliberately stigmatising, because that is part of the reality. I hoped to give a different slant on why people are as they are: some explanation which may influence practice. Social workers can become institutionalised in thinking and action. We need to be moved by those we work with: a colleague was in tears on reading *Evelyn*, whom she knows well. It is personally fulfilling for me to *paint these pictures*.

Rosemary Willett

Fiction

Stories are not 'true'

These stories are not reconstructions of chunks of *real life*. They cannot be. The *truth* in stories, as in ethnographic writing (Clifford 1986) can only ever be *partial*. No account, however carefully constructed, can ever be *true*. It will be told from the narrator's point of view, with the details they noticed and remembered; a different narrator would tell a different story. Even a video would only record what came within its field – no smell, taste, sense of touch, or sight and sound material outside its range. 'People talk about true stories. As if there could possibly be such things as true stories; events take place one way and we recount them the opposite way' (Sartre 1938, p. 62). The belief that any study can be objectively true, with a single 'teleological meaning' (Barthes 1977, p. 146), is itself a fiction. Everyone has their own way of seeing a situation; we all perceive selectively:

Selective hearing syndrome: female:

He: You are the most beautiful, fascinating, intelligent, witty, sexy, well-balanced, creative woman I have ever met, even if you are a bit moody sometimes.

She: Me? Moody?

Selective hearing syndrome: male:

She: You never take the children to the park, or read them a story; you never even cook an egg, and have never made the bed.

He: Bed? Now?

There are many occasions when a reflective practitioner needs to examine a particular incident, exploring only that event – their motives, feelings and thoughts, their actions and those of others, recording it as accurately and as widely as possible from their own memory, and possibly also consulting others for their perceptions. And there will be times when it is useful to explore scenarios fictionally – what might have happened, what others might have thought, and so on. And on occasion a reflective practitioner will want to explore attitudes and motives, ideas and feelings completely fictionally – as in a fairy story. None of these, however, can be *true* accounts: they will always recount experience from a point of view.

Stories might be what we live by. But the events to which they relate in our lives are not stories in the way we understand the word. Life as lived is viscous, it has no shape, certainly not the comforting fictive form we all recognise from infancy – with a beginning, middle and end, and a clear set of characters and sense of place. The function of the endless *stories* we tell and write is to give life a spurious and satisfying sense of shape. The identity, or *character*, of a person similarly is not static or fixed, as it is has to be in a *story*. 'We all talk about "me". How do we know that there is such a person as "me"? (Chuang Tsu trans. 1974, p. 136). In life as lived, we all have serial identities – changing and developing over time; our telling and writing of our stories enables us to celebrate this, and understand it better.

Stories only happen in the recounting of the events of our lives. We turn bits of our lives into adventures, or stories when we recount them. The ancient Greek tragedians Sophocles, Aeschylus and Euripides knew this. The great events of the dramas (generally very bloody) all happen offstage, recounted by such as a messenger. The murder of Agamemnon (Aeschylus trans. 1999) is foretold graphically, immediately before it happens, by the prophetess Cassandra. These episodes are all told as stories – a story within the story of the play – for dramatic effect.

Sartre's hero in *Nausea* (1938) suddenly realises that his greatest dream – to have adventures – is actually impossible: adventures only happen in the recounting, or remembering. In life 'we always begin in the middle' (Lyotard 1992, p. 116), and according to the fourth-century BC philosopher Chuang Tsu: *we are always in the middle*. Here is the hero of *Nausea*, in the process of realising that those essential aspects of adventure – beginnings and endings – are only to be found in story, in the recounting of a life, rather than in life-as-lived:

> First of all beginnings would have had to be real beginnings. Real beginnings, appearing like a fanfare of trumpets, like the first notes of a jazz tune, abruptly cutting boredom short. . . . Some thing begins in order to end: an adventure doesn't let itself be extended; it achieves significance only through its death. . . .
>
> When you are living nothing happens. The settings change, people come in and go out, that's all. There are never any beginnings. Days

are tacked onto days without rhyme or reason, it's an endless mono-
tonous addition.

Sartre 1938, pp. 59, 61

Trying to live our lives as if they were a series of *adventures* or *stories*
could only lead to depression or mental instability: 'I wanted the
moments of my life to follow one another in an orderly fashion like
those of a life remembered. You might as well try to catch time by the
tail . . . You have to choose: to live or to recount' (Sartre 1938, pp. 63,
61). Virginia Woolf had a similar experience:

> The past is beautiful because one never realises an emotion at the time.
> It expands later, and thus we don't have complete emotions about the
> present, only about the past.
>
> Woolf, quoted in Holly 1989, p. 26

Hélène Cixous makes another distinction; she says it is only masculine
stories which have beginnings and endings. 'A feminine textual body
is recognised by the fact that it is always endless, without ending . . .
at a certain point the volume comes to an end but the writing con-
tinues and for the reader this means being thrust into the void.' And 'a
feminine text starts on all sides at once, starts twenty times, thirty
times over' (Cixous, 1995 p. 175).

Why fiction?

Realising that stories of practice do not always need to stick to what
happened in life-as-lived can offer confidence in the expression of
experience, and widen the range of possible ways of reflection. Fiction
can omit slow episodes or effectively combine events which took place
at different times and with different people. Writing fictionally from
deep professional experience can be more dramatic, leap over the
boring bits, tackle issues head on; convey multiple viewpoints; sidestep problems of confidentiality, fear of exposure, and some of the
inevitable anxiety which accompanies the exploration of painful
events. Writing a story about 'she' or 'he' rather than 'I' can be liberating, for example. Fiction can feel safer to write – less personally revealing; later reflection upon the fictional writing can offer the writer a
slower, more staged way of exploring areas which might otherwise
seem too painful to address.

A fiction can be a vehicle for conveying the ambiguities, complexities and ironic relationships that inevitably exist between multiple
viewpoints. It can offer an intelligible research summary of the huge

body of data that qualitative research tends to provide. The creation of a fiction, with the awareness that it is a creation, can enable the writer to head straight for the heart of the matter (see also Rowland 1991, Winter 1988, 1989, 1991 and Rowland (Bolton) *et al.* 1990). 'Thinking up a plot and a range of characters in a certain context is analogous to formulating a theory of that context' (Winter 1988, p. 241).

In fiction, characters and situations take on a life of their own – a novelist or short story writer cannot decide on their plot and characters before they start, and expect them to stick to a plan. Characters have minds of their own: if the writer tries to discipline them to do what she wants, the writing will be flat, lifeless and dull.

This creative process allows expression to the non-logical, non-rational parts of the writer's mind; it allows the writer contact with other voices within themselves of which they might be unaware.

I'm not interested in it if it's not **true!**

Critics have been dissatisfied with forms of research or reflection upon practice which make overt use of fiction. Just as a visitor to a museum is disappointed when the exhibit they look at is a copy (however exact), they feel cheated. Few people are satisfied with the copy of Michaelangelo's *David* which stands in a Florentine piazza for anyone to gaze at with no charge and no queues; they need to see the very lump of marble from which Michaelangelo himself 'released' David.

A story, however, is not an *object* like the *David*, or a museum exhibit; it is a construction mediated through the writer or narrator. A collection of letters – transcribed exactly – between two or more parties is perhaps the closest to being a written *real thing*. But any account, however much the writer attempts to stick to what actually happened, will always be partial and biased – from the writer's point of view.

Writing and Reading

Stories written by practitioners are, of course, pieces of creative writing with a value all of their own. We do not relate to an effective novel, film or play because of what it overtly teaches us, but for its beauty, and insight into human nature and the human condition, as well as its power to reinforce our sense of social order. All these are implicit, intrinsic to the story and the relationship between story and audience. That writers take part in a creative process must not be forgotten in our enthusiastic embracing of the narrative form for professional development. The satisfaction and self-esteem of having created an object with enduring value, even if only to themselves and a tiny audience, is a very important element in the effectiveness of the reflective practice offered by this book. But how do practitioners initiate themselves as creative writers?

It is simple. They put pens to paper and write freely with no planning or forethought, on a fairly open theme such as 'a time I learned something vital', or 'a person who has been important to me'. An effective piece of writing, which communicates both back to the writer and to their audience, can take no longer than it takes to put the words on the paper. The immediacy of the process fosters the creation of writing that is fresh, invigorating and fascinating. The forms tend to be poetry, drama, or story based on experience, the latter being the most common. Practitioners discover that writing need take neither genius nor a willingness to spend hours filling the waste-basket.

The writers then often write further stories based upon the issues, themes or situation of the initial or core story. These are often imaginative explorations into aspects which the writer cannot *know* about but can fruitfully explore, such as what other characters were thinking at the time.

Plenty of time is then taken to read and reflect silently upon what has been written before sharing it with anyone (occasionally the writing is too personal for any to be shared). If the writing is done in a group, it is better closed and small, ideally no larger than eight, to foster confidence, confidentiality and trust.

In sharing writing with another it is useful to focus on the content of the writings, not the writers themselves. Helping a writer clarify their writing, in order to improve the form, can sometimes be useful. For example, a clumsy and involved passage often indicates a confused or poorly grasped incident in the writer's mind; readers helping to clarify the issues has the additional benefit of improving the quality of the writing.

Some writings may appear to be personal rather than professional; but the personal affects the professional, such as Mark Purvis' poem about the death of his brother, and the way the writing and discussion of this facilitated his dealing with child deaths in general practice.

The ancestry of this process is a mixture of *creative writing* tutoring, therapeutic principles (unconditional positive regard for the writers and their writing, for example), and the theory and practice of small-group work facilitation. The last of these is as vital as the first two. An effective group is not just a bunch of people who happen to be in a room together: the process needs to be fostered.

Other Uses of Storying

The place of narrative, particularly autobiographical, in initial and in-service teacher training has been explored extensively. Story telling has been used by Reason (1988) as a research method, dealing with personal rather than professional development. Abbs (1974) and Lewis (1992) both use personal and autobiographical writing with trainee teachers.

Jean Clandinin *et al.* write of an Alternative Programme in teacher education (Clandinin *et al.* 1992), set up to explore the potential for collaboration between students, schools and universities by making spaces for the stories of each to be shared. This proved a dynamic ground for understanding, assessing and reassessing experience. 'It is in restorying ourselves that it is possible to remake experience' (Clandinin and Connelly 1990, p. 31).

Neither Clandinin *et al.* nor Lewis (1992) call the writing they are engendering with their students 'fiction'. Yet Clandinin *et al.* put no emphasis on 'telling the truth' because they point out (as I have argued above) there is no ultimate truth to be told:

> What matters is that lives do not serve as models; only stories do that. . . . We can only retell and live by the stories we have read or heard. We live our lives through texts. . . . Whatever their form or medium these stories have formed us all; they are what we must use to make new fictions, new narratives.
>
> Heilbrun 1988

Synthesis, as well as Analysis

Writing a story or poem is a synthetic, organic process. It draws together elements from the muddle of experience, weaving them to create a coherent artifact which communicates a seemingly single strand – an experience. Sharing this text with peers, and restorying the same incident from different angles in ways suggested by these peers, can enable both writer and reader to perceive the core experience or incident as a synthesis of a multiplicity of stories and potential stories. If this is associated with a reading and discussion of significant related material from their larger professional, social and political world (journal papers, more popular material such as magazines or TV programmes, views and opinions of colleagues), then the experience will be deepened. This perception takes place because the professional experience is not only examined across a range of levels of reflection (as in Mezirow 1981), but more importantly refracted through different lenses, in different lights, and with different senses predominating, as well as material considered from psychological, social, political and spiritual arenas. This process is, then, a critical-synthetic one, rather than a critical-analytic one.

Kant used the word 'synthesis' to indicate the process by which the two sources from which our knowledge is drawn are combined. 'Judgement requires what Kant calls a "synthesis" of concept and intuition, and only in this synthesis is true experience (as opposed to mere intuition) generated' (Scruton 1982, p. 25). Kant argues that imagination has a central role in this 'synthesis'.

The synthetic process taking place in writing as a reflective practitioner explorations is between cognitive understandings of events (the rational discourse of Mezirow 1991, quoted above) and intuitive perceptions (sensibilities): between what appear to be facts and our feelings about them. Our feelings and ideas about an event are multifaceted. We can only assume the feelings and ideas of the others involved are just as complex. We cannot *know* these, but we can project, or imagine ourselves in their place by writing fictionally from their point of view. We can also explore our own feelings and ideas further by writing fictions in which the events are altered in some specific way. And we can draw upon the wider field of knowledge and opinion – through reading and discussion. There will then be a multiplicity of stories and themes perceived within a single incident.

Writing fictionally is one way of gaining a sight of this multiplicity, of being aware of the embeddedness of so much of our knowing in our experience. We know things in so many different ways. Marshall and Reason report a PhD student responding to her supervisors' anxiety that her thesis did not have 'a sufficiently wide-ranging exploration of literature'. The student:

> told us forcibly. 'There is a lot of theory in this, and you will find it integrated throughout the text. But more importantly, what I have written here is known through my body, my imagination and my practice. The quality of my work is in its integration with my whole being, not simply in academic theory.' We accepted her argument, as did the external examiner.
>
> Marshall and Reason 1997, p. 240

Writing in the voice of the student, for example, or recasting the situation as one in which both doctor and patient experience a positive outcome, or restorying with some of the genders switched, can give tremendous insight and release of emotion. An allied approach is to collect written stories from all the actors in a situation, as Mavis Kirkham has done with those present at a series of births (mother, midwife, doctor, etc.) (1997).

The reflective writer is then likely to be faced with there being no single answer to such questions as 'how could I have done better?' In place of answers there will probably be yet more questions, such as 'if I had done this, which I think would have been better, what would the patient/doctor have felt?' As Ann commented: 'no wonder it all takes so much time!'

Exploring issues in depth and width can take time. On the other hand, enlightenment can arrive after a 15-minute writing session. Re-reading written experiences can help enable the writer-reader to 'own' the experiences depicted, to recognise and begin to accept and work on them.

> Staff who learn on courses to take more responsibility for their suc-cesses, weaknesses, actions and feelings, and to relate their course functioning to their work context are in fact developing competencies that are readily available for transfer to their work-settings. At worst, staff thus empowered may offer a challenge too threatening to be coped with by an unempowered organisation and management struc-ture. At best, they can become a stimulating and thoughtful resource for their agencies.
>
> Hughes and Pengelly 1995, p. 170

Or at very best they thoroughly shake up their work organisation, or seek a new and much more dynamic post.

Image and Reflection

The reflection in Van Eyck's convex mirror in *The Arnolfini Portrait* (National Gallery, London) allows the picture to give a view of the couple from both sides. Our night sky would be denuded without the power of reflection: the moon and the planets are only visible because they reflect the sun's light.

Those who do not undertake reflection to illuminate practice are rather like the 'Lady of Shalott' (Tennyson 1832), cursed only to expe-rience mirror images, weaving them into a tapestry, rather than live her life directly. When handsome Sir Lancelot appears in her glass she can stand it no longer:

> She left the web, she left the loom,
> She made three paces thro' the room,
> She saw the water lily bloom,
> She saw the helmet and the plume,
>   She looked down on Camelot.
> Out flew the web and floated wide;
> The mirror cracked from side to side;
> 'The curse is come upon me!' cried
>   The lady of Shalott.
>
> Tennyson 1832, part 3, p. 82

She dies of course. She dies because it was her curse only to live at second hand. Reflective practice can enable fully rounded experiences, and therefore more effective and enjoyable practice.

8

How to Begin Writing

I learned the science of letters . . . and this opened before me a wide field for wonder and delight.

Mary Shelley 1820, p. 119

But Eeyore was saying to himself, 'This writing business. Pencils and whatnot. Over-rated if you ask me. Silly stuff. Nothing in it.'

Milne 1928, p. 153

Words can be taken for granted so easily, as the tool we use every day. After all *in the beginning was the Word*. We were taught to write through school and college. And then stopped. Yet writing has as complex a form, process and set of variations as any other cultural form, say music or algebra. There are many more different ways to write than there are writers, because each writer can tailor their writing style appropriately to the work in hand. And each piece of writing belongs to the writer, while it is being crafted – an adventure into their own thinking. When shared it becomes a joint journey: reader and writer together. Cavilling at this approach as arty-farty and touchy-feely is being like Eeyore – self-protective and afraid of what the process might reveal.

This chapter is a practical guide to writing, either for an individual reflective practitioner, or for a group facilitator. It will help unpick assumptions, and support a rediscovery of the *wonder and delight* of Frankenstein's monster. It covers what reflective writing is; for whom; and why, how, where and when it might be written. Reflective writers have the right to take ownership of their writing, and only share it with a reader when they are ready. Above all it is not only a learning tool, but to be enjoyed for its own sake.

Introduction To Writing
Trust the authority of the writing hand.

The process of writing recommended in this book is creative, a way of gaining access to each practitioner's deep well of experience not always accessible to everyday channels. It is akin to that used by the novelist, poet or playwright (Goldberg 1986), the diarist (Rainer 1978), or for personal exploration (Schneider and Killick 1998).

Writing is a valuable mode of expressing, sharing, assessing and developing professional experience; it is one of the best ways of reflecting solo, and stimulating effective shared reflection with colleagues (Rowland 1993). It has been used as an effective research tool (Winter 1991). Students, moreover, write in order to: express themselves, store an *aide-mémoire*, present an argument, demonstrate knowledge, explicate experience, or create a piece of literature.

Educators and professionals are also involved in the same processes. If not, then something is wrong. Students and colleagues are most ably supported if tutors have first-hand knowledge and experience of the processes themselves (Murray 1982).

Artistic (creative) writing is the mode used because: 'art takes one over a threshold, out of the rut, it questions custom, the "taken-for-granted" ', and 'writing taps tacit knowledge – brings into awareness that which we sensed but could not explain' (Holly 1989, p. 75). 'The function of art in the full extent of its expressions includes the deliberate and subversive challenge to every-day understandings and interpretations of events' (Smyth 1996, p. 937).

Writing is used because it is essentially different from talking. It can enable writers to make contact with thoughts and ideas they did not know they had, with completely forgotten memories, and enable the making of leaps of understanding and connections. It can also enable the expression and exploration of issues of which the writer is aware but unable or unwilling otherwise to articulate, communicate and develop. Writing has this power for a range of reasons:

- Speech or thought can be forgotten, or shift and change like *Chinese Whispers*, and then vanish on the air. Conversations about which both parties have a completely different memory, and each party is certain their recollection is correct, are only too common. Writing leaves clear footprints on the page.

- These footprints aid progressive thought. Writing stays in the same form to be worked on whenever the writer is ready.

- Rewriting and redrafting, to get closer and closer to what needs to be expressed, is a self-educative process.

- Writing is private, a communication of writers with themselves until they are ready to share it with another – a safer process than talking. Since something said and heard cannot be unsaid, spoken utterances are habitually severely edited, usually unconsciously. Writing can, to a degree, evade this policeman-editor; it can be creative and rewarding, tending to increase self-confidence and be a pleasure in practice.

- Writing can be torn up or burnt unshared with anyone, even the writer themselves, if that is required.

- Writing is a longer, slower, more focused process than thinking. It is more laborious, a writer is much less likely to 'rabbit on' than a talker. This encourages greater depth and breadth, and more immediate access.

- Images or tropes such as metaphor are appropriate and readily used in writing; these can give indirect access to feelings, thoughts, knowledge, ideas, memories not accessible to non-image contact which would be risky because such material can be too full-frontally direct.

- Fiction is an appropriate written form. It can protect confidentiality, be less exposing, more dynamic, and can convey ambiguities, complexities and the ironic relationships which exist between multiple viewpoints. Furthermore the recreation of a situation exactly as it happened is unlikely; it will be recounted as experienced through the writer's own senses, as felt and thought about by them. This can allow the exploration of the experience without worrying about getting the *facts* just right.

- Self-confidence and self-esteem can be increased by involvement in a creative process.

Why Writing?

Suspend your disbelief

This writing process is essentially playful. Creativity is playful: one of the aspects of its appeal to audiences and artists (musicians even 'play' their instruments). This does not denigrate art; rather it grows up the role of playing from the purely childish arena to which our modernist culture has relegated it. Writing can be enjoyable, but it also requires courage to plunge into it wholeheartedly. The serious (but safe) and too heavily enforced rules for writing we learned at school have to be unlearned, as Jenny wrote: 'it's not easy is it to unlearn bad learning?'

Might we not say that every child at play behaves like a creative writer, in that he creates a world of his own, or, rather re-arranges the things of his world in a new way which pleases him?

Freud 1995, p. 54

Freud reckoned the grown-up version of playing is fantasising. Creative writers surface fantasies and rid us of some of our tensions around fantasies – about which we are ashamed and secretive; we vicariously enjoy writers' fantasies. How much more powerful not to have to wait for a writer to tackle our fantasies, but to write our own, however big or small, in a playful way.

> The sound of pencils on paper
> An occasional sigh, or sniff, a page
> Torn roughly from a notebook, or
> Scrunched and discarded
> I twist a lock of hair around my finger and glance up.
> Someone is frowning,
> Another, smiling . . .
> Everyone concentrating.
> Time's up. (But this isn't an exam and doesn't feel like one)
> There's a growing excitement – like that moment when someone is about to open the present you've given them . . .
> My gift to them, theirs to me— words on paper.
> We're sharing very private thoughts . . .
> Thoughtful silence and lots of laughter too.
> It's a kind of communion.

Becky

Writing is a staged process, and the initial stages can too easily be left out, to the detriment of skill and confidence. To be literate and make full use of that literacy requires confidence. Writing does not come easily to many because of our early didactic training. We have all spent many years learning *proper* ways to write: the essay with its sequenced argument; the sonnet form; the short story's beckoning beginning, slick middle, and sting-in-the-tail end; the punchiness of the journalistic voice. Writing, for most professionals, is for reports: a burdensome and long-winded, hated but essential means of justifying work to authorities. All too often we strive to imitate successful writers, to please our teachers, editors, line managers: we have lost ownership of writing, forgotten we have our own voices.

One of the aims of this process is to encourage reflective writers to trust themselves to go back to the very first vital stages of writing. Engaging in these stages can transform that hitherto frustrating time of seeming to have an empty head with no writing in it at all, to writing a telling account. Never again (well, not quite so much) that 'Oh no!' fear of a clean sheet or empty screen.

The first two stages of writing will be discussed in detail, partly because they are the vital self-explorative, self-expressive stages required for reflective writing. And partly because they are the stages all too often skipped over. The later stages of writing relate to preparing work for publication: ensuring the writing communicates to a published audience; editing for grammar, syntax, clarity, appropriateness to audience, and so on. These are beyond the scope of this text (but see, for example, Albert 1997, Wade 1994, Doubtfire 1996). Suggestions are made as to how a reflective piece of writing can be developed.

First Stage

Your writing is a gift to yourself.

- Choose a comfortable uninterrupted place and time, and writing materials you like.
- Make sure you have everything else you need to hand – like coffee and chocolate biscuits.
- Be able to time yourself to write without stopping for about six minutes.
- Allow another 30–40 minutes or so after the six, in order to do the next bit.

Without stopping to think too hard about it, jot down right now:

- your feelings about undertaking a piece of writing
- your thoughts on the advantages and disadvantages of writing reflectively.

Adam's reflection upon writing

Take time to calm down, sit back, change gear. Nice and comfortable in here. Quite a few things I've thought about writing today. Nice to just let things just come out and sit on paper for a while. Not quite sure what track I'm on at the moment but don't worry something will come along in a bit. Good technique this. Doesn't matter. No one's going to read this later on – so don't worry about it – so can write anything.

Adam, undergraduate writing group

How to Start

You can't write the wrong thing. Whatever you write will be right – for you.

The initial stage of writing need not be shared. The act of committing words to paper can be a valuable communication with the self. Not all the initial words will be useful in themselves (you may never need to read them or allow others to, or you may redraft and edit them out of recognition). Writing is a staged process: every written word does not have to be public and perfect.

This first stage of writing is invaluable for reflective writing. It is also fundamentally the same for a story, a report or an essay. Some lucky people create everything clear in their head before beginning to write, and then write their complete piece without having to alter a word; their first draft is also more or less their last. But most of us feel we have nothing, or just a jumble, in our heads initially. Further to this, when confronted with a blank sheet of paper, I think all sorts of things need to be done before I can begin to write (like looking up just one more reference, or watering the plants). Although it is possible I am not ready yet to begin on this dangerous journey, these are usually mere delaying tactics.

The method below can help prevent the dither: 'what am I going to write?' It dumps mind-cluttering bits and bobs onto the paper. Some of these will be useful for the project in hand; some might be only a shopping list (or a scurrilous moan about the head of department). But the writer can move on more readily with that list safely on paper. The method can also capture invaluable elements the writer might not have known were there. Here is novelist Mario Vargas Llosa describing his first stage of writing:

> I write without thinking much, trying to overcome all kinds of self-criticism, without stopping, without giving any consideration to the style or structure . . ., only putting down on paper everything that can be used as raw material.
>
> Llosa 1991, p. 45.

Begin, as Llosa does, by allowing the pen/cil to cover the pages on its own:

1. Write **whatever is in your head**, uncensored.
2. Time yourself to write **without stopping** for about **six minutes**.

3. Don't think about what you are writing, it will probably be disconnected and might seem to be rubbish – but **don't stop to think** or be critical.
4. Allow it to flow with **no reference to spelling, grammar, proper form**.
5. Give yourself permission **to say anything,** whatever it is. You don't even *have* to reread it. Whatever you write it can't be the wrong thing – because no one will read your writing in this form.

Quite a lot might be written, or only a little seeming rubbish – it doesn't matter. The six minutes' writing sometimes turns up gold, sometimes dross. It is always useful, however, for beginning to scratch the surface.

Six minutes
I'm clearing out the rubbish
I'm emptying my mind,
The trouble with this task is that
I don't know what I'll find.

I came because I want to write,
I wanted to move on,
And if I keep on writing,
Maybe I can move the stone.

Perhaps what lies beneath is ore,
Of course it may be dross,
But let the chance go just once more,
And all there'll be is loss.

Janet Tipper

Six minutes
Here I am
Now.
It's hard – Something
I don't know what
Yet I know
I feel and yet I cannot
Say – or write
the words too slow the thoughts
Who – am I and why I think
that I can come and give.

It's clear – I think – I don't
know, I'm not sure
Will it be OK, can I do
this – I am there – or – here?

So hard, too easy to fill all
the spaces – a thought in
a word it can go to all places!
A life, that is mine, I want
To be known – my heart it is
beating through gates that
are open.

John McAuley

Writing a Reflective Splurge

Forget about grammar, syntax, spelling – for now. They block the inspirational flow. Correct them later.

The next stage is to write straight away about *a time when I learned something vital*. Focusing on a particular occasion is particularly facilitative for reflective writing. Alternatively a theme may have arisen in the *six minutes*. This is still first draft writing: it can be redrafted – no one else need read it. What matters is capturing what is there to be written.

- Write in the same way as the *six minutes*: allowing the words to arrive on the page without planning or questioning. Don't look over your own shoulder, questioning what you write.

But this time:

- **Write with a focus** – the story of a vital occasion. Try not to ask questions – yet. The most common blocking query is: *why have I chosen **this** to write about; it's not nearly important enough?!* Well, everything is important, try to ignore this policeman trying to prevent you starting.
- **Choose the first event which comes to mind**. Try not to reject it, for whatever reason. The more anxiously the *right* account is sought, the more the really right one – the one thought of first – will slide away from view. Choose the first one which comes to mind.
- **Only allow about twenty to forty minutes in which to write**. This is a good way of ensuring a start is made, rather than anxiously casting around for the best *time when*. . . . The more time wasted thinking, the less time there will be for writing. I have known students set an alarm clock, and stop when the bell rings. On the other hand, if you find you want to carry on, and on, then do so.

- **Recreate the situation as memory gives it**, with as many details, as far as possible for this first write, rather than an idealised *what you would rather have happened*.

- **Consider it fiction**. Even if the situation is recreated as closely as possible to the memory, thinking of it as fiction can relieve embarrassment or fear of confidentiality loss: these things happened to a character. It can also allow experimentation with elements at the hazy edge of memory. Or if it seems less important to explore the actual event, considering it fiction can offer freedom of expression, rather than *what really happened*.

- **Spelling, grammar, syntax, usually flow very well**, naturally, in this kind of vitally charged writing. If infelicities or repetitions do occur, they can be left until the end, when they are easy to correct.

- **The writing does not need a set *good story form*** (or poem, if that's how it seems to be coming out). Stories have proper beginnings, middles and ends. Life doesn't, as Sartre pointed out. The same sort of glorious muddle format as it originally had is appropriate to this stage of writing. Musings on the event (what you should/should not have said, for example) may seem to interrupt the narrative flow. But writing is endlessly plastic, and can be altered and tidied up later, before anyone else has to make sense of it, or embarrassingly read innermost feelings.

- **The pen/cil can effectively notice details**: tone of voice, clothing, spoken words, seeming incidentals, and feelings. As the experience is replayed, details begin to emerge which were ignored at the time of the experience, or only noted in passing.

- **Allow reactions, emotional responses, feelings.**

- **Refrain from judgements at this stage.**

Write for about twenty minutes according to the above *Reflective Splurge* way of writing. Remember this writing is for you. You need not share it with anyone.
  Write about:

A time when I learned something vital

Be as creative in your understanding of what constituted *vital* in your choice of *time when . . .*, and in your understanding of *learned* – there are many many ways to learn.

Bev's Story

The Midwife's Story

It was 1971 and I was working on the labour suite in Xmouth. Sister was a bossomly, matronly figure called Miss Lane, with iron grey hair and a face carved in granite. She exuded no warmth but appeared competent and in control. She certainly liked to control her flock of sheep – her nurses – and also her flock of rams – her doctors.

We were all in fear and awe of her; she had favourites and could be extremely sarcastic and make life difficult for those she did not like and her voice lashed out at people. Unfortunately this extended to the patients and she could be very prejudiced.

The girl was young and unmarried, scared to death and in labour for the first time. An enema was ordered for her – 'high, hot and a hell of a lot' – by Sister Lane. She was subdued and in misery, kept in isolation because she was socially unacceptable.

Her pain was intense and the medication seemed to be slow in appearing and the support she was offered was peripheral and mini-mal. Sister was in total control and had decided to make this young girl her mission.

I felt excluded and unable to offer support – we all did, we all stood on the periphery – watched and observed what this youngster was subjected to.

Sister did the delivery and everything was clinically correct and cold, cold, cold as ice – she allowed no family support into the deliv-ery room.

I don't know what trauma was taken away by this young girl and what processes were set up for her in her future. I do know that the scenario had a profound impact on myself about what to do and how to be with women in labour. About power, dominance, control, exclusion and the withholding of warmth and love to anyone in distress.

From another source years later I learnt that Sister had had a break-down of some description. Part of me thinks this was divine retribu-tion and another part reflects on what we do to ourselves as human beings when we become so rigid, fixed and inflexible. And part of me reflects that had I made different choices at certain times of my life that that could have been me.

Bev Hargreaves

Further Writing: Read, Extend, Vivify
Trust the process; have faith in yourself.

When first *dash* is finished, reread everything (including the six minutes scribble), taking notes:

- with an attentive yet open, non-judgemental mind, looking out for content rather than form;
- with an openness to *divergent connections* – things previously perceived as separate, or inappropriate together;
- and with an openness to underlying links and to fresh understandings and awarenesses;
- additions, alterations or deletions can be made;
- connections between the *six minute mind-clearing* and the *time when* . . . can offer insight;
- fill out the narrative with as much detail as possible: remembering we have **five senses** – smells and sounds as well as what things looked like can give vital clues, as can: time of year; discomforts; intuitions; what people said, and the tone of voice they said it in.

Everything is significant.
Ask some of these questions:

- **Is the nub of the situation pinpointed**? Or is it skirted around? The most vital issue might be located or clarified by looking down the wrong end of the telescope at a seemingly mundane trivial matter. As with fractals, the tiny recapitulates the great; and it is a great deal easier to concentrate on the small than the unwieldy.
- Notice **contrasts** within the story.
- Note the way **officialese/jargon** can be used to conceal.
- **Try not to come to an answer**, or even a definitive question – yet.

Bev Hargreaves' Sister Again

Bev reread and thought about the midwifery sister and the young unmarried mother, and the point at which she had ended her first story – wondering about the Sister's mental breakdown. The reflective practice group discussed it with her, sympathised with her pain at the memory. Bev felt guilt because she had not attempted to make things better for the patient. She was, of course, comforted by the thought that there was nothing she, a young student, could have done. But she wanted to try to get to the bottom of what was driving this Sister in her cruelty. She decided to attempt to see the story through her eyes:

Story from Sister's Perspective

I trained in the days when nurses were real nurses – the nurses today don't know what hard work is and are frequently cheeky so need to be kept firmly in their place.

The medical staff need organising, but I usually manage to keep them doing what I want them to do.

I'm responsible for the Labour Suite and feel proud of the lying-in ward and our suite of delivery rooms. I run the department like clockwork and I like the routine of the place. I live in here so am always able to keep an eye on the place.

Some of the nurses are good and I get on well with them, but others need to be kept firmly in their place at all times.

I love my work, I'm really dedicated to it, I've given my life to it and have no family of my own.

Midwifery has changed a lot since I came into it and the mothers now have better analgesics during labour – mind you, some of them still scream and shout and need firm handling.

I don't like messes in my delivery area, the clutter of husbands or other family members, and if I had my way I'd ban them all; but there is this growing tendency to ask the husband to be present at the birth.

I like things to be orderly, to have well-behaved mothers doing what they should do, and I don't agree with children out of wedlock.

I remember this young girl came in – she must have been 17 years, arrogant and demanding – I thought I'd soon knock the stuffing out of her, lick her into shape. Anyway it was not right that she should be with the other married mothers so I decided that I would look after her.

She wanted pain relief far too early and started yelling and screaming, so I had to be really firm with her, she was not going to get the better of me. She had medication when I deemed it was the right time, anyway she soon didn't have the energy for arrogance – and such a noise she made at the birth I couldn't let her hold the baby until she had calmed down.

Anyway that's my role, to keep control – control of everything, I'm not here to be liked, I'm here to do a job.

Bev Hargreaves

Types of Writing, and Topics

Autobiographical narratives, fictional stories with plots, poetry or songs, dramas or descriptive passages are all appropriate. Detailed accounts of experience may be followed by a piece of reflective interpretative thoughts; or these may remain unwritten until discussion with group or mentor.

Subjects for writing may well be suggested by a group. Each piece of writing will also generate ideas for fresh writings. Here are some thought of by my groups:

changes
a conflict
in control
taking care
a dilemma
a celebration
a moment of joy
a sensitive subject
a clash of interests
a conflict of loyalty
a misunderstanding
a frustrated episode
a missed opportunity
a parting or beginning
a case for compassion
an evocative occasion
an extremity of emotion
the most dangerous time
a breach of confidentiality
a time when I was incapacitated
the blowing of the pressure valve

Fiji and Reflective Practice

It's at 4 o'clock in the morning, when I can't sleep, that's when I get the pen and paper out.

Working as a counsellor at the University of the South Pacific is an idyllic experience in lots of ways. The Rogers and Hammerstein set every time I look out of my office window, tropical colours and scents. But, the sheer cultural complexity of the university community here at the main campus in Fiji is enough, add to that race, gender, sexuality, status and other aspects of diversity I'm meeting every day in the job and the lack of professional consultation and the isolation from any group of counsellors with a Code of Ethics and Practice is enough to keep me awake. So, I write it all down. The feelings of inadequacy, of excitement, the confusion and doubts, contradictions and discoveries.

Some of the writing I've kept, some was torn up into very small pieces, too awful to re-read, the thoughts too negative to carry around any more. Scribbling it all down, in complete privacy acted as a safety valve. I could be my own 'supervisor' and avoid the worst of the isolation. I also started to suggest writing to some of the staff and students who came for counselling. Some were using their third language, English, to speak to me and were thousands of miles away from their village in another remote part of the Pacific. The writing gave us the possibility of a bridge.

Mustn't grumble, that so very English maxim is turned on its head. You must grumble, I would say, but do it on paper and in your own language.

Jeannie Wright

Share your Writing with a Peer
Your writing has the power to influence another, and them you.

A peer's thoughts on reflective writing can open up fresh avenues of thought. They will be able to support in perceiving aspects, which even the illuminating process of writing hadn't highlighted. They can also support towards deeper levels of reflection, as well as see accounts in wider institutional contexts, or even on the national social and political stage.

Seeking just the right person or people can be a worthwhile endeavour. Writing to each other can be just as good as face-to-face contact. A colleague at work might be right, but they or a partner at home *might* be the *wrong* person: emotionally charged relationships may not offer the distance required for observation through a different pair of eyes.

> Reflecting on a critical incident is still within the confines of one's own perspective. Reflecting with another person, with the written incident before you, can bring added insights.

Jane

Here are suggested guidelines, or boundaries, for a discussion:

- Be positive and supportive. Negative opinions are more likely to be productively received when accompanied by positive approaches for dealing with the situation.

- Read and comment on the writing, rather than on the person who has written it. An engagement with writings in order to suggest useful and developmental avenues of thought is the focus, rather than therapy or personal support for the writer. If the writing is considered to be fiction, if the characters and their actions are fictional, then the reader has as much right to suggest ways of thinking and of developing them as the writer. The likelihood of hurt or loss of confidentiality is reduced.

- Safety for participants to say what they feel and think is offered by written or oral discussion being confidential to the parties involved, unless they specifically decide otherwise.

- A writer can usefully make it clear to the reader/commenter if they have any particular parameters for the discussion.

- Everyone usually feels everyone else's writing is wonderful and their own rubbish – an unfruitful competition can begin as to who can apologise the longest and most convincingly.

- Choose a colleague, friend or fellow student with whom to share writing.
- Use the above guidelines to support the development of other appropriate ones.
- Enjoy deepening the reflective process – whether verbally or in writing.

Developing the Writing
Thinking inhibits creativity: believe it or not. Let it flow.

Rewriting stories, or writing additional ones which reflect upon them (like Bev's), can deepen and widen the scope of understandings. This can be rather like a harnessing of transference and counter-transference. In transference the client transfers emotions and feelings from their original object (their mother perhaps) onto the therapist: the therapist can take on a role of as-it-were-mother to help the client deal with difficult or painful emotions. In counter-transference the therapist transfers feelings and emotions from their own life onto the client. In this *what if* writing, the writer is trying out being the *other* in the experience being explored, just as Bev projected herself into the sister.

Here are some developmental ideas. A group or a mentoring pair will develop their own, appropriate to their own writing:

- Give the story a title.
- Have protagonists other than the main character aired their opinions and standpoints? How might they have told the original story? Try writing from a different or opposing point of view.
- Write a similar story from the point of view of one of the other characters (like the client, or an observer to the main events).
- Rewrite the story with the gender of the main character(s) switched.
- Write the next chapter.
- Write a commentary on your own or another's text, either as yourself or as one of the characters.
- Retell the story with a different ending or focus, e.g. happy for sad.
- Write what a particular character is thinking at any one moment.
- Write about a (some) missing character(s). Like a photograph, a story is always an unreal and slim slice of reality – think of the area beyond the frame.
- Rewrite the story in a different style/genre – a newspaper article/fairy story/narrative poem/children's story. . . .
- Write *thought bubbles* for vital (or puzzling) characters at significant points in the narrative.
- Rewrite the story with the focus of control/power altered.
- You are a reporter: interview a character from the story.
- Take a character who's just left the action; what might they be doing/thinking?
- Write a letter from yourself to one of the characters, expressing your puzzlement/anger/sympathy. Write their reply.
- Write a letter/transcribe a phone conversation between two characters.
- List the objects/colours in the story. Are they significant?
- Write the story in a range of different genres (e.g. romance, detective, sci-fi, adventure . . .).
- Write a film/dustjacket blurb for the story.
- Continue the story six months/a year later.
- Consider asking someone who was involved in the *real* situation to write their own version; or interview them.
- Explore the area which puzzles you.
- Ask *what if*!

Write the next piece. The best things in life *are* free.

Bev's Final Story about Sister

Bev still wasn't satisfied she'd understood what might have embittered this Sister so deeply. The reflective practice group encouraged Bev to work on trying to get inside her mind better – to imagine she was Sister and write another account from her point of view. So Bev had another go at writing in Sister's voice; this time it was important to Bev to concentrate on her past:

Sister Lane's Memories
I had to write the first chapter: I don't want people to get beyond the shell that I now am. And as I reflect on the hardness, rigidity and controlled automaton that I have become I am upset and scared, scared to remember what used to be – I was in another life and country then and I don't know if I can bear to remember . . . to feel again.

Once upon a time there was a bubbly friendly five-year-old called Mary Ellen Rose. I was brought up in the country and loved animals, ponies, rabbits, badgers and foxes and knew where to find all of them.

I was one of two children, Robert was younger than me by two years and I idolised him. He was a blond, blue-eyed cherub, into mischief and dragging me with him.

My father was a clothier and worked long and hard hours. My mother was one of those delightful, warm, cuddly people who give a lot to others – we were a small family in a close-knit community – a happy and exuberant family, not at all remote as happens in some families.

I had many friends and we were a large and boisterous group who loved to go dancing, hiking and cycling together. I also had a special friend called Joe, who became my sweetheart and life-time partner. He was tall, dark haired, rather serious and intense and we had long involved conversations about the meaning of life – the sort that you have at that age. He was my best friend and eventually my lover.

I don't know when I decided that nursing was for me. It was hard work in those years, but I always wanted to care for anyone who was sick, so I went and started at the local cottage hospital – so young and naïve and green, but so proud of my uniform.

And then the war came and so many of my childhood friends went marching off, including Joe and Robert.

I haven't let myself dwell on the last time I saw them both, especially the last time I was with Joe – too bitter-sweet and it hurts, I hurt even after all these years. I hurt more and more after the news came that they had both died together in the same battle – I felt old and cold and grey, a bone-deep coldness that I couldn't shake off – the same coldness I felt when I had the miscarriage which was hushed up and never spoken of . . . I had almost forgotten . . .

Life had to go on; I buried myself in my work; everyone around me was suffering losses; there was no time for grief – self-indulgent nonsense. No nurse could be selfish: too much to do, so many broken bodies and souls – no, don't think, just concentrate on this job in hand, survive.

And so I lost my ability to be, to fully live my life, to allow myself to feel – too painful to feel.

I never again met anyone I fell in love with, or anyone I have been close to. I have just buried myself in my work.

Bev Hargreaves

A reflective writing course evaluation

It was a new experience for me to be able to share experiences in the written form in a trusting and stimulating place. I was surprised how easy it was to write about previous experiences, and, once the setting was right, how the ideas flowed. Over the months we laughed, cried and discussed our work together and I found I gained confidence both in my ability to write but also the value of it. Somehow writing it down enabled me to get to the essence of past experiences and events in a way that discussion alone cannot. From the beginning Gillie encouraged us to write whatever came into our heads; this felt very different from the prescriptive writing I had been doing as part of my Masters.

I discovered I wrote about the more profound and painful experiences and sometimes wondered if I wanted to share them; however, whenever I did it was very valuable.

Shirley

Suggested Further Reading

Albert, T. (1997) *Winning the publications game*. Abingdon, Oxon: Radcliffe Medical Press.

Bolton, G. (1999) *Writing Myself: The Therapeutic Potential of Creative Writing*. London: Jessica Kingsley.

Clough, P. (1996) 'Again fathers and sons': the mutual construction of self, story and special educational needs. *Disability & Society*, **11**(1) pp. 71–81.

Doubtfire, D. (1996) *Teach Yourself Creative Writing*. London: Hodder Headline.

Goldberg, N. (1986) *Writing Down the Bones*. Boston, Mass: Shambhala.

Greenwood, J. (1995) Treatment with dignity. *Nursing Times*, **91**(17) pp. 65–66.

Holly, M. L. (1989) Reflective writing and the spirit of inquiry. *Cambridge Journal of Education*, **19**(1) pp. 71–9.

Jackowska, N. (1997) *Write for Life: How to Inspire Your Creative Writing*. Shaftsbury Dorset: Element.

Lane, B. (1993) *Writing as a Road to Self Discovery*. Ohio: Writers Digest Books.

Landgrebe, B. and Winter, R. (1994) Reflective writing on practice: professional support for the dying? *Educational Action Research*, **2**(1) pp. 83–94.

Murray, D. (1982) *Learning by Teaching*. N. Jersey: Boynton Cook.

Paterson, B. L. (1995) Developing and maintaining reflection in clinical Journals. *Nurse Education Today*, **15**, pp. 211–20.

Progoff, I. (1975) *At a Journal Workshop*. New York: Dialogue House.

Rainer, T. (1978) *The New Diary: How to Use a Journal for Self-Guidance and Expanded Creativity*. London: Angus & Robertson.

Richardson, L. (1999) Writing: a method of inquiry. In N. K. Denzin, Y. S. Lincoln (eds), *Collecting and Interpreting Qualitative Materials*. London: Sage.

Rowland, S. (1993) *The Enquiring Tutor* (particularly Chapter 3). Lewes: Falmer.

Rowland, S. (1996) Lost for words. *Academic Development*, **2**(2) pp. 125–9.

Sansom, P. (1994) *Writing Poems*. Newcastle upon Tyne: Bloodaxe.

Schneider, M. and Killick, J. (1998) *Writing for Self-Discovery: a Personal Approach to Creative Writing*. Shaftsbury Dorset: Element.

Sellers, S. (1989) *Delighting the Heart: a Notebook by Women Writers*. London: Women's Press.

Snadden, D., Thomas, M. L., Griffin, E. M. and Hudson, H. (1996) Portfolio-based learning and general practice vocational training. *Medical Education*, **30**(2) pp. 148–52.

Tripp, D. (1993) *Critical Incidents in Teaching*. London: Routledge.

Tripp, D. (1995) SCOPE facilitator training. *NPDP SCOPE Project Draft*. Western Australia: Murdoch University.

Wade, S. (1994) *Writing and Publishing Poetry*. Oxford: How To Books.

Winter, R. (1988) Fictional-critical writing, in J. Nias and S. Groundwater-Smith (eds), *The Enquiring Teacher*. Lewes: Falmer. pp. 231–248.

Winter, R. (1989) *Learning from Experience* (particularly Chapter 10). Lewes: Falmer.

Winter, R. (1991) Fictional-critical writing as a method for educational research. *British Educational Research Journal*, **17**(3) pp. 251–62.

9

Writing as a Reflective Practitioner

> We write before knowing what to say and how to say it, and in order to find out, if possible.
>
> Lyotard 1992, p. 119

The process of writing for reflective practice is a first order activity. The writing, the essential discussions, and the writing of associated stories from different angles with the support of others is a creative explorative process in its own right, not a mere tool in professional reflection. Practitioners do not think and then write; the writing is the vehicle for the reflection – reflection *in* writing. This is an activity which facilitates a wider view from a distance, and an attitude of authority over practice.

Fictional reflective writing can create informative, descriptive material from the mass of ideas, hopes, problems, fears and images that our everyday working lives provoke. Shoppers filter out the reflection they don't want when looking in a shop window – by pressing their noses close to the glass and cupping their eyes with their hands to block out unwanted light. Similarly a reflective practitioner uses writing processes to help exclude all sorts of other issues and events which took place at the same time in order to focus effectively. The level of concentration for this kind of writing tends to be high. One practitioner likened it to a long refreshing swim, another to a deeply dreaming sleep. I remember overhearing someone whispering 'disgusting' as she wrote, hunched over her page. She was so deeply *there* – where she was writing about – we had all disappeared from her consciousness.

On reading their drafts, writers interact with and respond to their writing. The initial concept is subjected to interpretation and analysis through the very process of writing, which clarifies and extends the writer's thinking and understanding.

> To write is to open oneself up to chance, to free oneself from the compulsive linking up of 'meaning, concept, time and truth' that has

dominated Western philosphic discourse. Writing involves risk, play, loss of sense and meaning.

Flax 1990, p. 192

All art is at once surface and symbol.
Those who go beneath the surface do so at their peril.
Those who read the symbol do so at their peril.

Wilde 1891, p. 6

Speakers cannot hold trains of events and thoughts in their heads in the same way as when writing. For this reason written language is considered to be more logical and clearly argued than spoken, usually when redrafted and edited. This is the case – in planning and drafting any piece of work, like a unit of teaching or a speech, we 'think it through' in writing. But writing can do so much more than this: 'the only time I know that something is true is at the moment I discover it in the act of writing' (Jean Malaquais, quoted in Exley 1991). Reflective practitioners have again and again said: 'I didn't know I thought/ knew/remembered that until I wrote it'. One said: 'it is an opportunity to inhabit the unknown'. Laurel Richardson advises a range of writing activities in order to acquire writing confidence and skills, such as joining a creative writing group (1998, pp. 363–6).

Taking Responsibility

Reflective practitioners write about their own experience; the writings are created for specific others (group or mentor) with whom they are read, discussed and developed. There is full interplay of story, teller and audience, or text, interpretation and intentionality, without alienation (Tyler 1986).

It has been argued that our meanings are formed by our language, that signs do not have innate meaning, but are part of an endless interplay or diffusion of signification, and writing is more important than the spoken word. If this is the case, then undertaking a conscious process of self-examination through writing must help us to become more aware of our language and meanings.

The constraints we experience are constructed around us, and by us rather than a given situation whose bars we can only beat against. The responsibility for our actions lie with all of us, not an inhuman, inhumane system out there. Sartre suggested that at every moment we are faced with a series of choices, although we rarely perceive our freedom to choose. If we can exert control over tiny everyday elements, then metonymically, we will have taken some control over the larger structure. In deciding to write, tell and take ownership of some of our stories we are exercising some choice positively and enjoyably.

The ability to write and to express oneself in writing and read critically is vital in our society. Paolo Freire (1972) has maintained that one can only be heard politically through the medium of the written word – that ignorance of the literary mode spells oppression.

The kind of writing outlined here resembles the feminine writing put forward by post-structuralist feminist theorists such as Irigaray, Cixous and Kristeva who have been reclaiming writing from the dominant masculine mode (Moi 1985, Weedon 1987). This type of expression has been kept almost completely suppressed in our society because of its dangerous power. Cixous suggests that patriarchal thinking rests on a series of binary oppositions, such as: good:bad. These dyads are essentially male:female, the female always being the chaotic dark side to be feared and kept down by derision and containment. The boundaries of our understanding and communication need to be pushed beyond what have for so long been considered its limits. 'In the struggle to reassert feminine values, feminine writing which draws on the unconscious is a key site for bringing about change' (Weedon 1987).

The confidence acquired in writing as a reflective practitioner can spill over into any other sort of writing. A student wrote that one of their 'benefits and achievements' was 'learning to write with freedom'; I would add – with confidence and authority.

The Discipline of Writing

The writing of a story or poem is a disinterested, distancing process in which the writer creates a work of art. Perhaps 'distancing' is not quite the right word: for what happens is that the writing goes beyond the emotions of the moment, taking on more universality, yet at the same time drawing upon deep experience. So in a way it distances (puts it out there, onto the paper), but also brings in closer by putting the writer in contact with more of their emotions, thoughts and experiences than they were aware of before. Some of the dynamic – immediate – properties of speech can seem to be lost in the writing process, which can appear to freeze or embalm the experience. But if an explorative and expressive mode of writing is used, then writing is seen to be as dynamic as speech, if not more so. The structured form of writing is sufficiently controlled to allow exploration without it being too scary or chaotic. This can be called an 'emotional discipline':

The imaginative structuring of experience, then, is not only an intellectual structuring but a response to an emotional challenge – a sort of emotional discipline.

Winter *et al.* 1999, p. 204

There is a paradox here, however: for this to take place, the writer has to allow themselves to be in 'circumstances in which it is safe to be absent minded (i.e. for conscious logic and reason to be absent from one's mind)' (Freud 1950, p. xiii). This does not sound like discipline, it sounds more like a letting go.

Well of course the writer has to surrender to 'safe' 'circumstances' which are an element of the creative 'discipline' in this sort of writing. The words of the Church of England *Book of Common Prayer* are a good example of this kind of oxymoron: [*Thy*] *service is perfect freedom.* The discipline of creative writing allows a far greater freedom of exploration and expression than can be obtained without it. Within a workshop, I create a very carefully boundaried space in which staff feel secure and confident enough to surrender to the structured discipline of writing. I encourage them to set up safe enough situations in their own space and time so they can continue writing.

Creating a 'safe enough', disciplined environment is fundamental to the facilitation of the process. Here is another group member commenting on what she found facilitative:

> One of the reasons people seem able to open themselves up in these sessions is that Gillie imposes nothing of herself when she suggests the writing. The suggestions for writing and introductory words are very open and opening, with no way of doing it suggested, nor definite subjects, etc.

The surrender to creative discipline can be neither simple nor straightforward; our minds are used to controlling us not to be expressive and explorative. The understandings created can be very unsettling: 'One ought to write only when one leaves a piece of one's flesh in the inkpot each time one dips one's pen' (in Tolstoy quoted in Exley 1991).

Ted Hughes referred to this: 'The progress of any writer is marked by those moments when he manages to outwit his own inner police system' (Hughes 1982). Wendy Cope immortalised this in her own inimitable way, capturing the struggle between the 'inner policeman' and creative expression:

> Oh once I was a policeman young and merry
>   (young and merry),

Controlling crowds and fighting petty crime
        (petty crime),
But now I work on matters literary (litererry)
And I am growing old before my time ('fore my time).
No, the imagination of a writer (of a writer)
Is not the sort of beat a chap would choose
        (chap would choose)
And they've assigned me a prolific blighter
        (lific blighter)
I'm patrolling the unconscious of Ted Hughes.

(Cope 1986, p. 15)

Giving in to this discipline when writing in a group can be positive; group members create remarkable pieces of writing. One reflective writer described it pleasurably: 'everybody writing alone yet together'. But many then find it difficult to go on to find ways of creating the discipline – or permission – in their own space and time.

An example of this was Penny, who wrote an effective piece for the group at the first session when we all wrote together, but could not write anything at home for the second. So I suggested she try somewhere else, other than in her home, or with carefully chosen material she liked, or at a different sort of time.

Penny then wrote two pieces for the next session – very warm and celebratory ones, and clearly got a great deal out of the process and very much enjoyed sharing them with the group. The first was written in a café, having bought a shocking pink folder, a new pad and a bright pink pen. Both stories were written in pink though only the first at the café. The café writing and the pink materials allowed her to get going and write at home.

Some people find it hard even to begin to think of writing. One new participant of a group billed as an experiential reflective writing workshop looked extremely startled when asked to write, rummaging in her bag, saying: 'I've only got a lipstick to write with'. Many professionals find it difficult to find the time, though are very glad when they do:

All of us lead busy lives, and a lot of the actual writing is done like naughty children's homework, at the last minute, yet it is also clear that the stories come into being in the context of our lives, though they may only be written down in haste under a Sunday morning deadline. I think this may be what gives some of our efforts an

immediacy and seriousness which is occasionally beautiful, and always interesting.

Seth

There are also many staff who find it much easier to write on their
own and find it more difficult to accept the structured discipline of the
group writing time. There are, however, also those who find it difficult
to start at all:

> I know this small group now in a deeper way than I could ever have
> done in a whole course worth of sessions. You (a colleague) *look* dif-
> ferent now. You have become a person for me. I'm so glad. I had been
> so nervous of writing when we started, feeling I can't write what
> comes into my head; I really can't. And Gillie said 'fine, we must all
> write in the way that suits us, you do whatever that is'. But having
> heard all your pieces I can now see how I can do it; I'm going to rewrite
> mine with all my feelings, thoughts, ideas and other things – some of
> them really personal.

Finding the Writer's Voice

People are often nervous about beginning to write; they don't realise
the ability to express themselves in writing is as innate as in speech. It
can take time for their writing to settle down, for them to begin saying
in writing what they want and need to say. For confidence to develop
– trust in the process of writing; faith in themselves – that they can do
it; and a desire and determination to write, are all helpful. Positive
encouragement while new writers are experimenting with different
voices is facilitative; of course some take longer than others to gain
sufficient confidence. However inexpressive, imitative or inauthentic
the writing of a beginner is, they will progress if they are not put
down, but offered a positive way forward. It is exciting for every
writer once they have found their 'voice', and found the power of its
expression:

> Finding a voice means that you can get your own feeling into your own
> words and that your words have the feel of you about them. . . . A
> voice is like a fingerprint, possessing a constant and unique signature
> that can, like a fingerprint, be recorded and employed for
> identification.

Heaney 1980, p. 43

Speaking of finding one's 'voice' is one way of expressing the experience of writing confidently and clearly. I think *writing with one's voice,*

in Heaney's terms, is very close to the *writing of the body* of writers such as Cixous. It is the confidence to allow the hand to do the writing without the interference of the brain. Of course any writer has many voices in them, all of them authentic, and may choose to write in the voice of many different characters. The use of Heaney's expression could be confusing; but I use it because it is commonly understood by writers.

Once a writer has begun *finding their voice*, they can explore what they think, feel, know, remember, experience – through writing. Seamus Heaney has likened this to dropping a bucket down a very deep well to draw up the purest and clearest drinking water:

> Usually you begin by dropping the bucket half way down the shaft and winding up a taking of air. You are missing the real thing until one day the chain draws unexpectedly tight and you have dipped into water that will continue to entice you back. You'll have broken the skin of the pool of yourself.
>
> Heaney 1980, p. 47

Writing Stories Rather than Abstractions

Here we come to one of the commonest mistakes beginning writers make – out of both lack of confidence and lack of understanding of what writing is about. The writing of stories or poems about actual events from memory, or fiction from the depth of experience, enables people to grapple with both the mundane and concrete issues of their lives, at the same time as the abstract ones (a sense of alienation, for example).

Writing an abstract and generalised piece about *making mistakes* without it being related to a mistake in particular does not help the writer or their audience to gain access to deeper levels of meaning and understanding. Memorable poems and stories are all about events and people, their thoughts and doings: never just abstract philosophising. The philosophy, or theory, is embedded. Sartre's philosophy (see pp. 108–109) from his novel *Nausea* (1938) is part of the story, spoken by a character; this makes the *theory* memorable and comprehensible. Here is a teacher talking about the process:

> We got so much further than I could have thought we might in one short session. We slipped between theory and story in the discussions about the writing. Somehow the stories seemed to open us up to the theory and to clarify it.
>
> Brian

And another:

> Writing about an incident clarifies thought. Instead of a rambling account that moves back and forth in time (which I'm particularly prone to, as I don't have the facility for precise language) writing tends to make one create a sequential story. In doing so, various particulars, or gaps may stand out as one tries to present a story that makes sense. 'The process of writing inevitably leads to a reformulation, added clarity and ideas for further analysis' (Miles and Huberman 1994).
>
> Jane

William Carlos Williams knew this when he said 'no ideas but in things' (Williams 1951, p. 231): in effective writing, 'things', events, experiences carry or infer the 'ideas' and emotions, rather than these abstract elements being expressed directly. Another writer's saying is: *show don't tell*. Within an effective story or poem, information lives, is demonstrated by characters, plot and place rather than being told by the authorial voice. For example, don't *tell* me the woman is pregnant, *show* me her ungainly movements, the swell of her belly, the way she puts her hand to her back as she stops to get her breath. Here is Primo Levi saying how he'd far rather tell a story of what happened than generalisations about 'the country':

> No, no I can't tell you everything. Either I tell you about the country, or else I tell you what happened. But in your place, I'd pick what happened because it's a good story. Then if you really want to write it down, you can work on it, grind it, home it, deburr it, hammer it into shape, and you'll have a story.
>
> Levi 1988, p. 7

Of course, by 'hammered' story he means a publishable one – and his stories are finely tuned indeed. Reflective practice writing does not need to go to those lengths, unless the writer wishes for a wider audience than their group.

Writing in abstractions is a *warding-off*, self-protective, tactic. My experience of teaching poetry is that beginners often write in this abstract way, and have to be gentled out of it. Such pieces are often quite clever, and the writers often feel proud they have created a piece of philosophy, or poetic form. And the group are often taken in by the cleverness, and don't realise they do not discuss it, just exclaim 'oh I wish I could write like that'. This pride in itself tends to prevent such writers from beginning to write the more simple-seeming but much more effective and deep, direct accounts of practice. If those who write in this way have it gently problematised for them, they may begin to tackle issues more directly.

Here is a piece of abstract writing which was wonderfully useful to the group because it was written as the final part of a pair of reflective stories. It is an example of the way abstraction can be very fruitful when it relates directly to an experience which has been explored. Such writing then can be opening to both writer and readers:

> So at the end of this I know where I started, and that is being a good creative confident practitioner is about love not fear. It's about looking at what we do and others do with honesty and loving criticism and not with a big stick. It's about learning from the good and bad bits even if it's painful sometimes. It's about the excitement and satisfaction of doing the job a bit better.
>
> Leaving aside the issues of resources, behind a lot of bad practice is fear. Fear of getting it wrong, fear of patients' strong feelings, fear of our own strong feelings, fear of the demons inside us, of change, of saying 'I don't know', of our own inadequacies, of being out of control.
>
> In making more and more rules and edicts perhaps we are in danger of making the fears more powerful. We build the rules, the threats, the edicts into huge castle walls to keep the fears at bay. What if we took the walls down stone by stone and invited the fears to come in? For within our castle walls are the good fairies, the kind caring fairies who have to live alongside the fears.
>
> If we dismantle the walls and let the fears come in they wouldn't go away because they are real, and many of them are necessary but they might mingle a bit better with the good fairies. The fears might spice us up a bit and the good fairies – care, compassion, love and laughter – would maybe be able to stretch their wings and fly about a bit better.
>
> What if, in taking down our castle walls, we started with a piece of paper and a pen?
>
> Lindsay Buckell

When I asked Lindsay if I might use the above piece in this way she responded: 'when I wrote it, it didn't feel like an abstract piece at all, more an expression of my passionate hatred of the current climate of fear and blame'. Hatred, fear and blame are all abstract, but here they have a strong effective meaning for Lindsay and her readers because she is writing not about hatred, fear and blame in general, but specifically related to the incident which brought these emotions so forcefully to her mind:

It is a summer's day and I am looking after Simon. He lies, poor young thing, deeply unconscious, the machinery puffs and blows, whirrs and chugs. I am concerned that all the machinery, which is keeping Simon alive, is working right; and yet I love this young man, not sexually or romantically but from somewhere in my middle. I am not accepting that he is as ill as he is, I am not denying it either. I do not believe in a miracle cure, I am simply not engaging with it. I am concerned, at this moment, with looking after him and his machines.

The door opens and the ward sister comes in. She has trust in me that I can nurse her patient. She asks if I would like her to help me turn him. It is a question, not an order, in the way she says it she acknowledges that today Simon is my patient and she is simply offering to help me. She is cheery and competent, not cheery which might suggest avoidance of the situation, she is just present but lightly so. She says 'wouldn't he have hated this'. She is right – he is a diffident and intensely private young man. His mother died of the same disease. He has that depth in people whom personal tragedy has robbed of that illusion we all carry that life is essentially benign. He is quiet and shy, but laughs and chats with the other patients who are all much older than he.

Now he lies, totally dependent, his body exposed to anybody. She is right: he would have *hated* this. As we turn him she is very careful with the body which is on loan to us, because he can't protect it himself at present, careful to protect his dignity. We talk to him, not across him. In this care of this young man is our understanding that he is still a person with right to care and dignity, whether he knows or not.

In that moment I learned the truth of empathy; I received permission to have empathy with my patients, to believe in their rights as individuals, to allow myself to love them, but as a professional, not as a friend. She didn't talk about it, she didn't analyse it, she simply modelled it and all I'd heard about *not getting involved* which had never made sense inside me fell away. I understood something profound about the nature of being truly involved in a professional relationship with my patients.

Lindsay Buckell

Story and Fiction

Lindsay's piece is undeniably a story. But is it fiction? In a way any writing about a situation is inevitably fiction, insofar as it reconstructs or recreates the incident: it cannot be a factual or true carbon copy. So it is fiction insofar as it relies on Lindsay's own memory and experience of the event: the ward sister or the patient would undoubtedly write it very differently. Lindsay may, furthermore, have embroidered certain bits, and downplayed others, for the sake of making an interesting narrative, and to make the point she wished to make. The general theme to which she was writing (given by me) was 'Write a story about an *aha moment*, an *epiphany of understanding*'; her own specific theme, which emerged as she wrote, was 'the time I learned about empathy'. She certainly left out some bits and altered others so that hospital, patient and sister were all unrecognisable, in order to preserve confidentiality.

All stories could thus be said to be fictions, however much based on the writer's memory of an actual event. The distinction between *fiction* or *fact* (true or false) is one of those artificial binaries which beset modern living, and have been argued against by the post-structuralist writers (see above), and over two thousand years earlier by Chuang Tsu. A story is a creative construct, whatever the material it draws upon. Attempting to create distinctions between fact and fiction is a waste of time with regard to reflective practice. Any writing is written from a practitioner's depth of experience, knowledge and skill. This experience, knowledge and skill is as *true* as you can get: in the way a straight line is *true*.

A story can create a telling situation, and give a strong immediate sense of people in relationship to each other. A writer can draw unconsciously on their own deep professional and personal experience to convey nuances of gesture, speech, intention, memory, thought and feeling. Rereading such an account therefore offers insight to the writer, as well as to their audience. The audience can then share their insights with the writer; thus expanding their knowledge gain.

Stories and the transmission of culture

Such stories can, moreover, give a picture of some of the unwritten social and professional rules and codes that people live and work by, as well as an implicit comment upon them:

> Fiction not only legitimises emotions and aspirations, it also, again particularly since the appearance of the novel with its devotion to the minutiae of personal relationships, gives models and patterns of acceptable and unacceptable behaviour. I have certainly noticed that

those who never read, or have never read, fiction, tend to be obtuse and insensitive in personal relationships. It does really seem as if the consumption of fiction is a part of the necessary education of modern people in the fine points of human relationships. So many examples are given of how people are, how they may be expected to react, and what the harvest is likely to be.

Rockwell 1974, p. 81

A clash of codes is embedded in one sentence of Lindsay's story: *We talk to him, not across him.* Aha, think I (non-nurse reader): some nurses would treat this nearly inanimate body as if it were an object. Perhaps, until this point, Lindsay had only experienced nurses who did exactly that. What she learned that day was the possibility that: *he* (the near inanimate body) *is still a person with right to care and dignity, whether he knows or not.* Though I, as reader, made guesses about what was the learning point for Lindsay (note my *perhaps*), she responded to what I said above like this:

> I like what you wrote about it except that the bit that was so unusual and liberating for me was her comment about 'wouldn't *he* have hated this?' I had, in fact, met many nurses who would treat unconscious patients well – in not talking across them, and so on. What was so unusual was this indication of her deep understanding of *him* as an individual in that sentence. It joined up with all the other things I wrote about her in her ability to treat patients as individual people, therefore with empathy, rather than as a collective noun *patients*: i.e. part of the institution and all alike to be worked round as if they were all identikit and those who wouldn't play ball being labelled *difficult* or *manipulative*.

This issue, and its corollary, has also been reflected upon through reflexive journal writing and discussion by a student palliative care nurse: 'patients must be seen as real people not just patients. Patients need to see nurses as people . . . not mere nurses doing their job' (Durgahee 1997, p. 141). The *harvest* of nursing with empathy, in the way the Sister did (and Lindsay and Durgahee's student learned to), is clearly greater personal job satisfaction (to use a crude and jargon term). The *harvest* for the patient, who could quite possibly hear and understand everything the two nurses said, is also fairly clear.

Stories can tell us how we might or ought to act, think and feel. Think of the great writings which have informed your thinking; I am sure you will find you have gained immeasurably. Think what arose from: the unloving stupidity of King Lear (Shakespeare); the selfishness of Henry James's Isobel (*Portrait of a Lady*); Agamemnon's selfish stealing of Achilles' girl, Briseis (Homer). The same is true of reflective story writing, such as Lindsay's (see also Winter *et al.* 1999).

Stories enable us to perceive and to ask questions

A story not only presents us with a comprehensible set of possible ways of being, it always leaves us with questions. Stories offer understandings, but also lead the reader on to want to find out more about such behaviour, such situations, such emotions.

> The truest respect which you can pay to the reader's understanding is to . . . leave him something to imagine, in his turn, as well as yourself.
>
> Sterne 1760, p. 77

Story writing allows the writer to explore their experience in a full and rounded fashion. Insights often hinge upon small details, such as the Sister relating to the patient as a person, rather than just another patient. These details often appear in the writing without the writer having planned them. It is like the opening of an inner eye to aspects of situations with which the writer has not hitherto fully grappled.

The practice of awareness of detail, inculcated by writing and discussing, then slips into daily practice more and more: everyday practice becomes more aware and reflective:

> This course helped me, encouraging me to be more aware of each day, and making me more observant.
>
> Brimacombe 1996, p. 15

Novelist Lesley Glaister says she gets her ideas from 'my eyes, ears and gut feelings'; she would advise writers to 'stare, eavesdrop, never stop wondering'. I would recommend the same to reflective writers. This awareness of others inevitably benefits practice. We get the impression that some practitioners never actually perceive the student (client, etc.) before them, but only what they themselves think, just as Virginia Woolf depicted Orlando:

> He opened his eyes, which had been wide open all the time, but had seen only thoughts.
>
> Woolf 1992, p. 101.

Stories and writings from varying perspectives

A story is always a fragmentary text. It can only offer a narrow slice of experience. This can be frustrating: how often have you turned the last page of a novel, or seen the final scene of a play, and wished for more?

Reflective practice writing can benefit over straight storying: the initial or *core* story is associated with additional writings which deepen the learning for both writer and reader. Lindsay's abstract reflective passage, above, shows her working out what she meant, and enables us further to grasp messages from the scenario she depicts. Bev (page 125) wrote her story from her own point of view, and then wrote further stories from the point of view of the other protagonist. This enabled her to begin to understand the kind of forces at work upon herself and the other woman. Readers not only gain from the learning contained in the story, but can also relate it to their own experience; they are given a window of understanding not only into the situation Bev has depicted, but also into parallel experiences of their own.

Some reflective writers find it easy to begin to create stories from alternative points of view, or fictions based on their own experience, and they love doing it from the start. Other practitioners do not find it so easy, and take some time to get used to allowing themselves to explore these forms of writing.

Telling the same story through different characters' eyes is currently common in novels. Jane Rogers' *Mr Wroe's Virgins* (Rogers 1991), the story of an eighteenth-century religious fanatic, is written through the voice of four of the virgins he asked to come and live with and care for him. This multi-voiced approach gives the text a depth and roundedness which could be achieved in no other way. Frankenstein (Shelley 1820) and Dracula (Stoker 1897) are both also written with the 'I' being several of the main protagonists in the story in turn (much of the texts being in the form of personal journal).

A range of reflective stories and writings are possible around a *core story*. I have given the examples here of reflective abstract, personal journal type musings on a story, and stories written from the point of view of one of the other protagonists. Practitioners with whom I have worked have been imaginative in interpreting whose voice they might write in; I well remember one doctor writing from the point of view of a sofa. He reckoned the sofa on which his patient sat day in and day out had quite a story to tell; and he was right. There are many many other ways practitioners might write associated texts to further their insights from their *core story*.

A range of different voices can speak through a reflective practitioner's nexus of associated stories and reflective journal musings. A butterfly's eye is made up of a myriad of tiny eyes, each one recording an image from a slightly different angle. Its mind interprets these as one rounded image. Bodies of reflective writings offer a texture of images rather like that. Reflective writers often also write stories which are not an account of an incident or occasion from their memory, but are fictional in the usual sense of the word: just as Woolf and James *invented* their plots and characters.

Two Folk Tales

Pat and John work as tutors in higher education on a part-time degree for adult learners. They have used writing fiction in the past as an opportunity to reflect on key episodes of the degree. These writing sessions have been used within the teaching team as a means to share professional issues and for students to evaluate their own learning experiences.

The texts were achieved in a half-hour *automatic* writing session. They agreed to use the folk tale genre as a means to distance the writing and use an objective voice. This was especially useful at a time when the staffing of the degree had become a tense matter. As it happens John chose to focus on the learner's experience while Pat's writing was particularly concerned with teaching.

Pathway
She sat in a small dark room. Scared. Bored. Miserable. Alone. The woodman had left for his day's work in the forest bolting the door firmly behind him. Clunk went the bolt. Clack went the lock.

She waited for the hours to pass. Heavy long hours. Darkness began to fall in the forest. Birds made wing in the thickness. Clack went the lock. Clunk went the bolt. The door of the room was flung open wide. She peered out. No woodman.

'Hello,' she called. No voice answered.

'Anybody there?' she called again.

Still nobody answered. She got to her feet and went timidly to the door. Nothing but blackness. Her foot hesitated by the open door. Dare she step out? He had forbidden her to do so yet forward went her foot and touched pine needles on the cold earth. An owl shrieked.

Earth shrank. Pine needles vanished. There was no forest now only a clear path onward which she began to step slowly along. Cautiously. Nervously. Then there were others walking along the path each like herself stepping nervously and holding themselves back a little. At both sides of the path plans sprang up. Each was in gold writing on rolls of parchment. Each had a big red wax seal on it stamped with a crest of arms.

Then the plans began to speak. Excitedly. Enthusiastically. Happily. They sounded like her. Yet it was a strange and mysterious language. A language she'd never known in all her life. How she wanted the language to go on and on. Never stop. All the others along the path were speaking in the strange new language and now her lips moved too just like the rest.

The pathway was pulling her on. So on she moved. Quicker. Easier. All the others were moving too with the same ease and comfort. The pathway climbed skywards. It twisted and turned and the going was harder. Some fell off and were not seen again.

She had climbed long and hard and when now she looked back at the way she had come all she could see was a mirror. On the mirror was a bold and clear image of herself. Oh how she had changed. There was no way back now to the forest. The lock and bolt were broken beyond repair.

John Goodwin

The Golden Palace

Once upon a time in a land not too far away there were three clever people who wanted to build a golden palace. They went to the Prince of that land and told him of their dream and when he heard their plans he was pleased and told them to complete them, and come back to him in six months' time.

When six months had passed the three clever people returned to the Prince who explained that he had had to promise the King and Queen half the profits from the golden palace, but permission was given for the palace to be built.

The three clever people were delighted and began at once their five-year task to build the golden palace. The Prince often looked in to lend a hand. The other Princes and Princesses dropped in but said it didn't look much like a palace to them and they would not help to build it. On one occasion the King and Queen visited and said that it didn't look much like a palace to them but they went home and began to calculate their profits. After four years the palace was nearly finished.

Times grew hard in the land. Then the Other Princes and Princesses took a keen interest in the golden palace. They took the plans of the three clever people and said they didn't make sense. It was rumoured that the three clever people were not real builders at all. Then the Other

Princes and Princesses borrowed the tools of the three clever people and forgot to put them back. Then they forgot to turn up for work saying the three clever people were being unhelpful and confusing them. Then the Prince was removed and the King and Queen took over saying that they had decided to take all the profits from the golden palace.

Sadly the three clever people packed away their plans and left the golden palace. They set off along the road to the next kingdom. As they glanced over their shoulders they saw all the people celebrating on the top storey of the golden palace but no one was working on the lower floors and from a distance it seemed that the foundations had slipped and the walls were rather crooked.

Pat Murgatroyd

Writing and Anxiety

The practitioner undertakes reflective practice to develop their practice. Certain personal issues, however, can get in the way of professional effectiveness, as shown by GP Mark Purvis' work on the death of his brother. Different groups draw these boundaries in different places, in my experience. Professional development very properly deals with such issues. Areas which practitioners feel are definitely personal can be tackled in a separate arena with therapeutic writing either as a solitary pursuit, or with a self-appointed personal supporter.

Writing has an evidence base for alleviating the symptoms of anxiety and depression. A report of a randomised control trial (Smyth, J. M. *et al.* 1999) shows how writing about the most stressful event of their lives can create clinically relevant symptom reduction in patients with asthma or rheumatoid arthritis. The opinion in the journal's editorial was: 'Were the authors to have provided similar outcome evidence about a new drug, it likely would be in widespread use within a short time' (Spiegel 1999, p. 1328).

Lepore has reported a trial in which people who engaged in expressive writing about 'their deepest thoughts and feelings' about a stressful event 'exhibited a significant decline in depressive symptoms' (Lepore 1997, p. 1030). These trials of the therapeutic effectiveness of disclosure writing follows on from a wide range of trials conducted by James Pennebaker *et al.* (e.g. 1988) and others (e.g. Brewing and Lennard 1999), all demonstrating significant health benefits to people after writing about their lives' most stressful time. Sandra Bloom discusses the impact of these research findings on the understanding of trauma and the unique processes of writing, and their implications for psychotherapy (Bloom 1999).

A study of palliative care nurses involved in verbal group reflection (von Klitzing 1999) concluded that over time they reflected less about themselves and more about the patients. This might have been because they withdrew and protected themselves in response to increasing stress. I wonder if they might have been able to tackle that stress directly and reflectively had they written and discussed instead of just discussing.

There are many books advising on the personal development power of writing (e.g. Bolton 1999a, Hunt and Sampson 1998, Schneider and Killick 1998), and others telling of the healing impact of writing story and poetry about medical work (e.g. Borkan *et al.* 1999, Belli and Coulehan 1998, Campo 1997, Williams 1951, Hilfiker 1985).

Is Reflective Writing an Art?

Art has always questioned the boundaries of our existence. Artists and certain ethnographers and philosophers put themselves in situations in which the conventional orderliness of their everyday systems of thinking about their lives are suspended. Artists cross dangerous mental and social barriers and create images that jolt or shock their viewers, listeners or readers into some kind of reassessment. Brecht, for example, used the form of his work to set his viewers questioning structures that they habitually took for granted.

'There is no such thing as a literature which is "really" great or "really" anything independently of the ways in which that writing is treated within specific forms of social and institutional life' (Eagleton 1983 p. 202). A popularly held belief is that only writers can write, that art is a God-given capacity. Poets are thought of as lying around (either luxuriously or starving in a garret) waiting for the muse to strike: *it's easy for them but impossible for me*. The way writers speak of their own process, however, gives a very different impression: 'I rewrote the ending of *Farewell to Arms* thirty-nine times before I was satisfied' (Ernest Hemingway, quoted in Exley 1991).

We believe we have no power from the moment we learn to speak as infants: that it is located in father, God, government, philosophers, and so on. Academic literary criticism is one of these authorities: policing *acceptable* language, policing writing itself as either *literary* or *non-literary*: and deciding who is allowed to create and take part in the discourse (Eagleton 1983). It is time we overthrew these gods and started to listen to the quiet voices within ourselves and our colleagues.

Writing as a reflective practitioner seems to be a force which develops confidence in writing, co-operating, and collaborating, encourages the sharing of skills and the development of team-building, and enhances the ability to deal with conflict. This is an artistic, aesthetic process.

Writing, an Ancient Form of Communication

The first known writing was practised in the near east in 3300 BC. A hieratic papyrus from Thebes from about 1850 BC, the teaching of Ptahhotep, says: 'It is good to speak to the future the future will listen'. And we can listen to what was written all those years ago, such as Butehamen writing to his dead wife c. 1075 BC: 'there is no one who stays alive. We will all follow you. If I can be heard where you are, tell the Lords of Eternity to let me, your beloved, come to you.' Because writing had this power to *enshrine* text, it was considered to belong to the gods. The ancient Egyptian god of writing was Thoth 'who knows the mysteries and sets the gods' utterances firm . . . who proclaims all that is forgotten'. Egyptian hieroglyphs were called 'gods' words' and were considered to have a numinous power and were used as amulets. They could also act as emblems and amulets; stelae were inscribed with magical texts so that water could be poured over them and then drunk to ingest the magic of the texts.

'Damnatio memoriae' – damaging or erasing a written name – could be a way of attacking a dead enemy. To destroy the written name of a person was to deprive them of their identity and render them non-existent. It is an old notion also in our culture that power over someone or something is gained by speaking, and more particularly writing, their name. Reflective practice writers gain power over their practice by naming it in writing.

Endnote

Theorising is a practice of writing. One writes about the meanings in practice and through writing creates the meanings of practice. Practice is itself always changing hence there are always new meanings to be written about. At the same time, through writing, the meaning of practice is re-created, always cast anew.

Usher 1993, p. 100

A reflective practitioner wrote:

I even enjoy the physical holding of the pen, the shaping of the words, and I like the way it unfolds before you, like thought unravelling. The rest of the book is blank; I wonder what the next chapter will be?

Jenny

10

The Learning Journal

The periods when I undertake this (writing) activity can be unsettling just as much as they can be therapeutic. They are vehicles for me to test out the very basis of my assumptions and re-evaluate significant portions of both personal and professional life.

Sonya

A learning journal is a particularly personal and unstructured form of reflective writing. As its name implies it takes the form of entries written as for a personal (rather than engagement) diary, when appropriate. The kinds of writing used in it will vary according to the needs and wants of the writer and their situation. It is a more an organic tool to support the processes of reflection rather than to be seen as a created product. Any and all of the kinds of writing suggested in this book are appropriate in a journal.

The secret to keeping an effective learning journal is to: write it for yourself; use the *how to start writing* method outlined on pp. 121–124; and write about episodes of experience, including:

- what was **done** on any particular occasion
- what was **thought** about it
- what was **felt** about it

and taking into consideration the following:

Writing a journal calls on students – and staff – to relearn a lost language. We are trained to favour academic over expressive language, which includes the use and valuing of the first person singular. Ironically, it seems that the very requirement to write in the first person singular may be an important reason why journals contribute to improved learning.

Moon 1999b, p. 34

I like this idea of writing. I wrote poems in my youth, like we all. Then, writing for what? But now it feels comfortable, like a silent friend, there unquestioning, uncritical.

Rita

There isn't anything else more important than these four things to keeping a journal. So if you want to *do* rather than *read about it*, put this book down, write an entry, enjoy the process, and then see what you make of it afterwards. What follows here might have more meaning then.

This chapter covers: an explanation of what a learning journal is and can be, and how to keep one; an overview from the literature of how journals have been used by practitioners and on courses; an extended example of a teacher's journal.

Logs, Diaries, Journals

These words seem to be used interchangeably in professional development. It is useful to distinguish between them, as each one has its uses (see Holly 1989).

A **log** is a straightforward recording of events, calculations or readings (such as meteorological), like a ship's log. Its content is limited and predetermined. Extraneous data would not just be irrelevant, but would confuse the issue. The usefulness is clear: it is an *aide-mémoire*.

The **diary** is at the other extreme and can contain anything, be a confidante like Ann Frank's diary (1947) or Virginia Woolf's (1977, 1978, 1980). The diary is one of the oldest forms of literature in the west (Simons 1990, Blodgett 1991). Women were traditionally the diary writers, presumably because they were less active in an outside life, and therefore needed someone (or something) to talk to privately. They also were more constrained than men and so therefore had more to confide. Early novels were written as diaries (e.g. Burney 1898), I think because they offered an illusion of illicit reading since a diary is generally written for the self alone to reread.

So a diary can be a confessor, a confidante or special friend (as Anne Frank called hers) for a writer trapped in a tiny social circle (like Anne Frank, and so many earlier lady diarists), or a place of creation such as a writer's diary (Virginia Woolf's, for example).

These diaries contain stories of happenings, hopes and fears of what might happen, memories, thoughts and ideas, and all the attendant feelings. They also contain creative material: drafts of poems, stories, plays or dialogues, doodles and sketches. Thorough information on how to keep an effective diary is covered in Bolton (1999a) and Rainer

(1978). Just like a reflective practitioner's writing, I can hear you thinking. Well, yes.

A **journal** is a record of happenings, thoughts and feelings about a particular aspect of life, or with a particular structure. A journal can record anything relative to the issue to which it pertains. So a reflective practice journal is like a diary of practice but in addition includes: 'deliberative thought and analysis related to practice' (Holly 1988, p. 78).

Ira Progoff developed a form of journalling for personal development. His method uses a structured series of sections under which the client writes, such as: *relationships, work, dreams, here and now, the more distant past* (Progoff 1987). Like the professional journal, Progoff's contains deliberate thought and analysis, as well as intimate explorations of events and feelings, and attendant thoughts. Many people have found it useful, some too structured.

Journals can be kept for a range of purposes, other than being an intensive structured personal adventure like Progoff's, or as a reflective practitioner. A qualitative research journal records a researcher's findings, and thoughts and feelings about those findings. It might contain quotes of exactly what people have said, quantitative data such as tables and figures, descriptions of focus groups or interviews. A politician might keep a journal of her years in office, or one might be kept to record a holiday or journey.

Unlike a diary, but more like a log, these documents (some might be virtual, others painted, for example), might very likely be written to be read by someone other than the writer. The politician, and some artists (authors, for example), have their eye on publication, but there are also many which are written for a very small audience: the research journal and the teacher's or nurse's reflective journal, for example. Practitioners keep reflective journals primarily for their own learning, but also to share parts with their supervisor, or portfolio group, reflective practice group, staff development group, Masters course group, or whatever.

Here are two Masters students reflecting in their journals on the process, and what it has meant to them:

> I now feel quite sad about this journal and the ending of the group. This journal represents for me the space which this course has given me for my 'whole' life so far. It has given me intellectual space and opportunity – physical space from work and social group – spiritual space . . ., also psychological space to rethink my responses, reactions,

motivations, expectations and hopes (this passage cut from journal, for personal reasons). I'm more able to take risks and I have thought of things I'd like to do which I've previously not thought as possibilities in the past. . . .

Elaine

The writing has been a real eye-opener for me. I was sceptical at first, partly because the *reflective journal* has almost become a cliché in nursing education, but also because I was anxious about others reading my gibberish. . . .

I will continue to write a log because Gillie was right. Things come out differently when written down. Feelings and thoughts can creep up and surprise you in writing. I will always be grateful to this course for giving me the space to discover this. And when you discover something for yourself you use it!

Ann

And an example – an extract from Dr Becky Ship's writing, in which she reflects upon the difficult interface between herself as a private person, and herself as a very public professional:

A Letter to My Patients

I am listening, really I am.

I have to be honest, though – sometimes it's hard to pay attention. If my focus seems to shift away from you to the clock, or the door, or the computer, please don't think it's because I don't care.

Let me tell you something, my friend. I've got problems, too. Sometimes my problems are bigger than yours and I'm hanging on by my fingernails. But I'm the one with the desk and the prescription pad.

And what am I doing while you struggle to explain yourself to me? I'm holding myself together, is what I'm doing. I might distractedly put my hand up to my face while your words hover between us. Just checking I'm in one piece.

I'm not painting my toenails, that's for sure.

I'm not snuggled up under my duvet, drifting off to sleep.

I'm not licking a rapidly melting chocolate ice cream cone.

I'm sitting here, listening to you.

So make the most of me.

Becky Ship

Becky explained that when 'I distractedly put my hand up to my face' it was to make sure she had put her *work mask* on that day, and to check it hadn't slipped or cracked. Working with patients without it would feel far too exposing and risky; she needs to ensure her professional persona is in place to protect the vulnerable private one.

The Learning Journal: an Introduction

Writing things down in itself sharpens perspectives, breaks things down into clearer 'elements' and brings up further questions which facilitate learning.

Liz

The learning journal is the cornerstone of reflective practice work. It includes *stories of events* (these could also be called *critical incidents* or *events*) as well as a myriad of other invaluable reflective material. If it is kept for the writer's eyes only, then elements can be taken out out for discussion with peers, mentors, supervisors, or to include in a portfolio. Keeping it private in the first instance can enable free expression: the telling of secrets to the journal, for example. As one practitioner said: 'writing things down without worrying what other people think is the most powerful thing about this kind of writing.' And: 'I must say I like this idea of keeping track of your thoughts'.

Reflection on practice or learning by keeping a journal is a fundamentally dynamic rewarding process (Benner 1984, Beveridge 1997, Bolton 1991, 1994, 1995, 1999a, Boud, Keogh and Walker 1985, Morrison 1996, Schon 1983). It is an interactive process requiring commitment and energy from the writer:

> By keeping a personal-professional journal you are both the learner and the one who teaches. You can chronicle events as they happen, have a dialogue with facts and interpretations, and learn from experience. A journal can be used for analysis and introspection. Reviewed over time it becomes a dialogue with yourself. Patterns and relationships emerge. Distance makes new perspective possible: deeper levels of insight can form.
>
> Holly 1989, p. 14.

Reflective learning journal writers:

- take responsibility for discovering personal learning needs, and attempt to ensure they are met;
- only learn in this way by examining vulnerable areas, the cutting edge;
- question, explore, analyse what *you* do, what *you* think, and what *you* feel and also what peers feel, think and do – no safe examples of the practice or learning of others here, or semi-safe role-play – but personal experience.

What is a learning journal?

It is a collection of expressions of thinking and explorations. Like a map, it could chart the personal reflective critical background to experiences and understandings. It might include narratives or story, reflective stream of consciousness, sketches, cartoons, descriptions of dance, diagrams. Experiment!

Types of writing

A learning journal contains all sorts of different types of writing. Normally when we write we have to constrain ourselves to the type of writing expected by our readers: letter form (business or personal), short story, journalism, shopping list, academic or professional article. A journal can shift and change between any kind of writing as it goes along. There are different kinds of ways these forms can be looked at.

A journal, for example, might contain free flow *six minute* type writing, stories, poems, musings or reflections upon an event, dialogues with the self, fictional dialogues or monologues with others such as patients, clients or students, analysis of motives and actions, philosophising on such as ethics, evaluation, assessment of practice, description, fantasy used to aid insight, cathartic writing, letters, extended metaphors, ethnography.

I could go on and on fitting into categories the different writings you will come across in this book. You will probably create your own quite different categories.

The thing

A journal is an object, a possession. I suggest investment in something which is not only appropriate but a pleasure to use. Mine is a loose-leaf folder which can hold all sorts of shapes and sizes – A4 sheets of my writing (handwritten or typed), letters, newspaper cuttings, journal papers, pictures, and all sorts of other items. And I like to write with a 2b pencil with a rubber on the end: I think I like the idea of being able to rub out my writing, though I never do; I also like the whisper a soft pencil makes on the page. Some people prefer to buy a nice book. In one group of nurses, one had a suede covered book, another a book with bright children's pictures on the cover, one a plain but glorious red, another a shocking pink folder and pen.

Typing is likely to produce a different kind of reflection from hand-writing; it looks more organised and thought-out, and invites immediate analytic revision. A pen feels more permanent than a pencil; a fountain pen feels more professional and sophisticated than a biro. Coloured pens and paper for particular emotions and feelings can take writing in interesting directions, as can different sizes of paper – a huge sheet of A1 for anger, the back of an envelope for a period of lack of confidence.

Try out different things; choose for yourself.

Areas which you might concentrate on

- The relative status and roles of – tutor and student
  – physician and patient
  – nurse and doctor
  – social worker/therapist and client.
- The effect of this sense of hierarchy on work/self.
- The balance of responsibility between peers.
- The influence of informal contacts between – peers
  – non-peers.
- Personal/professional gains from supervision/courses/groups.
- Personal objectives and how these have been achieved.
- Taking responsibility; the role of shame and guilt.
- The match between – expectations/hopes and reality
  – clients/patients and you
  – students/staff and you.
- The effect of the forces of anger, compassion, denial, etc.
- Discussion/conflict – has it been useful/destructive?
- The difference between a goal-directed project and a process-focused one.
- The value of uncertainty in a world where science knows the answers; are there even a few right questions?
- Changes and developments in professional practice.

These reflections might make us more accountable to
  – ourselves
  – students/patients/clients
  – society and superiors
by developing greater:
- self evaluation/knowledge
- flexibility (more able to perceive the other point of view)
- critical awareness of dilemmas rather than being overwhelmed
- willingness to collaborate and learn from colleagues.

Why a learning journal?

We take in new things (from experience, inspiration, learning, practice, research . . .) all the time; these affect us in all kinds of ways. There's sometimes a muddly period while we accommodate (particularly if the new thing is big). This is a positive developing process.

The learning journal is a flexible tool in the process of learning, which helps in the grasping or filling out of vital issues which might otherwise become lost. It charts the development of personal learning. Parts of it may be shared with tutor or colleagues, but for it to be useful, try seeing it as being for *you* in the first instance. It:

- helps you clarify your own thinking
- allows you to express feelings about yourself/peers/tutors/course content/your writing/others' writing
- helps you identify misunderstandings/non-understandings
- can help you identify needs
- can inform a dialogue between you and your tutor/peers
- allows you to perceive links between knowledge/experience – past/present.

How?

A *learning log* could be reflective running notes on:
- any situation of practice – with colleagues or the home/work interface as well as directly with the clients or students with whom you work
- group sessions
- interactions with peers/tutors
- any other learning/teaching situations – past or current
- things you did/would not *say*, but did *think* – for whatever reason
- feelings about your writings
- comments on things you have read
- any increase in your knowledge
- increase in your ability to articulate and identify issues
- the expansion of your depth of vision and understanding
- changes in beliefs, theories, attitudes, relationships or practices
- anything else you want to get off your chest.

These notes might include:

- your fears, hopes, anxiety, expectations, values, beliefs
- comments on ideas or methods you think useful, would like to try out for yourself, consider irrelevant/impractical
- development of arguments or opinions not fully developed or expressed
- explorations of your changes of opinion
- details of what you found difficult to understand or do.

Useful tips

- Think of this as being for you – not to be shared at first.
- Try to write in a free-flow way (see pp. 121–124) for at least part of this – a good way of discovering what you think.
- Try writing in different ways: exploratory, descriptive, judgemental, story, poetry, anecdote, generalisation, lists, interview yourself, write vignettes or portraits. . . .
- Always date entries – you won't remember.
- Try to make entries soon after significant events – you are bound to forget.
- Take notes during teaching/learning sessions to fill out later.
- Use the learning journal to think through, to muse, to try out ideas – since it is for you, you can explore one idea and then its opposite – trying to work out which fits you.

When?

Any or every time: when you want to. The most creative times might be when your cognitive powers are at their least able, such as midnight or 4 a.m.:

> 'Aren't you going to bed *yet* Mum? Are you *still* working?'
> 'No, I'm not working. I'm just writing.'

Timing is vital with regard to how long after an event it is appropriate to write about it. If it is left too late, the event might well have lost its impact, no longer become a vivid piece of writing, and therefore not able ultimately to affect practice: it has passed its 'eat by' date. If it is attempted too soon, the event may still be too raw for an effective focus:

> If the experience is very close, I feel inhibited. . . . If the closeness of the real reality, of the living reality, is to have a persuasive effect on my imagination, I need a distance, a distance in time and space.
>
> Llosa 1991, p. 44

For whom?

For you, primarily; for your colleagues; some of it possibly for tutors or supervisor, or for assessment.

With whom?

Co-mentoring, paired support with a colleague each reading the other's material and supportively commenting, can be extremely useful, as can belonging to a group. Or your journal may be part of your work with a supervisor/mentor.

Where?

Anywhere: in a café, in bed, perhaps difficult on a bike.

A Counsellor and Academic's Journal

Here is a passage from Colin Feltham, the head of an academic counselling department (written in a café):

> I am oppressed by the cancer of bureaucracy and, too, by galloping technology. As a lecturer in counselling, I am not a good example to students or clients. Divorced, demoralised, struggling to survive everyday anxiety, nobody's model.
>
> I am in the business of teaching others how to help people suffer less, be more resourceful. I know all the theory. I've had the therapy. But I'm suffering more than ever. The training, the theory, the professions of counselling and higher education, parasitic pretenders to being on the side of the suffering and the hungry for knowledge, they make me sick. Yet, one of the most influential of counselling concepts tells me that it is I who make myself sick, I who 'perpetuate my psychological disturbance'. When things are at their grimmest, even beyond panic and piercing gloom, I find myself indulging in 'suicidal ideation'. To whom then do I turn? It would be great if counselling or therapy worked as neatly or reliably as it's said to in the books. It would be nice if God existed for me, but s/he/it doesn't. Pained instinct turns me towards poignant music and stillness. I listen and I sit,

alone. Even in the midst of panic, the shadow of the bureaucrat's axe falling on me, I yield to the simplicity of my body's sitting breathing. Sometimes facial muscles twitch oddly; sometimes tears spring forth, roll down; often worries echo through my head. I am not exactly my own best friend, it's rather that now I am briefly reminded that life itself is friendly. Beyond the crucifixion of everyday adversity, there all along, is original peace.

A student tells me she is experiencing severe insomnia, and I feel helpless, feeling only inner compassion. A colleague, in the canteen, looking ashen, laments his own bureaucratic burden and his impotence about finding any end to it. Again, I can only feel for him, sit in silent solidarity. Sometimes, with a client, while listening to a complex narrative of inescapable suffering, I will become aware of some stillness, in me, between us, a sensed original sanity.

Is this what is meant by a wounded healer? Wounded, yes. Healer, I'm not so sure. We seem to have created and live in such a wounding, adversity-generating culture, that healing – wholemaking – often seems a forlorn hope, empty slogan, uphill struggle, aspiration rather than reality. Perhaps healing, counselling at its best, is only found in timeless moments. The sacred fifty-minute hour, oasis in today's wilderness, symbolises – and occasionally is – such a moment.

And then there's the question: must life be an endless round of tolerating bureaucracy, suffering, complaining, and reflecting on it all? Where's the light, levity, light-heartedness? If bureaucracy is absurd – it is, it is – then one sane response must be laughter; and if counselling lifts even a little heavy-heartedness, couldn't we allow a few guffaws into the process? In this age of accelerating techno-toxicity and feverish (so-called) quality control, runaway consumerism, worship of entrepreneurs and lurching cognitivisation, who will cut through the Kafkaesque nightmare? If counselling isn't the place for lachrymal freedom, where is? If counsellors become tame, professionalised, 'audit-minded' rulekeepers, how can they free? If I can't overturn my adversity, de-oppress myself, practise what I teach, and practise what I feel, who can?

Colin Feltham

Learning How to Use Journals with Students

Stephen Trotter has been using learning journals with his prospective and veteran teachers, and to examine his own professional actions since the mid-1980s. His use of journals developed considerably as he came to understand the process of reflection better, and to perceive the potential of journals:

Engaging in reflective practice requires individuals to assume the perspective of an external observer in order to identify the assumptions and feelings underlying their behaviour and then to speculate about how these assumptions and feelings affect practice. . . . However I have found this process may be hampered by 'Fundamental Attribution Error' whereby the student places too much responsibility for causality on external factors rather than personal volition . . .

Examining 'personal volition' however, and the attendant feelings and experiences, seemed to me as a behavioural psychologist initially not only foreign, but fraught with miscues. However I now consider the miscues an essential process in the construction of a *Teaching Schema*. I initially chose to have my students report in a *Dragnet* style of *Just the Facts* [but] I came to realise this emphasis on objectivity and emotional distance was counterproductive to my instructional goals.

I slowly found myself more interested in the Journals of students who had violated the rules and strayed into the subjective meadow. The entries were both enlightening and in many instances poignant. I began to see the Journal entries as a mirror of a student's ever increasing awareness of the act of teaching. . . .

The examination of one's teaching behaviour may [however] be so painful as to serve as a disincentive and foster a defense mechanism of denial. Therefore in the teaching of the reflective process I find it helpful to try and increase the focus on positive behaviours and the identification of replacement behaviours. . . .

I have [also] found that without prior training, entry content is likely to be observational and reactionary rather than reflective.

Stephen Trotter 1999

The use of an effective approach to journal writing does need to be taught and fostered by individual or group education or supervision.

Some Reports of Journal Use

Journals are used in many different ways in professional education. Rita Charon's medical students are each given a new blank book in which to write their journal. They then very fruitfully share extracts with her and each other in seminars. Learning journals have also been well reported in the literature in education and nursing. Kember *et al.*'s (1996) qualitative and quantitative examination of how effective reflective journal keeping can enable education students to be prepared for far more fruitful tutorials and seminars plugs a gap in the literature. Jennifer Moon offers a thorough analysis of the work of educators in this area (Moon 1999a). Paterson has published a deeply enquiring, theoretically and methodologically thorough study of how to set up reflective diaries (including critical incidents) in nurse training (Paterson 1995). Glen *et al.*'s (1995) analysis in nursing is equally useful. Christine Love (1996) describes a very fruitful study in which student nurses and patients kept parallel diaries, and compared them at the end of the period. GPs (family practitioners) kept diaries of their emotional response to situations in order to reflect upon them, in a study by John Howard (1997).

An in-depth study of preservice (student) teachers' journals concludes they 'provide occasions for students to find their own voices to explain, describe, challenge, or question their experiences in the field' (McMahon 1997, p. 211). Taleb Durgahee reports wonderful work using journals and reflective groups to foster awareness and understanding of ethical issues with palliative nursing students (Durgahee 1997). Students wrote: 'because I had to write my diary, I was much more aware of the issues before making decisions', 'being aware of my beliefs, actions and my practice are crucial in ethical decision-making, I have learned to reason and think clearly'. Taleb comments: 'the students are helped to realise that there is no magic formula for ethical decision-making. Instead, the process of writing in the diary followed by group discourse enables the analysis of relevant and important factors to be considered in morally challenging decisions' (Durgahee 1997, pp. 140–1).

Best stresses the value of a journal 'as a process of integration'; for *containment,* and *therapeutic space*: it is a safe place to put experiences and emotions, however bad. These can then be reviewed more safely at a later date: the material will have remained the same on the page in the interval, but the writer will have moved on and be able to reassess the situation, their feelings and thoughts about it. She also calls it a *play space*: 'space to explore and confirm' (Best 1996, p. 298).

Mathematics undergraduates' use of reflective journals has been reported by Beveridge. 'Students are expected to write 1–2 sides per week on selected topics of interest', and develop 'their ability to think deeply about their own needs' (1997, p. 35). The students hand in a version of their journal for assessment after the module. Interestingly about half the entries concerned 'controlling their learning environment' (p. 38). Beveridge reports: 'The need to work at their own pace on individual skills was presented so forcefully through the journals that I reworked the second year module to include a significant amount of individually learned material.' It is not only the students who learn and change. He concludes: 'those students who are better able to notice and feel their successes learn more' (p. 42).

A reflective journal writing project in business management is described by Rigano and Edwards (1998). The employees of a particular company kept journals which they called *thinkbooks*: 'participants were asked to record significant events, make observations on their performance, analyse their actions, draw conclusions, note learning points, and make suggestions for further action' (p. 436). Vincent was an employee who undertook *thinkbook* writing with vigour. After the first three months he realised the impact of reflective journal writing, and his daily entries changed from 'organising daily routine . . . to a process of reflection leading to growth' (Vincent's own journal entry, p. 440). Vincent carefully structured this 'process of reflection leading to growth' himself, using readings about reflective practice to support him, as well as other texts on effective behaviour, such as de Bono. The researchers concluded that one of the reasons for Vincent's successful use of the journal was that he came to *own* the process himself completely. Towards the end of the project he realised he had reached a stage where he needed to share his reflections with a mentor or a group in order to develop further. One other conclusion was that the company was farsighted in allowing staff time, and in facilitating them in reflective writing practice.

Reflective journals can have a particular use for international students, if the journals are read by tutors. Hancock (1998) has used journals with such nursing students and reported their value in cross-cultural communication, in increasing facility with the language, and in fostering critical thinking. They are also useful for maintaining 'a student-driven view of coherence to taught modular higher degrees', given the fragmentation, loss of continuity, and problematic choice of modules occasioned by modularisation (Morrison 1996, p. 322).

Morrison has introduced all Durham School of Education higher degree students since 1991 to in-depth reflective journal writing throughout their period of registration. The contents are discussed with a named tutor, and they have to do an assignment which draws upon the journal data and their reflections upon them. The evaluation of the use of these journals with over 150 students has shown they report 'increased skill in articulating and crystallising issues and arguments'; 'increased confidence and ability to interrogate and critique issues'; 'a growing self-awareness'. They have appreciated the opportunity for 'self-analysis as a basis for planning for self-development', and 'enhanced enjoyment and satisfaction in the course', and the 'openness to self . . . as an opportunity to recharge themselves'. They even reported 'they were initially prisoners of their own expectations and perceptions and how the process of reflection has been an enabling and liberating experience – freedom *for* self-realisation' (Morrison 1996, pp. 323–4).

Journals Need to be Part of a Wider Reflective Process

Journals need to be carefully introduced and facilitated when they are used on a course: 'The act of writing alone does not move preservice (student) teachers beyond a preoccupation with themselves toward a broader conceptualisation of critical enquiry into the practice of teaching and their roles as educators' (Hoover 1994, p. 92). This is the conclusion of Hoover's study of reflective journals. The teachers wrote about day-to-day frustrations and problems but the journals did not seem to 'encourage reflectivity, particularly thinking about teaching and learning in light of theory, contextual factors, and ethical issues' (p. 92). Kruse (1997) has also found that teachers make variable use of journals. A few can maintain deep focused reflection within their writing: 'They look for innovations and new pedagogical forms of practice with a specific purpose in mind.'

However: 'Teachers who are less focused in their reflective activity concentrate on the enduring dilemmas of classroom practice. Their reflection is cyclical in nature, never resolving the issues that plague them; thus they remain 'stuck and searching for new ideas' as they struggle to maintain their professional self-esteem' (1997, p. 56). Hoover (1994) suggests dialogue journal writing, teachers reading and commenting on each others' journals, or teacher and supervisor might overcome this problem, as trialled by Staton (1988) and Bean and Julich (1989). I would suggest carefully facilitated group work is needed as well.

Some Ineffectual Support of Learning Journals

Deeply reflective writing and understanding does not come readily to graduates of our schools and universities. The barriers are high (Newton 1996). There is evidence in the literature of trainers and facilitators having difficulty in facilitating journal and story writing, and therefore finding it ineffectual. Bellman gives three-quarters of a page to exposing her own inadequacy in introducing and supporting this valuable mode of reflection. She quotes her co-researchers' reasons for not writing their journal, e.g.: 'embarrassing', we 'reflect anyway ... over a drink with the girls', 'couldn't see the relevance', 'too depressing', 'you forgot to give me one', 'I find it a threat because someone could read it', 'no one else was doing it', 'I don't see the point really' (Bellman 1996, p. 136). Wellard and Bethune (1996) report similar lack of success, unwittingly giving an example of how *not* to facilitate reflective journal writing, and blame the students.

Journals can be in danger of being used in inappropriate ways, if they are read or assessed by superiors. A practitioner can feel under pressure to *confess* or disclose professional or personal material.

One Teacher's Journal

Stephen Rowland runs a Masters in Education for university lecturers. In teaching other academics to teach, he is reflexively doing what he teaches his students to do. Here is part of his journal:

Module 1, Session 3

I have always felt uncomfortable about the fact that being a teacher places me in a power relationship in respect of my students. I think I used to feel that I could try to get rid of this by 'handing over' power to the students. In fact, this is never possible, however 'liberal' or 'student-centred' I am in my approach, because the teacher–student relationship is socially constructed to be one of power: the power to make the final judgement concerning the value of the students' work; the power that arises from having greater knowledge. This is the case whether my student is a four year old child (I once had an infant classroom) or a professor.

In principle, I believe that learning is more likely to be effective when students feel power or control over the conditions of their learning. I therefore try to engender that sense of control on the part of the students. In a enquiry-based course such as this, this means attempting to achieve equality between the contributions that participants and I make, so that we can all equally be critical of one another. These questions suggest the difficulty of achieving this:

- Do participants attach a greater significance to my contributions to the group discussion than to those of their colleagues?
- Might they not be wise to do so since I shall be making the final assessment of their work?

- Don't I know more about 'education' than others in the group? And if so, isn't it right that I should have more influence on both the content and process of our work? And isn't what I have to contribute of more value than what others have to contribute?

In spite of the difficulty of such questions, it is necessary to work towards equality so that people can learn through a critical engagement, because being critical in an appropriately supportive way presupposes some sense of equality. But the attempt to work towards equality of the learner–teacher relationship raises a host of dilemmas.

As a teacher, perhaps I want to have authority but not power?

Stephen Rowland

Rowland's Masters in Higher Education students kept parallel journals:

During each module participants were encouraged to keep a research diary of observations and interpretations they have made of an aspect of their teaching; accounts of their thinking in response to the discussions of the group; critical responses to any of the literature encountered; evaluative comments about the course itself; and so on. They were private documents to which no one else, including the tutors, had any rights of access. The material from them might be used in informal seminars on the course; it might be used as a basis for later publications; or to identify issues which require further exploration with other participants or the course tutors. The research diaries would also be a major source of material for compiling a portfolio of work relating to each module. . . .

We were concerned that these portfolios should be seen as working documents, as tools for thinking through ideas about practice, rather than as final products. . . . What seemed to be of immediate importance was that participants should see their own regular writing to be a fundamental part of the enquiry process.

Writing in such a way as to explore the professional values which underlie practice is not easy. Such values are always difficult to express. Their articulation needs to be retraced as they become questioned and new experience is brought to bear on them. Thus we would expect the participants to refine those ideas in one portfolio which may initially have been raised in an earlier one. They would pursue themes of enquiry across consecutive portfolios.

Rowland and Barton 1994, p. 371

Writing a journal enables a dialogue with the self which lasts over time. You will have noted Stephen Rowland's dialogues with himself; he tells me his students also engage in such internal discussions.

Journal writing encourages an awareness of the different voices in one's mind (for a discussion of this see Rowan 1990, Bolton 1999a), and what they have to offer in terms of different knowledge, intuitions, skills in analysis and thought, and feelings. It also enables the writer to stand back from experiences, thoughts and feelings, take a long thoughtful look at them, and form fresh views upon them:

> This writing process is really helpful. It enabled me to find a synthesis of all those things going round and round in my head.
>
> A group member

All this will inevitably affect future actions.

> Writing taps tacit knowledge; it brings into awareness that which we sensed but could not explain.
>
> Holly 1989, p. 78

11

Writing in Genre

Life never does more than imitate the book, and the book itself is only a tissue of signs, an imitation that is lost, infinitely deferred.

Barthes 1977, p. 147

Man is an animal suspended in webs of significance he himself has spun.

Geertz 1973, p. 5

Different forms of writing are there to be picked and chosen from – the right form for the right piece of writing. We have many selves and many potential voices, one perhaps clamouring vociferously to be expressed as fantasy story, another wanting nurturing towards haiku (tiny Japanese poem). 'Writing "works" because it enables us to come to know ourselves through the multiple voices our experience takes, to describe our contexts and histories as they shape the many minds and selves who define us and others' (Holly 1989, p. 15). This chapter looks at examples of practitioners' poetry (both formal and free verse), and different genres of prose.

Poetry

The inexplicable importance of poetry

Cocteau 1930, p. 128

Poetry is an exploration of the deepest and most intimate experiences, thoughts, feelings, ideas: distilled, pared to succinctness, and made music to the ear by lyricism. For those who write poetry, it is the only way to explore and express certain things – because it makes a direct dive for the heart of the issue, with no messing around with sentence structure and having to make grammatical sense. It can be a way of saying exactly what you want to say, and also of finding out what you need to say (Abse 1998). Sir Philip Sydney was desperate to 'faine in verse my love to show', yet could not find a poem good enough: ' "Foole," said my Muse to me "look in thy heart and write" ' (Sydney 1965, edn. p. 165, *Astrophel and Stella*, Sonnet 1) – he had to write it himself. The right words can be used in the right place, and only them; and these right words might be ones no prose writer could possibly put together.

Finding the right words and the right place is not easy – but once found they can offer expressive insight to the reader, and clarity of understanding to the writer. This happens partly because the poetic writing mind knows better than the more conscious mind, as one of my group members, just starting out, realised: 'I like poetry because I can't make it do what *I* want it to do, it will only do what *it* wants. I didn't want to write the poem I did write, I wanted to write a nice glowing poem about being a mother.'

Poetry often uses image, such as metaphor or simile, to express vital experiences in a few words. Many poets use strict form, such as sonnet or villanelle, when writing about their deepest experiences. The strictness of the form (whether to do with rhyme, rhythm, syllable counting or repetition) seems to contain the otherwise uncontrollable unlimitedness of grief for a friend's death from AIDS (Hamberger 1995), the work of a busy clinician (Campo 1997), and unrequited love (Shakespeare's sonnets). But 'Poetry should be . . . unobtrusive, a thing which enters into one's soul, and does not startle or amaze it with itself, but with its subject,' and: 'if poetry comes not as naturally as the leaves of a tree it had better not come at all' (Keats 1818).

Poetry writing is compulsive, utterly absorbing for these reasons, and therefore tends to be self-affirming, and self-confident making, as well as challenging and demanding. Poetry can offer startling insight as well as refreshment to the busy practitioner.

Maggie Eisner's Villanelle

On a muggy Saturday afternoon after a busy week at the Health Centre, I sat down with two hours to do my homework for the next day's meeting of the Reflective Writing Group for GPs [family medicine]. It's one of my very favourite things – I wonder why I always leave the writing till the last minute. I felt exhausted, uncreative and devoid of ideas. Six minutes *free writing*, recommended by our facilitator as a kind of warm-up, produced a long moan about how tired I was. Then I remembered reading how to write a *villanelle*, and wrote this:

A therapeutic villanelle

I'm spending too much time on work, I know,
The pressure's putting lines upon my face.
I'd like to sit and watch the flowers grow.

Sometimes I feel the tears begin to flow:
I'm leaden tired, I'm desperate for some space,
I'm spending too much time on work. I know!

Do they want blood? Why don't they bloody go?
I'll crack if I continue at this pace.
I need to sit and watch the flowers grow.

Those piles of paperwork oppress me so,
They never seem to shrink, it's a disgrace.
I'm spending too much time on work, I know.

If I could take my time and take it slow,
If life could be a pleasure, not a race,
Perhaps I'd sit and watch the flowers grow.

If I got bored, there's places I could go,
I'd stretch my limbs, write poetry, find grace.
Must get to spend less time on work – although
I might do more than just watch flowers grow.

When I'd finished it, I felt rejuvenated and alive. It's always good to express my feelings in writing, but I was surprised to feel so dramatically better. Possibly the villanelle, or the challenge of writing in a tight poetic form, had a specific chemical effect on my brain (maybe serotonin reuptake inhibition like Prozac, or dopamine release like cocaine).

Maggie Eisner

Robert Hamberger: At the Centre

Robert reflects upon the role of poetry in his life and work:

I've been a social worker for twenty years, and have viewed myself as a poet for about seventeen of those years. I've usually perceived these two aspects of my life as quite separate. The American poet Mark Doty said 'I write . . . to try to figure out my experience by shaping it' (1995, p. 24). It may simply be that figuring out most of my social work experiences doesn't require the shape of poetry. It may be that I find the ways of shaping reflective practice available in the workplace sufficient for most of the time. I've also attempted to shield my writing as something precious for myself, not for my work. I retain a fear of using the experience of others in a voyeuristic way; but the social work poems I have written are usually tributes to people, respecting their courage or their individuality in the way they deal with adversity.

At the Centre (for Kettering MIND)

When we all went on holiday they put a photo in the paper. My husband was embarrassed. He said you with all those mental people. I said I'm not ashamed. I've had a breakdown and that's me. Like it or lump it. People think you should hide coming here.

celebrate the woman
scabbing her skin with a matchbox edge
to make her husband listen
celebrate the man
who cracks jokes at the kettle
on bad days

Anyone can get depressed. I can, you can. They want me to have injections. I'm allright without it. If you go in the sun you've got to cover your arms. Who needs that?

they build their paper-maché time
carefully
shred by shred
so it won't unglue again

This isn't me. I had a job. I had a laugh. Look at my hands now. Mornings are worse. I take another tablet, go back to bed. I want to wake up and be like I was.

at the centre
you can tell your life
to whoever sits beside you
you can touch the shaking woman
say I've been there
and I know you will be well.

At the Centre was written towards the end of my first placement, when I was qualifying. I think writing it helped me to achieve two things simultaneously: to attempt to make sense of meeting a large, varied group of so-called 'mentally ill' people for the first time, and to – as some lines say – *celebrate the woman . . . celebrate the man*. The dedication to Kettering MIND was also important, because I was bowled over by the positive, supportive work they do. I hope that reading the poem feels like meeting a group of new people collaring you, the reader. If it does, that mimics the experience that led to writing it.

A recognition I channelled into writing the poem was that the people I met felt a compelling need to tell their stories: this is my life, my perspective, my experience of the mental illness I'm currently going through. The busy Day Centre was full of voices – sometimes competing against each other and arguing, but usually sharing a joke, a laugh, and literally supporting each other by their presence. I suppose the poem attempts to give both voice and shape to those voices. The prose sections are simply transcriptions of statements made to me.

The last stanza concerns a creative writing workshop I held at the centre. Two seriously ill women attended regularly. We would all read out the work we'd produced at the end of each session. After Christine read hers, she was shaking and saying that she felt she would never get better. Gillian, who sat beside her, and whose mental illness was as serious and long-standing, calmly said what became the last lines of the poem.

This generous and supportive statement was not only moving, it seemed to sum up the ethos of MIND – of mentally ill people helping each other to attempt to become well again – so forcefully that it stayed with me. It reverberated and I couldn't let go of it. During the placement all these statements dropped into my ear and fizzed inside my head, showing me glimpses of other lives and perspectives, trying to tell me something I didn't know before. Writing them down towards the end of the placement got them out of my head and gave them shape. By setting them on paper, I could let them go.

Robert Hamberger

John Graham-Pole: Through the Looking-Glass

John reflects how writing is at the centre of his practice:

Sitting down to my journal at 6.30 of a Friday morning I jog myself to remember that the first words spilling onto the page are the real ones. I've had that habit for so long of screening out first thoughts and feelings, settling for safe but second-hand ones. Today I get it though: the thought on the top is the ripest. Like salmon breaking the surface as though pleading: Hook and pluck me, strip and fillet me, serve me up for your brekker.

I'm as much writer as doctor [professor of paediatrics] nowadays. I don't separate them much. If William Carlos Williams could write the first fragments of his poems on patients' charts during house calls, then I can transpose my scribbled stick-it notes into my journal and onto my word processor and call them poetry. When I get up the next day, lo and behold, there they are – my little buddies grinning right back at me. And hey ho, off to work we go together, like Snow White and her dwarfs.

A lot of my work time I spend sitting around on beds. In the bone marrow unit my charges don't say much: their tongues and throats and palates are too sore from their chemo. First do no harm went out of the twelfth-floor window of our modern medical sky-scrapers before I'd even made it to houseman. We devastate our patients' body, mind and soul in the name of curing them of the utterly dreadful diseases besetting them. The children at least bounce back, forgetful and forgiving. Meanwhile I talk to their mums and dads. When I take the time to listen well, poems come. The words I hear are not ones heard in the shopping mart.

I have to remember though to value every relationship enough to stop and sit and see (not easy in an environment that often values only what it can bill for). When things are going a bit easier for everyone, I listen to myself making small talk. Not much about the illness or its treatment; they've heard that enough. I try to stay light. No data I know proves solemnity ever cured anyone. I share a bit of my homelife and hear about the homes I've never seen of all these people whose children's illnesses I know so intimately. This is when funny poems come, and sometimes I share them.

Mostly though I don't write poems for my patients to hear, although I do write for their benefit – perhaps as much as my own. Poetry seems the very art of service, when it helps me attend, listen, intuit, love. If I take my average clinic experience – yesterday for instance – the twenty children and their families got only a few minutes each of my really seeing them. Too much noise, too many pulls to the phone or to mini-crises, the ever-present time crunch, and sometimes anxiety intruding about what to do with a new symptom or a low blood count. Only a couple of jots made it to my stick-it notes yesterday. But at those moments I had the unveiled sight of a baby; and those children and their mums really got my attention.

I write poems for other people too, especially care givers. Their conciseness helps me make a point in a talk to medical students or nurses or hospice workers. I hope some of my poems are teachers, especially about things hard to put into more words, like this one:

Slant
I'd read them the poem about the nine-year-old
I'd told was going to die. His parents' wish, so
There'd be no conspiracy of silence between them.
How he'd howled for three minutes, then stopped
on an in-breath, played the stand-up comic, offered
jokes. The point about truth-telling opening the
sluice gate to emotion, trust-building, those things.
Afterwards two surgeons addressed me separately,
confidentially. One as much as to say: How dare you?

The other tenderly: Sorry, I couldn't do that:
'Tell the truth but tell it slant.' That's me, my
failure perhaps. Surgeons are really softies.
Acknowledging poems compress: Perhaps you'd
worked up to it a bit. Yes: I'd beat about the bush
a bit, but came at last to it: 'Joey, you're going to die,
go to heaven.' Candour I'd called the piece. Was I
too candid? They'd thought so. For me, I knew
he knew. He knew I knew it: Straight, no slant in that.

Writing this apology for the other poem I'd read and which had upset those surgeons was a good way to think and talk about the issue of candour with children. It's a hard idea to discuss, almost like religious belief. It helped me sort out on paper what I believe about this aspect of doctoring. Perhaps it can help another facing such a dilemma – or at least provoke some lively dialogue.

John Graham-Pole

Story

Things come out because the story lets them out.

A reflective practice writer

Life happens so fast there's no time to see the connections or consequences; there's too much noise everywhere. But in my work there is no noise. Everything has a ripple effect in a book; in the years of introspection, I grow. For me, it's like meditation or prayer.

Allende 2000, p. 6

Unlike poetry, in which from the first word to the last you are placed in a world of extraordinary sensibility and delicacy or dynamism, a novel or a short story is a text in which it is impossible to be intense and creative all the time and to sustain vitality and dynamism in the language. When you tell a story, the moments of intensity must be supported by episodes that are purely informative, that give the reader essential information for understanding what is going on . . . [It] is not possible in a novel, as in a poem, to use only intense, rich language.

Llosa 1991, p. 95

There are stories and stories – so many genres – fantasy, whodunnit, social realism, sci-fi, thriller, comedy, aga-saga . . . I can only represent so very few in this book. A writer's chosen genre will give a specific slant on the story told, an awareness of which adds an extra dimension to reflective writing work.

Each individual professional, furthermore, has a limited range of ways of viewing the world: comic, epic, soap, satire and so on. Think of a colleague – when they tell stories of their life, are they the hero(ine) of a romance, moral tale or tragedy? Few people realise they can play around with their habitual genre; but you can – to startling effect. I find that as soon as I suggest writing in different genre to a group, several will set off instantly and unthinkingly towards *romance* or *detective* or *fairy story*; a particular genre will grab them. One of the funniest times was when a nurse tried to write a *doctor–nurse romance*, swapping the roles to a male nurse and woman doctor. She couldn't make it work – the genre relies on a power structure of habitual male dominance. We all laughed a lot, but we learned a great deal about medical–nursing relations, and the way they are seen by 'the public'. Here is Amanda's genre story:

Strange Love

A good looking patient – that's a change. And smart – so why is he living round here? New patient card – always a frisson of expectation, so easy to impress on first acquaintance by a charming manner and efficient style.

He tells me he's in a hurry – 'got to get to London on business, just needs some antimalarials' as he's off to the Far East tonight. Exotic lifestyle then – and wonderful scent, Opium for Men? His shirt is white, bit creased, touchingly ruffled. Does he smoke? No. Keep fit? Yes. Drink? A smile – eye contact – 'now and again, how about you?'

He's flirting! But I don't mind. Married? No. Lives alone? Mostly. Will he be in Sheffield long? No, 'fraid not, just passing through.

I take a chance and suggest he might like a blood pressure check 'since he's obviously a busy man and probably doesn't get much chance to look after himself'. An excuse really. I see a masculine forearm, and some rather stylish leather braces, but not much flesh. Oh well – this is feeling rather unethical anyway.

He leaves, thanking me, shaking my hand – the firm dry grip of all romantic heroes. After he's gone, I notice the name on the computer. It reads Bond, J: patient I.D. number 11 – 007.

Amanda Howe

Fantasy and Fairy Story

Now that we have no eternal truth we realise that our life is entirely made up of stories . . . truth is made of stories. So we can rehabilitate myth . . . myths are the stories people live by, the stories that shape people's perception of life.

Don Cupitt 1991

Fantasy is particularly appropriate currently. Cultural, professional, political and familial forms all seem to be in flux – we constantly have to change how we do things, our colleagues, and to whom we are answerable. And we are increasingly working on rather a moveable stage. No longer can one be a GP to the same families, a village schoolteacher teaching children whose parents they also taught, or a midwife remembering the birth of the mother. Fantasy deals with people not knowing in what dimension they are living, nor what kind of being they will meet, nor what kind of communication is appropriate. The only thing which remains constant is the values of the main characters. These, as in *Startrek*, are usually strong and moral; and things turn out right in the end; though sometimes they turn out very wrong – there's never any half measures in this genre. It is part of our relentless attempt to create moral order in a chaotic world.

Fairy stories or folk tales have a similar function, and always have had. They use archetypes, as the Greek stories and plays did, to help us to make sense of our world. Just as people tend to tell their lives according to a particular genre (see above), so they relate to particular archetypal characters. Are you, or a colleague, wily beautiful Scheherazade, Baba Yaga the witch, Anansi the tricksy spiderman, the boy who knew the king was wearing no clothes and wasn't afraid to say so, or perhaps 'Mudjekeewis,/ruler of the winds of heaven' (Longfellow 1960, p. 37)?

Practitioners accordingly enjoy writing fairy stories, which can carry feelings, experiences and ideas in a telling fashion. This process of confronting elements in our everyday world by exploring fantastic ones has been called 'structured fabulation' (Gough 1998). Huxley's *Brave New World* (1932), Orwell's *1984* (1949), and Shelley's *Frankenstein* (1820) are all examples of fantasy which both create and critique our own world.

Jacky Martin's Fairy Story

Jacky works for NHS Direct – a British National Health Service nurse-led telephone consultation service, using computer health information, recommended by British premier Tony Blair. People can ring up at any time for immediate and appropriate advice and assistance, enabling some to look after themselves at home. Many GPs (family practitioners) have been very supportive, but some have expressed initial reservations very volubly.

Once upon a time there was a land where the fairy people lived. It was a happy and prosperous land and all who dwelt there lived long and well.

Some of the fairies had the gift of healing and they spent much of their time visiting the babies when they became hot and spotty, and they would dispense kindly words of advice and wisdom. The healing fairies were easily recognised with their dark blue shiny wings and their red lined navy blue capes.

The ruler of the land at that time had caused much of a stir. Everyone felt certain he was a leprechaun, but some felt he was a bad leprechaun turning good, and others felt he was a good leprechaun turning bad. His name was Tonicus Blair and one day he had an idea.

'Aha,' he said 'I will take some of the very best healing fairies to a special clearing in the woods because I have a very special job for them.' And so he did. The clearing in the woods had seven spotted toadstools for sitting on, seven magic screens for looking deep into, seven magic pointing mice and seven sets of magic earmuffs for hearing voices far away.

But the healing fairies were anxious and worried about the magic in the clearing in the woods. Tonicus Blair, however, had another idea. He called for an older fairy who knew the magic of the screens. Seven long days and seven long nights she spent with the fairies and she whispered her secrets and she passed on her knowledge behind the ancient symbols and rituals.

Soon they all grew to know and understand the magic. From then on the healing fairies could still talk to the mothers when the babies became hot and spotty, but now they could dispense their kindly words of advice and wisdom from far away. And the folk of the land continued to be happy and to prosper.

There was another more ancient breed of healer who lived in the land. They looked like dwarves but everyone knew they were really of the goblin race. And that is how they were known: the Goblin People or GPs for short.

They were generally very hairy, had very long beards and were nearly all men.

The art they practised was very different. They would stomp around, in and out of the houses, muttering into their beards and dispense potions and lotions to heal the sick.

The GPs were very frightened of the fairies in the woods. They thought they would drain their power and banish them to the dark side of the land where the rivers were dry and the flowers did not grow. So when they went stomping and mumbling into the houses they said, 'Don't speak to the fairies in the woods. They will turn you to stone!'

Some of the GPs were younger and a bit brighter in expression. Their beards were shorter, and some of them were women – their beards were hardly visible at all! All of the GPs, however, bore a secret burden – they were all afraid of the dark.

When dusk fell they would all stomp back to their dwellings and liked nothing more than to lock their doors and bolt their windows until dawn turned the sky golden. They were fearful of the shades of night whom it was said might follow a stranger and freeze him with their cold breath and dead eyes.

One day one of the younger GPs had a very good idea, and so he called a meeting with all of his colleagues. 'What if,' he said, 'What if, in the dead of night when the night shades are abroad and the fairy babies become hot and spotty, what if the fairies in the woods could talk to the fairy mothers and dispense their kindly words of advice and wisdom. Then we could stay safely locked and bolted in our dwellings until dawn turns the sky golden.'

'Aha,' said the GPs very loudly together. 'What a VERY GOOD IDEA.' And so they all did just that and everyone in the land continued to be happy and to prosper.

The fairy mothers were very happy. They had a kindly person to talk to anytime, day or night.

The fairies in the wood were very happy. They could dispense kindly words of advice and wisdom from far away and they never had to get off their toadstools.

The GPs were very happy. They could stay safely locked away from the shades of night until dawn turned the sky golden.

Tonicus Blair was happy. He had become acquainted with the Wizard in the West and now he planned to be King of All Lands.

But the happiest one of all was the older fairy who knew all the secrets of the magic screens. She had stumbled over a pot of gold on the way home, and now she lived in a beautiful cottage by the edge of the river, where the woods met the fields and where the sun always shone.

She baked bread, she made wine and she sat in her garden and watched the flowers grow. But she never ever forgot the secrets of the magic screens.

Jacky Martin

Parody

Parody is part of our lives: used to help us understand (or make fun of) an everyday matter. 'Shall I compare thee to a heap of shit . . .', parodying Shakespeare's *Shall I compare thee to a summer's day* [sonnet 18], is the kind of thing students have often written. Like fairy story and fantasy, parody often uses archetypes to which we all relate.

Problem-Solving
I did once and once only use a form of writing to help me resolve a problem: and it was amazingly effective – so rather surprising perhaps I've never used it since. It used the simple device of taking the A. A. Milne, *Winnie the Pooh* (1928) format and style, and using his characters – Tigger and Eyeore and so on – as a sort of allegory to represent the various people and their relationships as I saw them in my own psychodrama. The extraordinary thing was, I started writing it in the vein of spleen and hurt and anger, a means of venting my spite against those who had hurt me. But as I went on, I found the very act of writing (and I suppose using that particular model) induced a feeling of generosity in me which spilled over not only in the little story (now lost!) but into the real-life relationships as well.

This actually did have a permanent effect on my working life, because it awoke me to an effect of creative writing I'd only intellectualised about before. I determined to introduce this form of writing into my English Literature students' experience, and from that small beginning a whole undergraduate degree course in Writing has now sprung.

Susanna Gladwin

Autobiographical reflective stories

A large proportion of reflective stories are based on the direct experience of the practitioner; there are several reproduced earlier in this book. The term autobiography was only invented at the start of the nineteenth century (Cox 1996). Such stories are inevitably only partial, in only representing the viewpoint of the writer, but are a way of exploring and making sense of impressions, understandings and feelings.

Mavis Kirkham: The Wisdom of Nausea

Here is Mavis, a midwife, reflecting upon experience:

> In recent years, I have cared for several women who have had long labours at home with successful outcomes. During these labours, I have inevitably become tired. In each case I have had a similar experience. After a long period with no apparent problems, I had to leave the room because of nausea. On some occasions I actually vomited. After a wash and a walk round the block to clear my head, I returned to the labouring woman. On each occasion she then started to push.
>
> My first reaction to this was the traditional female response of blaming myself. I concluded that I am getting old, tired and possibly past coping well with long labours. I arranged better back-up against my own exhaustion and need to leave women at a crucial time.
>
> Then I heard Susie Orbach give a lecture in which she described physical experiences of counter-transference in her practice as a therapist. This, and subsequent discussion with her, led me to realise that my nausea occurred at the same point in each labour.
>
> My next labour was a forty-one-year-old primigravida, at home, and the pattern recurred.
>
> My stomach somehow picked up that the woman was approaching second stage well before I could see or hear any signs. Because I learned this through my stomach, rather than my intellect, I had to leave the room, later returning with fresh energy that was picked up by the tired woman and her tired supporters.
>
> This experience led me to ponder a midwife's ways of gaining knowledge, which are discounted because they do not appear in textbooks and are not congruent with measurable medical knowledge. I discussed this with colleagues and became aware how different midwives pick up knowledge from women in different ways. A colleague with an astute sense of smell told me how she is aware of changes in the smell of women as they progress in labour.
>
> The rhetoric of reflective practice takes place within the accepted sphere of authoritative knowledge. Therefore it does not seem to have had much impact upon what we accept as knowledge or our recognition of patterns in our own experience. As women caring for others, we tend not to see our own feelings as important enough to reflect upon.
>
> Reflecting on bodily knowledge has made me aware of the wisdom of my own perceptions and of the ways in which I can learn that are

not intellectual. It has also made me aware that I am trained in ways of knowing that prevent me from acknowledging my own wisdom, which made me initially think I was old and inadequate rather than growing in awareness.

Mavis Kirkham

A version of this appeared in *Midwifery Today* 1999, **52**, p. 15.

Lane Gerber: We must hear each other's cry

Lane is a psychotherapist with Southeast Asian refugees:

> For me the whole 'business' of my writing and the vignettes I use is an attempt to find out what I am thinking/experiencing – which I don't know except as I begin to reflect and to 'talk' in written form about what is moving around inside me. It doesn't take full shape and meaning until I begin the writing process, which creates the meanings out of what has been inside me, unbirthed in thought or language.
>
> I got into writing about refugees for many reasons I suppose. I felt very strongly that I didn't want to separate my professional life from my personal life. It's been a thing for me since graduate school but I haven't always known how to do it and haven't found a lot of role models at close hand. So my writings about therapy have been about the interaction and wondering about who I am as I am in relationship with the other at the same time I am trying to understand their world.
>
> I remember seeing the Joseph McCarthy hearings on the TV and my mother's involvement in it: her tears and anger at seeing this demon destroying lives just for the fun of it while no one for the longest time spoke out against it. This laid down an important experience and value for me as did the heritage of my grandparents escaping Russian pogroms at the turn of the nineteenth century. So this social political line combined with me, finally, in finding, almost accidentally a Medical Refugee Clinic at the large county hospital which saw SE Asian and African patients. I wanted to work with survivors of political torture from South and Central America. One experience sitting with a Cambodian woman as she began to talk about her 'medical symptoms' led to part of her story as a survivor and I was found by and found myself something beyond me while being with her . . . and then went somehow on from there.
>
> And before this I was struggling in medical school which I hated and began writing letters to friends trying to find my way out of the career morass – really trying to find who I was. And 'writing', such as it was, enabled me to make a bit of sense out of what was inside me that I hadn't been able to do in any other way. Certainly not by talking. And

it was the letters and then papers I wrote for grad school in which I found subject matter that counted for the course, but more importantly helped me express my despairs and longings and hopes. For me the writing was discovering something that felt real and true about me at a time when I felt on the verge of losing myself.

The following is an extract from Lane Gerber's paper: We must hear each other's cry: lessons from Pol Pot survivors:

> As she ran down the road with her two remaining children and her friends from the camp, she noticed a woman sitting on the road holding and nursing her infant and crying. . . . With gunfire going on all around her, N stopped. She told her children to go with their friends into the forest and then she covered the woman and infant with her own body. She noticed that the infant was dead, yet the mother still was trying to nurse it. She stayed in that position sheltering the woman with her body until the shooting and fighting finally ended. They were the only ones left alive on the road into the jungle which was now littered with dead bodies.
>
> 'The woman was in pain (N said). I knew crying and pain too. That made us relate to each other.' . . .
>
> The Cambodian survivors' stories evoke not only pain and horror in the hearer, but also a compassion that links the speaker to the listener in a bond that is powerful and also inclusive – that seems to go beyond the two people involved. For the listener, the experience can be one of hearing and responding, becoming more fully human. If we can allow their voices to really reach into our ears, we are reminded that we too have been vulnerable and cried out for another. Out of the pain of all the senseless violence, death, and isolation of their life stories the survivors themselves can sometimes feel heard and those of us who are privileged to sit with them can sometimes hear their cry. A cry that on being heard seems to lift the two of us beyond the constraints of our individual selves to humanity in general. In this cry and hearing a more hopeful vision of our self and our species seems to emerge.
>
> Gerber 1996, pp. 3, 14

12

A Story of Writing
by Sue Gee

The captain unlocked his word hoard.

Beowulf, p. 12

This chapter charts the development of three published novels, showing that the form and process of *writing as a reflective practitioner* is similar to that of the novelist (or short story writer). It moreover demonstrates the rootedness of literature in everyday life. The reading of literature offers deep insight into a range of experiences as wide as life itself; the knowledge and experience gained thereby is invaluable to the effective practitioner. **Sue Gee** is a novelist and a lecturer at Middlesex University, where with colleagues she is devising London's first MA in writing.

Falling in Place: The Growth of a Novel

Growing a novel is mysterious and elusive. Light gleams on water and is gone. In the silence of the study, little may happen for a long time; away from the desk, engaged with the world, a second, secret life courses through your bloodstream, and offers, when you are fortunate, moments of revelation.

The beginning of my last novel, *The Hours of the Night*, lay in a photograph. The ending came long before I had reached the halfway mark on the page, in a meeting at work on a summer afternoon. People I knew only a little were sitting round a conference table; windows were open in the heat; outside, two formal conifers cast long shadows on the grass. Beyond them, birch trees were motionless; the light was rich and intense.

The air was so still, so still.

In the middle of a meeting I found difficult, this line offered itself as a glimpse of something radiant and pure. I knew that the novel would move towards it, and that the sense of timelessness and peace it gave me would be as important to my characters, gathered in a garden after much upheaval. Their garden, out on the Welsh borders, was quite unlike the one beyond the conference room window: it was unkempt, with apple trees. I thought of a postcard pinned above my desk, a painting by John Piper: stooks of corn on stubble in a sloping field; late evening; stillness, deep shadow. I thought of the visionary seventeenth-century poet Thomas Traherne, whose voice is at the heart of 'Hours', and who, in a Herefordshire childhood, saw *orient and immortal wheat, which never should be reaped, nor was ever sown. I thought it had stood from everlasting to everlasting.* . . .

Two gardens on a summer afternoon, one real and one imagined (and much more real to me); a harvested cornfield, a poet's childhood vision –

The air was so still, so still. This simple and unbidden line drew everything together, sank deep within me, and remained. It was well over a year before I came to write the novel's last scene but when I did so that silence and stillness found their place as I had known they would, offering moments of perfection between people who had come through anguish.

And so. An image comes, and when it has a real connection with some part of me, it stays. From here, like most people, I imagine, I make notes, and follow possible lines of thought, and write what seems to be the right opening. Eventually, when much has been discarded, a first skeletal plan is pinned above my desk. Gazing at it, I begin to feel as if something might happen. New scenes disclose themselves behind it, and new connections gradually become evident. I write them in – just a line or a few words which might, one day, become a chapter. This plan is continually revised as the novel develops: I heap up notes in a file, and new outlines are pinned up; but generally I have found that the overall shape remains clear, and what I therefore hope for is to be surprised.

It is within this rare but astonishing moment of discovery that the whole point of the novel can reveal itself: a deep skein or muscle connecting my own inner life and that of the people I am both leading and following through the events on the page.

The most concrete example I can give of this came in the writing of my third novel, *The Last Guests of the Season*. Set in Portugal, it draws on a real house, where I had stayed with my own family and friends. At its centre are a bisexual woman, obsessively in love, and Tom, her disturbed young son, whom nobody really understands or can handle.

Early in the writing, I visited an exhibition of Jewish art at the Barbican: mostly of paintings, but including, for a reason I can't recall, a small wooden house on a pedestal. I looked at this, and thought: Tom will find a doll's house, within the house in Portugal. It will represent all that he is longing for: order, stability, a contented family. Back at the desk I made a note, and waited for the moment when he would discover it.

This came down in the cellar, where he has wandered while everyone else prepares for a trip on the river. Exploring dusty shelves and alcoves, he finds what he realises is a replica of the house he is staying in (which we later learn had been made by the architect owner). He moves to unfasten the hook at the side which will open the whole of the front. What happened as I wrote this scene? Tom discovered that with the opening of the house a lid in his head yawned hideously open, and I had a violent blackout which sent me halfway across the desk. Recovering, I typed at the top of the page: he's epileptic: that's what this is about.

I am not epileptic, but from adolescence, after a long period of petit mal and a convulsion, until well into my twenties, there was a question that I might be. This is something I rarely talk about, but used to think about a great deal, and I am sure that the petit mal experience, in which you are briefly 'absent' from your surroundings, has a profound psychological effect on your apprehension of what is real and not real, something else which exercised me greatly in adolescence.

What happened at this stage in the writing of the novel was the realisation of how deep the quasi-epileptic experience still lay within my own psyche and, within the fiction, how crucially it explained much about Tom's personality and behaviour: his sense of apartness, his physical clumsiness, the alienating effect his strangeness and periodic absences had on those around him. It also put him – the undiagnosed son of parents whose own distress at their failing marriage made them blind to his needs – at real physical risk, and this sense of impending danger became the driving force of the novel, building towards a climax of which, when I began writing, I had no idea at all. Finally, the image of the lid in his head clearly presented itself as the symbol of repression which was already a key theme for every character.

Looking back on all this, I realise that *Last Guests* was a place where something whose importance in my life I had underestimated could be explored, and fall in place within it. And it represents the first time I fully realised the power of the unconscious in writing, and how deeply the creation of fiction is a two-way process: in which you are both feeding into and drawing from an imagined world. Perhaps only when the two come together, as I felt I did then, do you begin to write anything worthwhile.

Something else I keep having to learn, over and over again, is how much stamina writing requires, and how much faith: events in the 'real' world made *Last Guests* go dead on me halfway through; this has happened with other novels, and produces those memorable occasions when you walk back into your study and behold only meaningless heaps of paper. There cannot be many writers who have pursued their path without such times and felt that the whole endeavour was pointless; my experience is that there is nothing for it but to grit the teeth. Slowly the life on the page begins to pick up again, and develop – or has done so far. There cannot be many writers who do not dread the time when this no longer happens.

In *The Hours of the Night* (the only one of my novels beside which I am prepared to stand or fall), I discovered that Gillian, the eccentric virginal poet at its centre, was descended from Thomas Traherne: this drew together and made sense of the whole spiritual theme of the book. What else? Something small but significant. Important from the beginning is a great pond, a symbol of holiness and hope, which is fringed with bulrushes and iris. It came from a real pond, fringed with yellow-flag, an exquisite wild iris. Towards the end of the novel, when Phoebe, a gardener, is dying of cancer, she searches in a herbal for a remedy. I searched in a herbal too. What was an ancient cure for cancer? Yellow-flag.

In everyday life I am sceptical of many things, and scornful of superstition. Writing fiction has taught me to respect what seems to be random, or coincidental; to have faith in small beginnings, and faith that the process of writing has its own alchemy.

Little of this bears much relation to the academic life, except in so far as one hopes to bring what intellect one has both to writing and to teaching. At Middlesex University, Susanna Gladwin has pioneered the country's first undergraduate writing programme, on which I feel fortunate to be teaching. Outside the university, people ask me: but can you teach people to write? After ten years in my study, and five on the campus, my only honest answer is: I don't know. I learned to write by writing: what other way is there? Sometimes I feel that all one can hope is that by giving people time and space and silence in which to grow; with models of good writing, an attentive eye and encouraging voice, they will find their own way, as we all must.

Above my desk is a note which I wrote to myself: The less I write, and the more I teach, the less effective I become as a teacher. It's true: the sense of authority, not to say identity, diminishes when you are not practising your art, and I imagine there are many writers and teachers who have the experience of trying to find the balance between such private and such public worlds.

I write to travel far from my desk. I write to integrate my life. I did not, of course, consciously set out with this in mind, but after a few novels I realise that this is what gives the activity meaning. There is calculation, and some coldness, in craft and technique, but there is also the sense of touching something both beyond and within myself which I can do in no other way: not through prayer, and not, entirely, through human relationships. Only through solitude, the tap of the keys, the discovery of some connection between inner and outer, intellect and emotion, body and spirit – feeling aspects of all these, and of the smallest and most everyday events, fall into place in silence and still-ness, striving towards a whole.

Sue Gee
(Adapted from Gee 1997a, pp. 20–2)

13

Reflection upon Medical Practice by Tom Heller

Life is short and the art long; the occasion fleeting; experience fallacious, and judgement difficult.

Hippocrates, aphorism 1

This is a story, but it is also about the meaning of life, and making sure that a life does have meaning. Our main character, Kurt, collects stories from people. Sometimes he does this in a conscious way, but mostly the stories just arrive at his morning or evening surgeries and spill out into the space between him and the people who come to see him. He works as a GP in downtown Sheffield.

Kurt the Doctor, Sheila the Patient

Let me tell you one of the stories, just to get you in the mood. It is by no means the most lurid story that Kurt will hear today. It is told by Sheila, who is exactly the same age as Kurt, fifty, but he thinks that she looks much older. Some of it is in her own words, because at a later date she wrote to Kurt about her own life. The deep and dirty lines around her eyes have an ingrained look to them and seem to indicate that she has been screwing her eyes tightly shut for long periods of her life. From a distance her skin could pass as being slightly sun-tanned and indeed there is a sort of pigmented look to the exposed skin on her face, but close-up it is not really healthy looking at all. Also, I am afraid that it is impossible to deny the fact that she carries with her a particular smell. It is not so much an unwashed sort of smell, but just that any underlying smell from her own flesh is covered by a general aura of cigarette smoke and the effects of standing too near a smoking-spitting frying pan. As she sits with Kurt it is almost possible to imagine the thin rashers of cheap bacon in bubbling fat being prepared a few inches from the front buttons of her mock leather coat. I suppose she has to cook in her coat because it is so persistently cold in her house. Sheila doesn't tell her story all in one go.

The delight (and the burden) of general practice is that people keep on coming back. They tell Kurt their stories in little spurts and great big gushes over the months and the years. The picture is always being added to, never taken away from. If the whole picture is not there now, don't worry, he knows that extra bits will slot into place sometime in the future. The way Sheila tells her story is to pin all her experiences onto one terrible decision. Her big mistake was to fall for the wrong bloke. She was a normal, slightly rebellious teenager from a loving family and she fell for the wide-boy on the block. He was so worldly-wise and knew how to get about and how to get what he wanted for himself and for the young Sheila he courted with such immediacy. He knew where to get his hands on things in times of shortage, and reading between the lines, he also knew where to put his hands on Sheila as well. Soon she was well and truly in love. It was to him that she related, rather than to her family or to friends of her own age, and she cut off her ties from all of them very quickly. For what could they offer that could compare to Jim's fast car and faster lifestyle?

> I was 13 years old and changed areas to Harrow where my parents bought a house. Met ex-husband (first boyfriend) at age of just 15 years. Engaged to be married for one and a half years. Fell pregnant at sixteen and a half years, but finished O levels and RSA in Commerce, Shorthand/Typing. Only worked for six months approx, then got married at age seventeen and had a baby boy and a girl two years later. At age twenty-two husband left me for another woman, came back but from then on always belting me. Tormenting me mentally as well as physically. My father had not long died aged forty-two. So husband got much worse then. Lost house as mortgage not paid because husband never kept up payments.

It can't have been much later that she discovered that Jim supported his lifestyle by being a drug dealer. A few years later Sheila had tasted a full-house of Hogarthian delights. She had had her children taken away by social services, become in turns and in various combinations a prostitute, a drug and heavy alcohol user, a battered wife, a drug courier, a convict in a foreign jail . . . banged up for being caught with two pounds of heroin in her knickers.

> Husband started dealing dope, started with just smoke, ended up dealing heroin. Got me smoking cigs aged sixteen, never smoked before, pushed them on to me then. Anyway got me started on marijuana

then progressed to cocaine then heroin. Whilst all this dealing by him was going on we were both well addicted to heroin by 1978. He was importing loads of three to four kilograms of heroin from Thailand. A syndicate he belonged to took me with them as cover. I was too gone and scared by this time to care. My kids went to private boarding school for a while as we went travelling all over while he was doing his dirty work. I kept out of his business as I didn't like it and never wanted to know, but I was an addict. Looking back on it I hate him for injecting me for the first time and taking me into it.

Well, no wonder she now needs a few painkillers to help her through the day in order to try to deaden the pain that screams within her when she thinks of her life. But what does Kurt do with her story?

Choices

Hey, Kurt! You have some choices to make here. What are you going to do, and how should you behave? What part of your training has helped you to cope with this dollop of stuff that has been dumped in your lap? Ah yes. You are supposed to stand back and make a diagnosis at this stage. Well, it must seem obvious to all you medical model, RCGP clones that this woman has a fundamental personality disorder. She has been incapable of making relationships with the right sort of person throughout her life. She has not had the psychological equipment to cope with the problems that have faced her and she has become dependent on various substances in turn. Previously opiates and alcohol, now she is dependent on painkillers. She is obviously depressed, not sleeping well and only just manages to look after her own needs for daily living. The diagnoses here are (1) depression, (2) addiction to painkillers (3) underlying personality disorder and addictive personality.

I fear that some of your mainstream colleagues would also question whether you are being too soft on Sheila. Why should she keep coming to you demanding painkillers? Isn't she becoming rather a drain on your scarce resources of time and money? Her regular painkillers are not cheap and you would certainly find it easier to keep within your medicines budget if you suggested that she find herself another GP list to join.

Or, wearing your more psychodynamic hat, you might begin to wonder what features of Sheila's life are actually the effect of her early upbringing. How come that she trusted Jim so completely? What sort of relationships does she expect from men and how was this expectation formed by her early childhood experiences? Could she even have been abused as a child as well as later as an adult? Even now she has come to expect that external others (in this case you, Kurt) will sort out her problems, dust her off and set her on the right path again, healed and mended. She does seem to find it difficult to take responsibility for her own actions and lacks the capacity to analyse or influence her own destiny. On the other hand, many of your psycho-analytical colleagues would doubt, especially at her age, whether she should be taken on in a psycho-therapeutic context.

You may remember some of the sociological theories that you read when you were a student, Kurt, which seemed to offer the answers to everything. Sheila is a victim of a patriarchal society that has expected her to be subservient to male needs and requirements throughout her life. In turn she has been a mother, prostitute, drug user, drug courier, etc. all demonstrating the way that dominant males use and then discard women. Her lower social class background and her drift further down the social scale have excluded her from many forms of help. Now, when she is no longer apparently of productive use within society, she is housed in substandard accommodation in the most deprived area of the town away from any significant resources. Her plight has become individualised and seen as her own problem rather than a problem that is a result of dominant forces within society.

Well it seems as though the standard (albeit stereotyped) models of general practice may not have all that much to offer either for Sheila, or indeed for Kurt himself. At some level Kurt has become affected by the things that Sheila has been telling him and he's still left wondering how he should respond? This is a human situation played out between two human beings, it's a relationship.

What is Kurt's role in all this? Now then, support groups for GPs or reflective writing courses are not the only answer to everything, but since this is a story let us transport Kurt to his group. He has written down his version of the story about Sheila and read it out to the group. The other members of the group remember other 'Sheilas' that they have met and how difficult they found them. But they start to gently probe why Kurt may have chosen this particular story from all the others he could have chosen to write about. What role does her age have in all this, does Kurt have a special empathy with people who are exactly the same age as him? And what about the role of that big decision in Sheila's life, is her decision to run off with Jim reflected in any way by big decisions in Kurt's own life? Is there an equivalent moment from Kurt's own past which, had it been different, would have changed his whole life? How does Sheila's experience relate to other things going on currently in Kurt's life? Well, this is the time that his own children are making choices for their own life's paths. Does Sheila, as a teenager, remind him of one of his own children and their current struggle for detachment from him and the family hearth? Does any of this give clues as to why he finds it difficult to remain detached from Sheila and why he has apparently become embroiled in her story-web?

What Difference Has Writing it Down Made?

The act of writing down Sheila's story has helped Kurt to empathise about her situation. It doesn't really matter that he was not clear about all the exact details, or the chronological precision of her life story. Indeed he fantasised and embroidered about some events and had forgotten or changed other things to make it into a story rather than a case history. The important feature seems to be that he was able to see the world through her eyes for a while. Before he sat down to write he was not at all clear why she stuck out for him from a whole week of other possibly equally compelling surgery attenders. The process of writing has clarified many things for him. What must it be like to live your entire life as Sheila has, with a major regret? How can that event have shaped everything else she did and the way she thought and felt about things thereafter? The feelings of guilt, self-loathing, remorse, hatred and despair are immediately transmitted through the written word from Sheila's own life in a very direct way into Kurt's consciousness. It is not that the written product is especially brilliant literature, it is just that it responds to the human dimensions of the situation.

By writing it down, Kurt has acknowledged the importance of the story to him and started to consider the things that happen when these two human beings meet. The story has established a grid pattern to start to make Sheila's life understandable and accessible to Kurt and to any others who take the trouble to read or hear the story.

Reading the Story to the Group

The work done in the group is important also. By opening himself and his emotions to the group through the writing, Kurt remains in control of what he says and how deeply he wants to take all this. It is possible to use it just as a story. It is fabulous and fascinating just at that level. Many writers would pay a lot to be fed the story lines that Kurt is given during his daily work. But the continued process of sharing the written work he has prepared usually gets the whole procedure down to other levels which individual, personal reflection may never approach. The group immediately establishes its caring credentials for Kurt and empathises with the difficulty that people like Sheila may present to doctors. He knows that in general they are going to help him in his quest for further enlightenment, this is the pattern that has been established in the group. The doctors are not competitive or aggressive, they will not laugh at him for getting something wrong, or leave him feeling exposed when delicate emotions are touched on. The group leader patrols the boundaries and asks the 'naïve questions' that no one else dares to ask. She pretends that she knows little about the work of general practice and is an interested outsider in the process. The group does not make suggestions or proposals, there are no conclusions, diagnoses or certainties. Various things are considered, mulled over and the enquiry moves on. This is very different from the formal, often rather aggressive approach of bog-standard general practice, where the drive for evidence-based, cost-effective interventions and the like leaves little room for philosophical ruminations, experimentation, or the following of feelings or hunches.

After the group Kurt feels that he really can understand at a greater depth both the way that Sheila's life has panned out for her, and what is happening in the interaction between them during the consultation. He feels that he has learnt as much about himself as he has about Sheila, and this is useful if not always comforting. It may have brought up quite disturbing things for him to think about and which may need resolution in other contexts and at other times. He has recognised that it is not possible to get help at this level with every person who comes to see him, but that selective, intensive work of this nature does help him understand at a general level what may be going on in the lives of people whom he has some responsibility to try to help. It is a valid and important form of training for all his work, not just a help for his work with Sheila. He thinks it might also help him in his way of being with other people (specifically his own children) at important times of decision in their lives.

The Reflective Writing Group

The 'isolation' of general practice is often acknowledged, but the solutions for it are less common subjects for discussion. In the reflective writing group we have started to develop a way of working together that looks at some of the institutional, structural and especially the personal strains involved in our jobs. When we sit down to write in the privacy of our own homes we focus naturally on events and situations that have affected us in some way. There is no point in writing about neutral events.

The process of writing gets Kurt in touch, very directly, with his feelings, and he imagines it is the same for the others in the group. Writing, the flow of words and ideas, thoughts and inner feelings . . . and then the editing and rewriting, polishing as best he can for presentation to the group, is a ritual that he knows will help him sort out and organise his feelings about the subject which he is preparing. The next stage is to bring the contribution to the group. It has become less scary to bring these little private efforts and lay them bare before the others. The group seems to be able to accept each others' imperfections and are relieved and strengthened to find that many of them are shared . . . and that all of them are understood by the group.

The levels of discussion that follow the presentations are important also: acknowledge the human being within the professional concretions; discuss the feelings behind the descriptions; empathise with the situation; ask a few questions to get to the nub of the problem. Ease and joke as well to relieve some of the intensity. All these techniques seem to have been developed unselfconsciously as a group together and they have arrived at levels of intimacy which are indeed supportive.

When next Kurt meets with Sheila he feels that a warmth and understanding has developed and deepened since their last meeting. He feels emboldened to suggest things that might never have been tried if he did not feel the support of his group behind him. . . .

Tom Heller is a GP in Sheffield, UK, and Senior Lecturer, School of Health and Social Welfare, Open University, Milton Keynes, UK.

14

Reflection on Reflection

'Would you tell me, please, which way I ought to go from here?'
'That depends a good deal on where you want to get to,' said the Cheshire Cat.
'I don't much care where –' said Alice.
'Then it doesn't matter which way you go,' said the Cat.
'So long as I get *somewhere*,' Alice added as an explanation.
'Oh, you're sure to do that,' said the Cat, 'if you only walk long enough.'

Carroll 1865, p. 54

This book began with the oxymoron of *certain uncertainty* which is at the heart of reflective practice. The only way to get anywhere in reflective practice is to do it – trusting the journey will be interesting and useful, having faith in and respect for yourself and your abilities to reflect as well as practise. But you do not know where you are going. You never will get to a definitive *somewhere* anyway, just as Alice got to the Mad Hatters Tea Party – an illuminating experience – but she had to move on again. She later met the Mock Turtle who helped her realise that the most productive journeys are undertaken without set purpose (see also Aristotle trans. 1953):

'I'd have said to the porpoise, "keep back please: we don't want *you* with us!" '
'They were obliged to have him with them,' the Mock Turtle said: 'no wise fish would go anywhere without a porpoise.' . . .
'Don't you mean "purpose"?' said Alice.

Carroll 1865, p. 88

Setting out into reflective practice with an open questioning mind, rather than with a set purpose, can take the practitioner into fresh and dynamic territory. But that is, just as Eliot pointed out, 'to arrive where we started/And to know the place for the first time' (Eliot 1936,

p. 222). We don't travel far in reflective practice: just make a great deal more sense of where we are.

This 'open questioning mind' implies another oxymoron: in order to undertake this enquiry we allow ourselves to be *thoughtfully unthinking*, in the way football players are taught not to think, or else they'll mess up their own playing, and the game. Reflective practice can be hindered by too much self-consciousness, and self-awareness.

But this process of *letting go* is utterly responsible. It is a letting go of hard and fast notions of myself in order to take responsibility for a greater range of my actions and thoughts and feelings, even ones I was not aware of before. We live in a culture where it's always considered to be somebody's fault; somebody has to pay; someone has the duty to sort me out – doctor, policeman, clergyman, therapist, counsellor, lawyer. I am not responsible for my self, and who is my self anyway? I no longer surrounded by a consistent nexus of family, neighbours, priest, the same boss and employees – these figures are always shifting and changing and cannot be relied upon. In the same way, I can always change my body with plastic surgery or drugs, and invent my persona differently every day by wearing bellbottoms or mini-skirt, cheongsam or sari.

An outward consistent sense of self cannot be relied upon. Instead I invent myself anew all the time by telling and writing stories about myself: to make some kind of sense. And I locate and shift this growing self alongside others: through discussion and hearing their stories, and in the wider world through reading and discussing as many relevant texts as I can. ' "I" doesn't exist, one constructs oneself' (Simone de Beauvoir, quoted in Guppy 2000). And: 'The unfinishedness of the human person [in] a permanent process of searching' (Freire 1998, p. 21). Perhaps *me* is not a noun, but a verb, a process – *to me*.

This can only be undertaken by the whole practitioner in a holistic process – one which is aesthetic and creative, and doesn't flinch from the range of human experience:

The states of mind or feelings that art can excite have been helpfully distinguished in Sanscrit aesthetics, where they are called *rasas*, from a word meaning 'juice' or 'essence'. A fully achieved work of art should flow with all nine of them: their names might be transposed in English as wonder, joy, sexual pleasure, pity, anguish, anger, terror, disgust and laughter.

Warner 1998, p. 7

Reflective practice will never offer solutions or final answers. If such are sought, and seemingly found, they will prove hollow – just as the *meaning of life* being 42 in *The Hitch Hiker's Guide to the Galaxy* (Adams, 1984) is meaningless.

The Ekoi people of Nigeria, says Alida Gersie (1992), have a tradition of *story children* from long ago. Each story has to be told and heard for both *child* and hearers to be nourished and run free. Once heard and known, however, the wisdom in each story can never be unheard or unknown: therein lies its power. Listening to and telling such stories changes the teller and listener irreversibly:

> They were not the same eyes with which he had last looked out at this particular scene, and the brain which interpreted the images the eyes resolved was not the same brain. There had been no surgery involved, just the continual wrenching of experience.
>
> Adams 1984, p. 493

Bibliography

Abbs, P. (1974) *Autobiography in Education*. London: Heinemann Educational Books.

Abell, S. K., Bryan, L. A. and Anderson, M. (1998) Investigating preservice elementary science teacher reflective thinking using integrated media case-based instruction in elementary science teacher preparation. *Science Teacher Education*, **82**(4) pp. 491–510.

Abell, S. K., Bryan, L. A. and Anderson, M. (1999) Development of professional knowledge in learning to teach elementary science. *Journal of Research in Science Teaching*, **36**(2) pp. 121–39.

Abercrombie, M. L. J. (1993) *The Human Nature of Learning: Selections From the Work of M. L. J. Abercrombie* (ed. J. Nias) Buckingham: Open University Press.

Abse, D. (1998) More than a green placebo. *The Lancet*, **351**(9099) pp. 362–4.

Adams, D. (1984 (1995)) So long and thanks for all the fish, in *A Hitch Hiker's Guide to the Galaxy: a Trilogy in Five Parts*. London: Heinemann.

Aeschylus (trans. 1999) *The Oresteia* (trans. T. Hughes). London: Faber.

Albert, T. (1997) *Winning the Publications Game*. Abingdon, Oxon: Radcliffe Medical Press.

Allende, Isabel (2000) The Guardian Profile, interview by M. Jaggi. *The Guardian*, 5 February, pp. 6–7.

Aristotle (trans. 1953 J. A. K. Thomson) *The Nichomachean Ethics*. Middlesex: Penguin.

Atkins, K. and Murphy, K. (1994) Reflective practice. *Nursing Standard*, **8**(39) pp. 49–56.

Barker, P. (1991) *Regeneration*. London: Penguin.

Barry, C. A., Britten, N., Barber, N., Bradley, C. and Stevenson, F. (1999) Using reflexivity to optimise teamwork in qualitative research. *Qualitative Health Research*, **9**(1) pp. 26–44.

Barthes, R. (1977) *Image, Music, Text*. London: Fontana/Collins.

Bauer, L. Duffy, J., Fountain, E., Halling, S., Holzer, M., Jones, E., Leifer, M. and Rowe, J. (1992) Exploring self-forgiveness. *Journal of Religion and Health*. **31**(2) pp. 149–59

Bean, T. W. and Julich, J. (1989) Using dialogue journals to foster reflective practice with preservice, content-area teachers. *Teacher Education Quarterly*. **16**(1) pp. 33–40.

Bell, J. (1992) Cross Cultural Studies. Paper presented to Teachers Stories of Life and Work Conference, Chester.

Belli, A. and Coulehan, J. (1998) *Blood and Bone: Poems by Physicians*. University of Iowa Press.

Bellman, L. M. (1996) Changing nursing practice through reflection on the Roper, Logan and Tierney model: the enhancement approach to action research. *Journal of Advanced Nursing*, **24**, pp. 129–38.

Benner, P. (1984) *From Novice to Expert: Excellence and Power in Clinical Nursing Practice*. Menlo Park: Addison Wesley.

Beowulf and Grendel (trans. 1973 M. Alexander) London: Penguin.

Best, D. (1996) On the experience of keeping a therapeutic journal while training. *Therapeutic Communities*, **17**(4) pp. 293–301.

Bettelheim, B. (1976) *The Uses of Enchantment*. London: Penguin.

Beveridge, I. (1997) Teaching your students to think reflectively: the case for reflective journals. *Teaching in Higher Education*, **2**(1) pp. 33–43.

Blake, W. (1958) *Songs of Innocence (The Divine Image)*. Middlesex: Penguin.

Bleakley, A. (1999) From reflective practice to holistic reflexivity. *Studies in Higher Education*. **24**(3) pp. 215–330.

Bleakley, A. (2000) Adrift without a lifebelt: reflective self-assessment in a postmodern age. *Teaching in Higher Education*, **5**(4) in press.

Blodgett, H. (1991) *Capacious Holdall: An Anthology of Englishwomen's Diary Writings*. University Press of Virginia.

Bloom, S. (1999) Give sorrow words: emotional disclosure and physical health. *The Psychotherapy Review*, **1**(7) pp. 312–13.

Bolton, G. (1991) Stories at work. *Writers in Education*, **8**, pp. 10–11.

Bolton, G. (1994) Stories at work, fictional-critical writing as a means of professional development. *British Educational Research Journal*, **20**(1) pp. 55–68.

Bolton, G. (1995) Stories at work, writing for professional development. *Issues in Social Work Education*, **14**(2) pp. 21–33.

Bolton, G. (1999a) *Writing Myself: The Therapeutic Potential of Creative Writing*. London: Jessica Kingsley.

Bolton, G. (1999b) Stories at work: reflective writing for practitioners. *The Lancet*, **354** pp. 243–5.

Bolton, G. (1999c) Reflections through the looking glass: the story of a course of writing as a reflexive practitioner. *Teaching in Higher Education*, **4**(2) pp. 193–212.

Borkan, J. Reis, S., Steinmetz, D. and Medalie, J. (1999) *Patients and Doctors: Life Changing Stories from Primary Care*. University of Wisconsin Press.

Boud, D. (1998) Use and misuse of reflection and reflective practice. Seminar at Sheffield University, February.

Boud, D., Keogh, R. and Walker, D. (1985) *Reflection: Turning Experience into Learning*. London: Kogan Page.

Boyd, E. M. and Fayles, E. W. (1983) Reflective learning: key to learning from experience. *Journal for Humanistic Psychology*, **23**(2) pp. 99–117.

Brewing, C. R. and Lennard, H. J. (1999) *Trauma Stress*, **12**(2) pp. 355–61.

Brimacombe, M. (1996) The emotional release of writing. *GP*, 13 December.

Brody, H. (1987) *Stories of Sickness*. Yale University Press.

Brookfield, S. D. (1987) *Developing Critical Thinkers*. Milton Keynes: Open University Press.

Burney, F. (1898) *Evelina or the History of a Young Lady's Entrance into the World*. London: George Bell & Sons.

Campo, R. (1997) *The Desire to Heal: a Doctor's Education in Empathy, Identity, and Poetry*. New York: Norton.

Carson, R. (1994) Teaching ethics in the context of the medical humanities. *Journal of Medical Ethics*, **20** pp. 235–8.

Carr, W. (1995) *For Education: Towards Critical Education Enquiry*. Buckingham: Open University Press.

Carr, W. and Kemmis, S. (1986) *Becoming Critical: Education, Knowledge and Action Research*. Lewes: Falmer.

Carroll, L. (1865 (1954)) *Alice's Adventures in Wonderland*. London: Dent & Sons.

Charon, R. (2000) Informed consent: the imperative and the therapeutic dividend of showing patients what we write about them. Paper presented at the Narrative Matters: Personal Stories and the Making of Health Policy Conference. Airlie Virginia, March.

Chuang Tsu (trans. 1974 Gia-Fu Feng and J. English) *Inner Chapters*. London: Wildwood House.

Cixous, H. (1995) Castration or decapitation? in Sean Burke (ed.) *Authorship from Plato to the Postmodernists: a Reader*. University of Edinburgh Press, pp. 162–77.

Clandinin, D. J. and Connelly, F. M. (1990) Narrative experience and the study of curriculum. *Cambridge Journal of Education*, **20**(3) pp. 25–37.

Clandinin, D. J., Davies, A., Hogan, P. and Kennard, B. (1992) *Learning to Teach: Teaching to Learn: Stories of Collaboration in Teacher Education*. New York: Teachers College Press.

Clarke, A. (1998) Born of incidents but thematic in nature. *Canadian Journal of Education*, **23**(1) pp. 47–62.

Clifford, J. (1986) Introduction: partial truths, and On ethnographic allegory, in J. Clifford and G. E. Marcus (eds.) *Writing Culture: the Poetics and Politics of Ethnography*. Berkeley: University of California Press, pp. 1–26 and 98–121.

Clough, P. (1996) 'Again fathers and sons': the mutual construction of self, story and special educational needs. *Disability & Society*, **11**(1) pp. 71–81.

Clutterbuck, D. (1998) *Learning Alliances*. London: Institute of Personnel and Development.

Clutterbuck, D. and Megginson, D. (1999) *Mentoring Executives and Directors*. Oxford: Butterworth, Heinemann.

Cocteau, J. (1930 (1968)) *Opium: The Diary of a Cure*. London: Peter Owen.

Coleridge, S. T. (1978 (1834)) *The Rime of the Ancient Mariner*. New York: Harper and Brothers.

Cope, W. (1986) *Making Cocoa for Kingsley Amis*. London: Faber & Faber.

Copeland, W. D., Birmingham, C., La Cruz, E. and Lewin, B. (1993) The reflective practitioner in teaching: toward a research agenda. *Teaching and Teacher Education* **9**(4) pp. 347–59.

Cox, A. (1996) Writing the self, in John Singleton and Mary Luckhurst (eds.) *The Creative Writing Handbook*. London: Macmillan.

Cupitt, D. (1991) Interviewed by Neville Glasgow. BBC Radio 4. 8 September.

Cutcliffe, J. R., Epling, M., Cassedy, P., McGregor, J., Plant, N. and Butterworth, T. (1998) Ethical dilemmas in clinical supervision. *British Journal of Nursing*, **7**(15) pp. 920–3.

Dante Alighieri (trans. 1985 Tom Philips) *Dante's Inferno*. New York: Thames and Hudson.

Deal, D. (1998) Portfolios, learning logs, and eulogies: using expressive writing in a science method class, in E. G. Sturtevant, J. A. Dugan, P. Linder and W. M. Linek. *Literacy and Community*. Texas: The College Reading Association.

Department of Education and Science (1978) *Primary Education in England*. London: HMSO.

Dixon, D. M., Sweeney, K. G. and Periera, G. (1999) The physician healer: ancient magic or modern science? *British Journal of General Practice*, **49** pp. 309–12.

Doubtfire, D. (1996) *Teach Yourself Creative Writing*. London: Hodder Headline.

Doty, M. (1995) An interview. *PN Review*, **21**(6) pp. 22–7.

Duffy, C. A. (1999) Mrs Midas in *The World's Wife*. London: Picador, Macmillan.

Durgahee, T. (1997) Reflective practice: nursing ethics through story telling. *Nursing Ethics*, **4**(2) pp. 135–46.

Eagleton, T. (1983) *Literary Theory: an Introduction*. Oxford: Basil Blackwell.

Eastaugh, A. (1998a) The pursuit of self knowledge through a study of myself as a member of a group of co-tutoring facilitators. Unpublished MA dissertation.

Eastaugh, A. (1998b) Abstract for paper presented to the International World Organisation of Family Doctors Conference, Dublin.

Eliot, T. S. (1936 (1974)) *Collected Poems*. London: Faber.

Exley, H. (ed.) (1991) *A Writer's Notebook*. Watford: Exley.

Ferry, N. M. and Ross-Gordon, N. (1998) An enquiry into Schon's epistemology of practice: exploring links between experience and reflective practice. *Adult Education Quarterly*, **48**(2) pp. 98–112.

Flax, J. (1990) *Thinking Fragments*. Berkeley CA: University of California Press.

Fowler, J. and Chevannes, M. (1998) Evaluating the efficacy of reflective practice within the context of clinical supervision. *Journal of Advanced Nursing*, **27**, pp. 379–82.

Fox, D. (1983) Personal theories of teaching. *Studies in Higher Education*, 8(2) pp. 151–63.

Frank, A. (1947) *The Diary of Anne Frank*. London: Macmillan Children's Books.

Freire, P. (1972) *Pedagogy of the Oppressed*. London: Penguin.

Freire, P. (1998) *Pedagogy of Freedom: Ethics, Democracy, and Civic Courage*. Maryland: Rowman and Littlefield.

Freud, A. (1950) Foreword, in M. Milner, *On Not Being Able to Paint*. London: Heinemann Educational.

Freud, S. (1910 (1962 edn.)) *Two Short Accounts of Psychoanalysis*. London: Penguin.

Freud, S. (1995) Creative writers and day-dreaming, in S. Burke (ed.) *Authorship from Plato to the Postmodernists: a Reader*. University of Edinburgh Press, pp. 54–62.

Gee, S. (1993) *The Last Guests of the Season*. London: Arrow.

Gee, S. (1997a) Falling in place. *Writing in Education*, **11**, pp. 20–2.

Gee, S. (1997b) *The Hours of the Night*. London: Arrow.

Gee, S. (2000) *Earth and Heaven*. London: Headline Review.

Geertz, C. (1973 (1993)) *The Interpretation of Culture*. London: HarperCollins.

Gerber, L. (1994) Psychotherapy with southeast Asian refugees: implications for treatment of western patients. *American Journal of Psychotherapy*, **48**(2) pp. 280–93.

Gerber, L (1996) We must hear each other's cry: lessons from Pol Pot survivors, in C. Strozier and F. Flynn *Genocide, War, and Human Survival*. New York: Rowman and Littlefield, pp. 297–305.

Gersie, Alida (1992) *Storymaking in Bereavement*. London: Jessica Kingsley.

Gibran, K. (1926 (1994)) *The Prophet*. London: Bracken Books.

Glaister, L. (1999) *Sheer Blue Bliss*. London: Bloomsbury.

Glen, S., Clark, A. and Nicol, M. (1995) Reflecting on reflection: a personal encounter. *Nurse Education Today*, **15**, pp. 61–8.

Goldberg, N. (1986) *Writing Down the Bones*. Boston, Mass: Shambhala.

Goodson, I. (1998) Storying the self, in W. Pinar (ed.) *Curriculum: Towards New Identities*. New York and London: Taylor & Francis, pp. 3–20.

Gough, N. (1998) Reflections and diffractions: functions of fiction in curriculum inquiry, in W. Pinar (ed.) *Curriculum: Towards New Identities*. New York and London: Taylor & Francis, pp. 91–129.

Greenhalgh, T. and Hurwitz, B. (eds.) (1998) *Narrative Based Medicine*. London: BMJ Books.

Greenwood, J. (1995) Treatment with dignity. *Nursing Times* **91**(17) pp. 65–6.

Grumet, M. R. (1981) Restitution and reconstruction of educational experience: an autobiographical method for curriculum theory, in M. Lawn and L. Barton (eds.) *Rethinking Curriculum Studies: a Radical Approach.* London: Croom Helm, pp. 115–30.

Guppy, S. (2000) Feminist witness to the century. *Times Educational Supplement*, February, p. 27.

Hamberger, R. (1995) Acts of parting. *New Statesman*, 24 November, p. 49.

Hancock, P. (1998) Reflective practice: using a learning journal. *Nursing Standard* **13**(17) pp. 37–40.

Hargreaves, J. (1997) Using patients: exploring the ethical dimension of reflective practice in nurse education. *Journal of Advanced Nursing*, **25**, pp. 223–8.

Hartley, L. P. (1953) *The Go Between.* London: Hamish Hamilton.

Heaney, S. (1980) *Selected Prose 1968–1978.* London: Faber & Faber.

Heilbrun, C. (1988) *Writing a Woman's Life.* New York: W. W. Norton.

Heller, T. (1996) Doing being human: reflective practice in mental health work, in: T. Heller *et al.* (eds.) *Mental Health Matters.* London: Macmillan.

Heller, T. (1997) A GP writes, in B. Mcdonnell (ed.) *Serious Fun: the Arts in Primary Health Care.* Dewsbury: Yorkshire & Humberside Arts.

Hesse, H. (1927 (1965)) *Steppenwolf.* London: Penguin.

Hildebrand, J. (1995) Learning through supervision: a systemic approach, in M. Yelloly and M. Henkel (eds.) *Teaching and Learning in Social Work: Towards Reflective Practice.* London: Jessica Kingsley.

Hilfiker, D. (1985) *Healing the Wounds: a Physician Looks at his Work.* New York: Pantheon.

Holly, M. L. (1988) Reflective writing and the spirit of enquiry. *Cambridge Journal of Education.* **19**(1) pp. 71–80.

Holly, M. L. (1989) *Writing to Grow: Keeping a Personal-Professional Journal.* Portsmouth NH: Heinemann.

Homer (trans. 1996 R. Fagles) *The Odyssey.* London: Viking Penguin.

Hoover, L. A. (1994) Reflective writing as a window on preservice teachers' thought processes. *Teacher and Teaching Education.* **10**(1) pp. 83–93.

Howard, J. (1997) The emotional diary: a framework for reflective practice. *Education for General Practice.* **8**, pp. 288–91.

Hudson Jones, A. (1998) Narrative in medical ethics, in T. Greenhalgh and B. Hurwitz (eds.) *Narrative Based Medicine: Dialogue and Discourse in Clinical Practice.* London: BMJ Publications, pp. 217–24.

Hughes, T. (1982) Foreword, in S. Brownjohn, *What Rhymes with Secret.* London: Hodder & Stoughton.

Hughes, L. and Pengelly, P. (1995) Who cares if the room is cold? Practicalities, projections, and the trainer's authority, in M. Yelloly and M. Henkel (eds.) *Teaching and Learning in Social Work: Towards Reflective Practice*. London: Jessica Kingsley.

Hulatt, I. (1995) A sad reflection. *Nursing Standard,* 9(20) pp. 22–3.

Hunt, C. and Sampson, F. (1998) *The Self on the Page: Theory and Practice of Creative Writing in Personal Development*. London: Jessica Kingsley.

Huxley, A. J. (1932 (1994)) *Brave New World*. London: Flamingo.

Hwu, Wen-Song (1998) Curriculum, transcendence and Zen/Taoism: critical ontology of the self, in W. Pinar (ed.) *Curriculum: Towards New Identities*. New York and London: Taylor & Francis, pp. 21–40.

Jackowska, N. (1997) *Write for Life: How to Inspire Your Creative Writing*. Shaftsbury, Dorset: Element.

Johns, C. (1995) Framing learning through reflection within Carper's fundamental ways of knowing in nursing. *Journal of Advanced Nursing,* 22, pp. 222–34.

Johns, C. and Freshwater, D. (eds.) (1998) *Transforming Nursing through Reflective Practice*. Oxford: Blackwell Science.

Keats, J. (1818). Letter to John Taylor, 27 February.

Kember, D. *et al.* (1996) Encouraging critical reflection through small group discussion of journal writing. *Innovations in Education Training International,* 33(4) pp. 313–20.

Keys, C. W. (1999) Revitalising instruction in scientific genres: connecting knowledge production with writing to learn in science. *Science Education,* 83, pp. 115–30.

Kipling, R. (1902) *Just So Stories*. London: Macmillan.

Kirkham, M. (1997) Reflection in midwifery: professional narcissism or seeing with women? *British Journal of Midwifery,* 5(5) pp. 259–62.

Kirkham, M. (1999) The wisdom of nausea. *Midwifery Today,* 52, p. 15.

Kolb, D. A. (1984) *Experiential Learning*. London: Prentice Hall.

Kruse, S. D. (1997) Reflective activity in practice. *Journal of Research and Development in Education,* 31(1) pp. 46–60.

Landgrebe, B. and Winter, R. (1994) Reflective writing on practice: professional support for the dying? *Educational Action Research,* 2(1) pp. 83–94.

Lane, B. (1993) *Writing as a Road to Self Discovery*. Ohio: Writers Digest Books.

Lao Tsu (trans. 1973 Gia Fu Feng and J. English) *Tao Te Ching*. London: Wildwood House.

Lepore, S. J. (1997) Expressive writing moderates the relation between intrusive thoughts and depressive symptoms. *Journal of Personality and Social Psychology,* 73(5) pp. 1030–37.

Levi, P. (1988) (1987) *The Wrench*. London: Abacus.

Lévi-Strauss, C. (1978) *Myth and Meaning*. London: Routledge & Kegan Paul.

Lewis, R. (1992) Autobiography and biography as legitimate educational tasks or pedagogic terrorism. Paper presented to Teachers Stories of Life and Work Conference, Chester.

Llosa, M. V. (1991) *A Writer's Reality*. Syracuse University Press.

Longfellow, H. W. (1960) *The Song of Hiawatha*. London: Dent.

Love, C. (1996) Using a diary to learn the patient's perspective. *Professional Nurse*, **11**(5) pp. 286–8.

Lyotard, J. P. (1992) *The Postmodern Explained to Children*. London: Turnaround.

Macnaughton, J. (1998) Anecdote in clinical practice, in T. Greenhalgh and B. Horwitz (eds) *Narrative Based Medicine*. London: BMJ Books.

Marrow, C. E., MacAuley, D. M. and Crumbie, A. (1997) Promoting reflective practice through structured clinical supervision. *Journal of Nursing Management*, **5**, pp. 77–82.

Marshall, J. and Reason, P. (1997) Collaborative and self-reflective forms of inquiry in management research, in J. Burgoyne and M. Reynolds, *Values and Purposes in Business Management*. London: Sage.

Marx, K. (1962) *Writings of the Young Marx on Philosophy and Society*. (ed. and trans. L. D. Easton and K. H. Gudat) New York: Anchor Books.

McKenzie, J., Sheely, S. and Trigwell, K. (1998) An holistic approach to student evaluation of courses. *Assessment and Evaluation in Higher Education*, **23**(2) pp. 153–63.

McMahon, S. I. (1997) Using documented oral and written dialogue to understand and challenge preservice teachers' reflection. *Teacher and Teacher Education*, **13**(2) pp. 199–213.

Meath Lang, B. (1996) Cultural and language diversity in the curriculum: towards reflective practice, in I. Parasnis (ed.) *Cultural and Language Diversity and the Deaf Experience*. Cambridge University Press, p. 160–70.

Mezirow, J (1981) A critical theory of adult learning and education. *Adult Education*, **32**(1), pp. 3–24.

Mezirow, J. (1991) *Transformative Dimensions of Adult Learning*. San Francisco: Jossey Bass.

Miles, M. B. and Huberman, A. M. (1994) *Qualitative Data Analysis: an Expanded Sourcebook*. London: Sage.

Milne, A. A. (1924 (1959)) *The World of Christopher Robin (When We Were Very Young)*. London: Methuen.

Milne, A. A. (1928 (1958)) *The World of Pooh (The House at Pooh Corner)*. London: Methuen.

Moi, T. (1985) *Sexual Textual Politics*. London: Routledge.

Montgomery Hunter, K. (1991) *Doctor's Stories: the Narrative Structure of Medical Knowledge*. Princeton University Press.

Moon, J. (1999a) *Learning Journals: a Handbook for Academics, Students and Professional Development*. London: Kogan Page.

Moon, J. (1999b) Reflect on the inner 'I'. *Times Higher Education Supplement*, 15 October, pp. 34–5.

Morrison, K. (1996) Developing reflective practice in higher degree students through a learning journal. *Studies in Higher Education*, **21**(3) pp. 317–31.

Murray, D. (1982) *Learning by Teaching*. New Jersey: Boynton Cook.

Newton, R. (1996) Getting to grips with barriers to reflection. *SCUTREA Conference Papers*, pp. 142–5.

Nias, J. and Aspinwall, K. (1992) Paper presented to the Teachers' Stories of Life and Work Conference, Chester.

Orwell, G. (1949 (1987)) *1984*. London: Penguin.

Paterson, B. L. (1995) Developing and maintaining reflection in clinical journals, *Nurse Education Today*, **15**, pp. 211–20.

Pattison, S., Manning, S. and Malby, B. (1999) I want to tell you a story. *Health Services Journal*, 25 February, p. 6.

Pennebaker, J. W., Kiecolt Glaser, J. and Glaser, R. (1988) Disclosure of traumas and immune function: health implications for psychotherapy. *Journal of Consulting and Clinical Psychology*, **56**, pp. 239–45.

Phye, G. D. (ed.) (1997) *Handbook of Academic Learning*. San Diego, California: Academic Press.

Pietroni, M. (1995) The nature and aims of professional education for social workers: a postmodern perspective, in M. Yelloly and M. Henkel (eds.) *Learning and Teaching in Social Work: Towards Reflective Practice*. London: Jessica Kingsley.

Pinar, W. F. (1975) Currere: towards reconceptualisation, in W. F. Pinar (ed.) *Curriculum Theorising: the Reconceptualists*. Berkeley CA: McCutchan, pp. 396–414.

Pinar, W. F. (ed.) (1998) *Curriculum: Toward New Identities*. New York & London: Taylor & Francis.

Plato (trans. 1958 W. K. C. Guthrie) *The Protogoras and Meno*. London: Penguin.

Prigogine, I. (1999) Review of *Doubt and Certainty* by T. Rothman and G. Sudarshan. *Times Higher Education Supplement*, 24 September.

Progoff, I. (1987) *At a Journal Workshop*. New York: Dialogue House.

Purdy, R. (1996) Writing refreshes my practice. *Medical Monitor*, 6 March.

Rainer, T. (1978) *The New Diary: How to Use a Journal for Self-Guidance and Expanded Creativity*. London: Angus & Robertson.

Reason, P. (ed.) (1988) *Human Enquiry in Action: Developments in New Paradigm Research*. London: Sage.

Reason, P. and Hawkins, P. (1988) Storytelling as inquiry, in P. Reason (ed.) *Human Enquiry in Action: Developments in New Paradigm Research*. London: Sage, pp. 79–126.

Rigano, D. and Edwards, J. (1998) Incorporating reflection into work practice. *Management Learning*, **29**(4) pp. 431–46.

Richardson, L. (1998) Writing: a method of inquiry, in N. K. Denzin and Y. S. Lincoln (eds.) *Collecting and Interpreting Qualitative Materials.* London: Sage.

Robertson, P. (1999) Talk to King's Fund 'Arts in Hospital' Forum. December.

Rockwell, J. (1974) *Fact in Fiction.* London: Routledge.

Rogers, C. (1969) *Freedom to Learn: a View of What Education Might Become.* Columbus: Charles E. Merrill.

Rogers, J. (1991) *Mr Wroe's Virgins.* London: Faber & Faber.

Rowan, J. (1990) *Subpersonalities: the People Inside Us.* London: Routledge.

Rowe, J. and Halling, S. (1998) Psychology of forgiveness, in R. S. Valle (ed.) *Phenomenological Inquiry in Psychology: Existential and Transpersonal Dimensions.* New York: Plenum, pp. 227–46.

Rowe, J., Halling, S., Davies, Leifer, M., Powers, D. and van Bronkhurst, J. (1989) The psychology of forgiving another: a dialogical research approach, in R. S. Valle and S. Halling (eds) *Existential-Phenomenological Perspectives in Psychology: Exploring the Breadth of Human Experience.* New York: Plenum.

Rowland (Bolton), G., Rowland, S. and Winter, R. (1990) Writing fiction as enquiry into professional practice. *Journal of Curriculum Studies,* **22**(3) pp. 291–3.

Rowland, S. (1984) *The Enquiring Classroom.* Lewes: Falmer.

Rowland, S. (1991) The power of silence: an enquiry through fictional writing. *British Educational Research Journal,* **17**(2) pp. 95–113.

Rowland, S. (1993) *The Enquiring Tutor.* Lewes: Falmer.

Rowland, S. (1999) The role of theory in a pedagogical model for lecturers in Higher Education. *Studies in Higher Education,* **24**(3) pp. 303–14.

Rowland, S. (2000) *The Enquiring University Lecturer.* Buckingham: Society for Research into Higher Education and Open University Press.

Rowland, S. and Barton, L. (1994) Making things difficult: developing a research approach to teaching in higher education. *Studies in Higher Education,* **19**(3) pp. 367–74.

Sacks, O. (1985) *The Man who Mistook his Wife for a Hat.* Picador, Macmillan.

Salvio, P. (1998) On using the literacy portfolio to prepare teachers for 'willful world travelling' in W. Pinar (ed.) *Curriculum: Towards New Identities.* New York and London: Taylor & Francis, pp. 41–75.

Sansom, P. (1994) *Writing Poems.* Newcastle upon Tyne: Bloodaxe.

Sartre, J. P. (1938 (1963)) *Nausea.* Middlesex: Penguin.

Schneider, M. and Killick, J. (1998) *Writing for Self-Discovery: a Personal Approach to Creative Writing.* Shaftsbury, Dorset: Element.

Schon, D. A. (1983) *The Reflective Practitioner: How Professionals Think in Action.* New York: Basic Books.

Schon, D. A. (1987) *Educating the Reflective Practitioner.* San Francisco: Jossey Bass.

Schratz, M. (1993) Researching while teaching: promoting reflective professionality in higher education. *Educational Action Research*, **1**(1) pp. 111–33.

Scruton, R. (1982) *Kant*. Oxford University Press.

Sellers, S. (1989) *Delighting the Heart: a Notebook by Women Writers*. London: Women's Press.

Shelley, M. (1820 (1994)) *Frankenstein*. Ware, Herts: Wordsworth.

Simons, J. (1990) *Diaries and Journals of Literary Women from Fanny Burney to Virginia Woolf*. London: Macmillan.

Smyth, J. M. *et al.* (1999) Effects of writing about stressful experiences on symptom reduction in patients with asthma or rheumatoid arthritis. *Journal of the American Medical Association*, **281**(14) pp. 1304–9.

Smyth, T. (1996) Reinstating the personal in the professional: reflections on empathy and aesthetic experience. *Journal of Advanced Nursing*, **24** pp. 932–7.

Snadden, D., Thomas, M. L., Griffin, E. M. and Hudson, H. (1996) Portfolio-based learning and general practice vocational training, *Medical Education*, 30, (2) pp. 148–152.

Sophocles (trans. 1982 Robert Fagles) *Antigone*. New York: Penguin.

Spiegel, D. (1999) Editorial: Healing words: emotional expression and disease outcome. *Journal of the American Medical Association*, **281**(14) pp. 1328–9.

Staton, J. (1988) An introduction to dialogue journal communication, in J. Staton, R. W. Shuy, J. K. Paton and L. Reed (eds) *Dialogue Journal Communication: Classroom Linguistic, Social and Cognitive Views*. Norwood NJ: Ablex, pp. 1–32.

Sterne, L. (1760 (1980)) *Tristram Shandy* (Vol. 2, chapter 11). London: W. W. Norton.

Stevenson, R. L. (1886 (1984)) *Dr Jekyll and Mr Hyde*. London: Penguin.

Stoker, B. (1897 (1994)) *Dracula*. London: Penguin.

Sumsion, J. and Fleet, A. (1996) Reflection: can we assess it? Should we assess it? *Assessment and Evaluation in Higher Education*, **21**(2) pp. 121–30.

Sydney, Sir P. (1965) *The Poems of Sir Philip Sydney*. W. A. Ringler (ed.) London: Oxford University Press.

Tennyson, A. (1932 (1886)) 'The Lady of Shallott', in J. Wain (ed.) *The Oxford Library of English Poetry*. Oxford University Press, pp. 79–83.

Thomas, R. S. (1986) Poetry for supper, in *Selected Poems*. Newcastle upon Tyne: Bloodaxe.

Tripp, D. (1995a) *Critical Incidents in Teaching*. London: Routledge.

Tripp, D. (1995b) SCOPE facilitator training. *NPDP SCOPE Project Draft*. Western Australia: Murdoch University.

Trotter, S. (1999) Journal writing to promote reflective practice in pre-service teachers. Paper presented to the International Human Science Research Conference, Sheffield, July.

Truscott, D. M. and Walker, B. J. (1998) The influence of portfolio selection on reflective thinking, in E. G. Strutevant, J. A. Dugan, P. Linder and W. M. Linek, *Literacy and Community*. Texas: The College Reading Association.

Tsai Chi Chung (trans. 1994 Brian Bruya) *Zen Speaks*. London: HarperCollins.

Tyler, S. A. (1986) Post-modern ethnography: from occult to occult document, in J. Clifford and G. E. Marcus (eds) *Writing Culture*. Berkeley: University of California Press.

Usher, R. (1993) From process to practice: research reflexivity and writing in adult education. *Studies in Continuing Education*, **15**(2) pp. 98–116.

Usher, R. Bryant, I. and Jones, R. (1997) *Adult Education and the Postmodern Challenge: Learning Beyond the Limits*. London: Routledge.

van Manen, M. (1995) On the epistemology of reflective practice. *Teachers and Teaching: Theory and Practice*, **1**(1) pp. 33–49.

von Klitzing, W. (1999) Evaluation of reflective learning in a psychodynamic group of nurses caring for terminally ill patients. *Journal of Advanced Nursing*, **30**(5) pp. 1213–21.

Wade, S. (1994) *Writing and Publishing Poetry*. Oxford: How To Books.

Warner, M. (1998) *No Go the Bogeyman: Scaring, Lulling and Making Mock*. London: Chatto & Windus.

Weedon, C. (1987) *Feminist Practice and Post-Structuralist Theory*. Oxford: Basil Blackwell.

Wellard, S. J. and Bethune, E. (1996) Reflective journal writing in nurse education: whose interests does it serve? *Journal of Advanced Nursing*, **24**, pp. 1077–82.

Wilde, O. (1891 (1949)) *The Picture of Dorian Gray*. London: Penguin.

Williams, W. C. (1951) *Selected Poems*. London: Penguin.

Winter, R. (1988) Fictional-critical writing, in J. Nias and S. Groundwater-Smith, (eds), *The Enquiring Teacher*. London: Falmer, pp. 231–48.

Winter, R. (1989) *Learning from Experience* (particularly chapter 10). Lewes: Falmer.

Winter, R. (1991) Fictional-critical writing as a method for educational research. *British Educational Research Journal*, **17**(3), pp. 251–62.

Winter, R. Buck, A. and Sobiechowska, P. (1999) *Professional Experience and the Investigative Imagination: the Art of Reflective Writing*. London: Routledge.

Woolf, V. (1977, 1978, 1980) *The Diary of Virginia Woolf*. (3 volumes) London: Hogarth Press.

Woolf, V. (1992) *Orlando*. Oxford University Press.

Yeats, W. B. (1962) *Selected Poetry*. London: Macmillan.

Yelloly, M. and Henkel, M. (eds) Introduction, in: *Teaching and Learning in Social Work: Reflective Practice*. London: Jessica Kingsley.

Index